LITERATURE AND CRIMINAL JUSTICE IN ANTEBELLUM AMERICA

Literature and Criminal Justice in Antebellum America

Carl Ostrowski

University of Massachusetts Press

Amherst and Boston

Copyright © 2016 by University of Massachusetts Press
All rights reserved
Printed in the United States of America

ISBN 978-1-62534-238-6 (paper); 237-9 (hardcover)

Designed by Jack Harrison
Set in Adobe Garamond Pro
Printed and bound by The Maple-Vail Book Manufacturing Group

Cover design by Sally Nichols
Cover art: Detail from a daguerreotype depicting Worcester city marshal
Frederick Warren with handcuffed prisoner, c. 1849. Courtesy, American Antiquarian Society

Library of Congress Cataloging-in-Publication Data
A catalog record for this book is available from the Library of Congress

British Library Cataloguing-in-Publication Data
A catalog record for this book is available from the British Library.

To Tina and Walt

Contents

Acknowledgments

I have the good fortune to work in a large and collegial department of English at Middle Tennessee State University, where a number of colleagues read portions of this book in manuscript, answered my queries regarding their particular areas of specialization, or otherwise fostered an atmosphere of intellectual curiosity. For these and other contributions to my intellectual growth and professional morale, I thank (chair) Maria Bachman, Allen Hibbard, Marion Hollings, Alfred Lutz, Philip Phillips, Mischa Renfroe, (former chair) Tom Strawman, Kathleen Therrien, and especially my son Walt's adoptive uncles, Will Brantley and Bob Holtzclaw.

For the gift of long-standing friendship, I am grateful to Margaret Doetsch, Michael Fulgenzi, Mark Graybill, Pat Hamilton (*il miglior fabbro*), and David Manchel. Special acknowledgment is due to two more recently acquired friends, Timothy Helwig and Magdelyn Hammond Helwig of Western Illinois University, for generously inviting me to join them for dinners, literary tours, and various social events at several American Literature Association conferences.

It is a great pleasure to express my gratitude here to editor Brian Halley of the University of Massachusetts Press for his faith in the project and his keen editorial insight. Thanks also to managing editor Carol Betsch for guiding the manuscript through the publication process and to copy editor Amanda Heller for her painstaking attention to detail and her forbearance with my stylistic bad habits. She may even have broken me of a few of them.

I am grateful to the anonymous readers at the Press for their remarkably discerning critiques. Their reviews opened up unforeseen areas of inquiry and saved me from embarrassing errors. The book's remaining faults and missed opportunities exist despite the readers' best efforts and are, of course, entirely my own responsibility.

Although I do not know him personally, I thank Christopher Looby of UCLA for uploading to the Web several years ago the early journalism of George Lippard. The chapter comparing Lippard's and Walt Whitman's journalism was the first element of this book to take shape, appearing (in slightly different form) in the journal *American Periodicals,* published by the Ohio State University Press. Thanks to the editors of *American Periodicals* for permission to republish that material here.

The MTSU Research and Creative Activities Committee provided a summer research grant early in the composition process, for which due acknowledgment is here recorded.

A very special category of gratitude extends to cover the work of Dr. Nishitha Reddy of the Vanderbilt University Medical Center on my behalf.

Finally, I thank my wife, Tina Stenson, and our son, Walt Stenson Ostrowski, for their love and support.

LITERATURE AND CRIMINAL JUSTICE IN ANTEBELLUM AMERICA

Introduction

Overlapping Spheres of Literature and Criminal Justice

The relationship between literature and criminal justice in antebellum America, the terms linked in the title of this book, eludes simple formulation. The parallel historical development of an expanding print culture and a changing criminal justice system created a distinctive contact zone where discourses and figures from the worlds of literature and criminal justice collided in productive new ways.

To get a sense of the fascinating overlap between these worlds in the 1840s and 1850s, consider, for example, the connections between Ned Buntline (the pen name of novelist Edward Zane Carroll Judson) and George Matsell. A soon-to-be inmate of Blackwell's Prison in New York, where he would serve a year for helping to incite the Astor Place Riot, Buntline fashioned his 1848 novel *The Mysteries and Miseries of New York* as a commentary on (and adjunct to) the criminal justice system.[1] While some parts of the novel are obviously fictionalized and contain plotlines typical of the city-mysteries genre,[2] Buntline also claims in his preface that he received help researching the novel from police officers who accompanied him on visits to the dens of vice depicted in the novel's pages, giving the novel a patina of true crime authenticity. The novel includes a lengthy nonfictional appendix, where Buntline rails against police and judicial complicity in allowing gambling halls and brothels to operate, publishes the addresses of known establishments, and calls on police to shut them down. George Matsell appears as a character in the fictional sections of *The Mysteries and Miseries of New York,* where Buntline lionizes him as an incorruptible public official who earns the grudging respect of criminals. But Matsell was a real historical personage who also embodies the period's literature–criminal justice nexus. Matsell had been a magistrate presiding over New York City's police court and detention facility, widely known as the

Tombs, before being appointed the city's first police commissioner. Matsell also made his mark in publishing as the author of *Vocabulum; or, The Rogue's Lexicon* (1859), a dictionary of "flash" speech used by members of the criminal underground, and later as the proprietor of a popular crime-related newspaper called the *National Police Gazette*.[3]

Or consider the textual links between crime novelist George Thompson and counterfeiter-poet Christian Meadows. Thompson (who, not incidentally, spent six weeks in Boston's Leverett Street Jail and wrote letters to a newspaper exposing its substandard conditions, leading to reforms) published *Life and Exploits of the Noted Criminal, Bristol Bill* in 1851.[4] Bristol Bill was the alias of William Darlington, a real historical figure convicted of counterfeiting and notorious for, among other things, stabbing the prosecuting attorney at the conclusion of his trial. *Life and Exploits* is something of a hybrid, insofar as the first half, set in England, is an obviously fictionalized story of Bristol Bill's life written in the style of the Newgate novel,[5] while the second half borrows heavily from nonfictional court documents chronicling Darlington's trial and conviction in Vermont. A subordinate character in the novel is Bristol Bill's accomplice, Christian Meadows. But Meadows, also a real historical figure and a former inmate at the Massachusetts State Prison, turns out to be the star contributor to an anthology of prison poetry, *Voices from Prison*, first published in 1847 to forward the goals of the prison reform movement.[6] The contributors to *Voices from Prison*, which was edited by prison reformer and anti-gallows activist Charles Spear, wrote poems about how the experience of incarceration had been redemptive, giving them time to reflect on their crimes and reestablish their moral character. A novelist (and soon-to-be prison inmate) who wrote a book about ineffectual police and judicial corruption featuring a real-life police officer, who himself became an author and publisher of crime-related literature; another novelist (who spent time in jail and tried his hand at the prison exposé format) writing about a criminal whose accomplice was a poet, whose own work had been published to lend support to the prison reform movement: the intricate Mobius strip relationships among these figures speak to a period when the criminal justice system and American literature experienced an intimate, experimental, and productive overlapping of spheres brokered by an expanding print culture. These overlapping spheres form the subject of this book.

One need not look exclusively toward such marginal literary figures as Meadows and Matsell, of course, to discover links between literature and criminal justice in the antebellum period. The surprising number of major American literary figures who were involved in or commented on the processes of criminal justice at some point in their careers offers additional justification for this investigation. Like their contemporary Charles Dickens,

George Lippard and Walt Whitman worked as journalists covering the criminal courts before they turned to more literary forms of expression. Among the New England Transcendentalists, Ralph Waldo Emerson visited a prison in New Hampshire to observe penal practice; Margaret Fuller's journalism included a number of pieces evaluating reform efforts in various penitentiaries and asylums; and Henry David Thoreau's most influential essay arose from the occasion of a night spent in a county jail.[7] In the fiction of the period, Nathaniel Hawthorne (whose close friend and literary patron John L. O'Sullivan was a founding member of the New York Prison Association, an organization devoted to helping former convicts reintegrate into the community) examined questions of criminal justice in all four of his major romances and chose a prison reformer as the quintessential example of an overzealous philanthropist in *The Blithedale Romance* (1852).[8] Herman Melville consigned the title characters of *Pierre* (1852) and "Bartleby, the Scrivener" to death in prison and denounced the nation's commitment to incarceration in his early novel *Typee* (1846). Edgar Allan Poe's tales have been read as an extended critique of Americans' belief in reform via incarceration and as responses to controversy over the insanity defense.[9] James Fenimore Cooper's final novel, *The Ways of the Hour* (1850), looks into such matters as jury tampering, jury nullification, popular election of judges, and premature conviction of defendants in the court of public opinion. Among the many popular but now lesser-known writers who pondered the implications of a changing criminal justice system were E. D. E. N. Southworth, Sylvester Judd, Edward Everett Hale, and Richard Hildreth, in addition to innumerable, often anonymous contributors to the periodicals of the era.

The argument unfolded in the pages that follow shows that in the three decades preceding the Civil War, a critical period of development in the nation's criminal justice infrastructure, a handful of tropes originating in crime-related discourse profoundly shaped the period's literature. I delve into antebellum print culture to identify the constituent features of key cultural narratives about criminal justice, and then explore the implications of their adaptation, manipulation, or rejection in a wide range of texts, from a work as canonical as *The Scarlet Letter* (1850) to far more obscure items, including the memoirs of prison chaplains and anthologies of prisoner-authored poetry. The existence of these latter items indicates another form that the relationship between literature and criminal justice assumed during this period: authors, editors, and publishers catered to readers' interest in criminal justice by collaborating in the creation of new crime-related subgenres. Examining these intersections of literature and criminal justice yields insights into a number of subjects, including reporters' and editors' understandings of the daily newspaper's social obligations in reporting on crime; the relationship between vigilantism's unpredictable distribution of judicial authority and fictional depictions of African American civic agency; the extent and limits of cultural authority available to antebellum women by virtue of association with the penal reform movement; the threat that discharged penitentiary convicts posed to a hierarchical distinction between free (white) and coerced (black) labor as they attempted to pass back into society; and the opportunities opened up for outsider authorship by widespread interest in American penitentiaries.

Of course, it is not entirely unexpected that so many literary authors wrote about criminal justice during the antebellum period. Criminality had been a prime subject of interest from the very beginnings of the modern novel in English as practiced by Daniel Defoe (who spent time in Newgate Prison), Henry Fielding (co-founder of an early urban police force, London's Bow Street Runners), and other eighteenth-century figures. I contend that the specific subject of communal and governmental responses to crime held special interest for American authors of the 1830s through the 1850s, however, because it was during this time that the institutions we now recognize as our criminal justice system coalesced. In the words of legal scholar William J. Stuntz, "While America's Founding generation and the generation that fought the Civil War and battled through Reconstruction crafted the nation's key constitutional texts, the generation that *preceded* the Civil War defined its key criminal justice institutions."[10] It should be acknowledged at the outset, perhaps, that any allusion to a criminal justice "system" imposes an inaccurate or anachronistic coherence on a range of institutions and officials operating independently of one another and at different levels of government: night watchmen, newly established urban police forces, overnight lockups, county jails, state penitentiaries, police court judges, city aldermen, trial lawyers, private prosecutors, district attorneys, state and federal courts, governors, and so on.[11] Whether or not they regarded such institutions as part of a coherent system, however, American authors, editors, and publishers closely scrutinized the changing procedures associated with criminal justice and addressed them in a wide range of printed forms.

A number of scholars working from varied methodological perspectives have directed attention toward the intersection of criminal justice and antebellum American literature and/or print culture. Studies by Caleb Smith, Jeannine Marie DeLombard, and Paul C. Jones, for example, have investigated the intertwined narratives of civil death and rebirth central to the poetics of the penitentiary, the role of African American criminal confessions in opening up a space for black civic agency, and links between the period's prominent anti–capital punishment campaign and American literature, respectively.[12] My debts to these works, which are cited repeatedly in the pages that follow, will be obvious to readers familiar with them.

Part of what I hope to add to this scholarship is a broadened base of evidence facilitating awareness of how deeply stories about criminal justice had penetrated into antebellum print culture and how influential they were in shaping the period's literature. This project's archive embraces major figures such as Whitman and Hawthorne alongside relatively little-known contemporaries including Judd, Hildreth, and Hale. Although Lippard, treated in three of my six chapters, has received significant critical attention, he is too often identified solely with his best-known novel, *The Quaker City* (1845), whereas some of his most revealing portraits of the criminal justice system appear in lesser-known works—starting with his early journalism and continuing through his novels *The Nazarene* (1846), *The Empire City* (1850), *The Killers* (1850), and *New York* (1853)—which receive attention here. A transatlantic dimension emerges from inclusion of celebrated British travel writers (Dickens, Harriet Martineau, and Frederick Marryat) who reported on their visits to American penitentiaries. I also analyze material from the era's periodicals, including arrest reports in penny papers (the *New York Herald,* Philadelphia's *Spirit of the Times,* and the *Brooklyn Daily Eagle*), articles in prison reform periodicals (*Prisoner's Friend* and *Pennsylvania Journal of Prison Discipline and Philanthropy*), reviews of crime novels in assorted periodicals (*The Knickerbocker,* the *American Monthly Magazine,* and the *Christian Examiner and General Review,* to name a few), and stories related to incarceration and discharge in popular literary magazines (*Godey's Lady's Book, Graham's Monthly Magazine,* and the *Atlantic Monthly,* among others). The present volume therefore profits from work in the growing field of periodical studies.

In focusing on literary depictions of (and challenges to) certain elements of the legal system, I ask questions associated with scholarship in the law-and-literature tradition. Brook Thomas's *Cross-Examinations of Law and Literature* stands out as an influence on account of its intensive treatment of the antebellum period and for the subtlety and complexity of its readings.[13] Colin Dayan's insights into "negative personhood," especially as applied to nineteenth-century penitentiary inmates, inform my discussion of discharged convicts.[14] One paradigm for studying law and literature is to trace the impact of literary culture on American jurisprudence, an approach that has been fruitfully pursued by Laura Hanft Korobkin.[15] In contrast, in the pages that follow I tend to look in the opposite direction, at how narrative patterns and rhetorical gestures that originated in discourse related to legal issues infiltrated the period's literary expression. Nevertheless, insofar as some of the authors discussed here intended their literary efforts to have public policy or jurisprudential implications, the relationship between the two modes of discourse was not unidirectional. In shaping the present book, I have drawn inspiration from Nan Goodman's belief that "neither literary nor legal narratives in nineteenth-century America can be understood without the other," as well as from Gregg Crane's postulation of "the intricate and multivalent interactions between law and literature" during this period.[16]

A brief overview of developments in the theory and practice of criminal justice from the Revolution through the antebellum era will provide useful orientation for the claims that follow. At the time of its founding, the United States had inherited various criminal justice practices from its colonial past, for the most part (depending on the region in question) rooted in the traditions of English common law. In the decades following independence, however, Americans aimed to institutionalize criminal justice in ways more closely aligned with Enlightenment theory and more consistent with principles of republican government.[17] By emphasizing the role of the environment in shaping personality, Lockean psychology had contributed to a softening of attitudes toward criminals. Eighteenth-century theorists of criminality disavowed physical torture, capital punishment, and other excesses of state-sponsored cruelty in favor of what they considered a more humane and rational approach to crime. The Italian criminologist Cesare Beccaria's 1764 book *An Essay on Crimes and Punishments* (which stressed certainty and proportionality of punishment) circulated widely in the early republic and was a mainstay of legislative libraries, found, for example, in the earliest catalog of the Library of Congress.[18] As evolving ideas about the origins of criminal behavior justified measures aimed at reform rather than retribution, liberalizing theological attitudes discredited the Calvinist conception of crime as an expression of innate depravity, allowing for the possibility that "human evil might be overcome by religious training."[19] Summing up these late-eighteenth-century developments, Louis P. Masur finds that "faith in the reformability and perfectability [*sic*] of man contributed to a redefinition of the causes of criminality . . . and elevated the reformation of the criminal into the principal end of punishment."[20] State constitutions formulated in the wake of the American Revolution reflected these beliefs, insofar as the number of capital crimes declined and incarceration in penitentiaries became the primary method of punishing—and, it was hoped, rehabilitating—convicted criminals.

The early decades of the nineteenth century witnessed the rise of an international penal reform movement. The famed Eastern Penitentiary at Philadelphia opened in 1829, operating on the so-called Pennsylvania (or solitary) system, in which prisoners worked alone and lived in virtual solitary confinement, conditions meant to encourage them to reflect on their crimes and, guided by chaplains and reformers, achieve penitence. Reformers associated with the Auburn Prison in New York took the lead in promoting the competing Auburn (or congregate) system of incarceration, in which inmates worked silently together during the day in factory-like conditions and retreated to individual cells at night. Developments pioneered in these institutions spread across the Northeast and Midwest, and, by the 1830s, American penitentiaries had attracted international praise for their purported advances in the rehabilitation of criminals. A penal reform debate between proponents of these two systems of incarceration continued until the Civil War.[21]

Enjoying a sudden vogue in the United States in the 1820s and 1830s (and considerable popularity with the general public thereafter, even as it was discredited in scientific circles), phrenology generated additional, if not uncontested, support for the rehabilitative ideal. Among the many social problems to which phrenologists applied their theory, notes Christopher J. Beshara, "none caught their attention quite like criminal vice." From a phrenological standpoint, criminal behavior resulted from a combination of diseased brain development and a morally unsound environment; phrenologists' belief in "the plasticity of the hereditable mental faculties" suggested that benevolent institutions might reform criminals by teaching them to cultivate and exercise their moral faculty.[22] The phrenological treatise *Rationale of Crime* by English journalist Marmaduke B. Sampson was published in the United States in 1846 with an introduction and extensive notes by Eliza Farnham, acclaimed matron of the women's division of Mount Pleasant Prison in New York State. Farnham justified an American edition of the book on the grounds that "the subject of Criminal Jurisprudence, at the present period, is claiming much of the public attention."[23] A reviewer in the *United States Magazine, and Democratic Review* endorsed phrenology's assumption that perpetrators of crime "are objects of sympathy and good will" whose punishment should be aimed at "reformation, and not the infliction of pain," while other reviewers strongly condemned the treatise, arguing that phrenology's attribution of individual criminal behavior to a physiological cause dangerously absolved perpetrators of moral accountability.[24]

A second, and related, transatlantic conversation about moral accountability and criminal psychology involved the insanity defense. Maine physician Isaac Ray, an early adherent of phrenology, published *A Treatise on the Medical Jurisprudence of Insanity* to wide approbation in 1838.[25] Ray encouraged jurists to apply a more up-to-date, medically informed understanding of insanity to criminal cases, in which partial (or moral) insanity, as determined by physician experts, was recognized as a legitimate defense. Several years later, in 1844, the murder trial of Abner Rogers, who had killed his warden in the Massachusetts State Prison, intensified interest in this area of jurisprudence when

Massachusetts Supreme Court Chief Justice Lemuel Shaw applied a novel standard of "irresistible and uncontrollable impulse" to the claim of exculpatory insanity.[26] Americans were also well aware of developments in Great Britain, where a panel of judges in 1843 clarified what came to be known as the McNaughton rule, by which the test of insanity was a defendant's inability to understand that what he or she did was wrong.[27] The *North American Review* took note of this medico-legal debate (and acknowledged occasional public outrage over acquittals by reason of insanity) in a lengthy review essay on the subject in 1845.[28]

Criminal trials did not have to involve the highly charged insanity defense, however, to arouse public interest. Spurred in part by the increasing professionalization of the American bar, courts evolved significantly during the antebellum period.[29] Newly complex criminal trials featured "closer cross-examinations, increasingly well-defined extra-statutory rules of evidence, multiple counsel, large numbers of witnesses, extended addresses to the jury, and a more thoroughly adversarial spirit than in 'traditional' trials."[30] Inevitably, public interest attended institutional change. Journalists attacked the integrity of criminal prosecution on multiple fronts, impugning individual magistrates whom they regarded as insufficiently tough on crime, criticizing grand juries as too beholden to the interests of social elites, and denouncing too liberal use of the pardoning power by state governors.[31] One of the period's primary debates relative to criminal trial courts had to do with the relative power of judges and juries; some legal theorists regarded juries as the essential safeguard of democratic liberties against tyrannical state authorities, while others saw runaway juries as a threat to social order.[32] These issues surfaced when juries refused to convict defendants on moral grounds (for example, when they acquitted abolitionists of violating the terms of the Fugitive Slave Law).[33] In the frontier regions of the West during the 1830s and 1840s, underdeveloped criminal justice institutions were frequently proffered as a rationale for citizens to take matters into their own hands through vigilante courts; vigilance committees achieved a new level of public acceptance with the actions of the San Francisco Vigilance Committees of 1851 and 1856. Collectively, these developments contributed to a "distrust of the judiciary" widely noted in scholarship on the period's legal history.[34]

The perceived urgency of the problem of urban crime was another factor directing Americans' collective attention toward the functioning of the nation's criminal justice apparatus in the antebellum era. In the space of a few decades, immigration and urbanization radically transformed the cities of the Northeast. Paul Boyer reports that in the thirty years preceding the Civil War, "the urban population increased by over 700 percent, from about 500,000 to 3.8 million. . . . Philadelphia grew from 161,000 to well over 500,000,

Boston from 61,000 to 133,000 and New York from about 200,000 to more than 800,000."[35] Extremes of wealth and poverty characterized these rapidly expanding cities, where the urban poor occupied overcrowded and unsanitary tenements. The volatile mix of (often Catholic) immigrants, African Americans, and Protestant working-class whites engendered ethnic, religious, and racial tensions that culminated in urban riots during the 1830s. The perception of disorder in American cities demanded a municipal response. New York constructed the Tombs to house its police court and local jail in 1838, and night watchmen gave way to professional police forces in various major cities during the 1840s and 1850s. In Samuel Walker's concise assessment, "the development of a criminal-justice system in the United States was a response to the extraordinary disorder wrought by social change."[36]

The industrial revolution driving social change in the United States caused similar unrest, of course, in the cities of western Europe. The transatlantic nature of antebellum print culture meant that attempts by Britons to understand their own nation's troubled industrial centers found a curious and receptive American readership. Edwin Chadwick's highly regarded *Report on the Sanitary Condition of the Labouring Population of Great Britain* (1842) attributed vicious behavior among the urban poor to overcrowding, unsanitary living conditions, intemperance, and a general cheapening of life which "appears to re-act as another concurrent cause in aggravation of the wretchedness and vice in which they are plunged."[37] Journalist Henry Mayhew's *London Labour and the London Poor* was published in parts in the United States beginning in 1851. Mayhew's eminently Victorian project involved using statistics and firsthand reportage to create an encyclopedic overview of London's destitute residents, including its criminals.[38] Whereas some American commentators saw Mayhew's compendium as reflecting strictly local concerns (it was a commonplace of American thought that British victims of the industrial revolution fared worse than their U.S. counterparts), others recognized that the conditions Mayhew observed in England also described American cities. Reviewing two books by the British reformer Mary Carpenter, a writer in the *North American Review* acknowledged in 1854 that "a great, banded community of criminals and outcasts is thus gathered in the heart of every populous city," among which the author included New York.[39]

Antebellum Americans therefore struggled to reconcile a legacy of Enlightenment faith in the reform of criminals with a growing fear that cities harbored a dangerously alienated criminal population. New York physician John H. Griscom (who cited Chadwick's volume on London as the inspiration for his own *Sanitary Condition of the Laboring Population of New York* [1845]) attributed the moral degradation of the urban poor to "the influence of degraded associations, of habitual neglect of cleanliness, and prostration of health by impure living," stressing, however, that such urban dwellers should be regarded as "the creatures of circumstances beyond their control."[40] In 1841, Unitarian preacher William Ellery Channing noted that urban centers housed "a horde of ignorant, profligate, criminal poor," but he charged society with having created these "monsters in its bosom" and urged listeners to mobilize their prosperity to improve social conditions among the destitute.[41] American social reformers generally retained their faith in the possibility of ameliorative measures to reduce crime even as they described the squalor of urban life with undisguised abhorrence. This tension between perceptions of a depraved criminal caste and middle-class faith in social reform may help to explain the complexity of the period's crime-related literature, in which one finds both credulity and skepticism regarding reform measures, sometimes residing ambivalently within a single text.

Scholars have documented the rapid expansion of American print culture dating from roughly the 1820s through the 1850s, driven by a number of demographic, technological, and cultural factors.[42] What is perhaps worth emphasizing is the close relationship between wide public interest in criminal justice and key sectors of this innovative, entrepreneurial print culture. The new penny papers of the 1830s owed their unprecedented success in large part to sensationalized coverage of local street crime and high-profile criminal trials, beginning with the trial of Richard Robinson for the murder of Helen Jewett in 1836 and continuing with the trials of John C. Colt (1842), Albert J. Tirrell (1845), and John Webster (1850). Pamphlet accounts of sensational criminal trials, which provided extensive transcripts of the proceedings, further stimulated public interest in the criminal justice system, encouraging scrutiny of its methods and verdicts.[43] The popularity of crime journalism in penny papers like the *New York Sun* and the *New York Herald* led journalists George Wilkes and Enoch E. Camp in 1845 to found the *National Police Gazette*, which simultaneously titillated readers with the exploits of criminals and purported to help bring criminals to justice. Based in New York, the nationally distributed *National Police Gazette* included physical descriptions of lawbreakers, accounts of sensational crimes, and a series called "Lives of the Felons," offering fictionalized biographies of notorious criminals.[44]

Publishers active in sectors as widely separated as cheap sensational fiction and evangelical writing came to recognize firsthand experience within the walls of the penitentiary as a potent marketing strategy. Buntline opportunistically turned his prison sentence to literary account by publishing *The Convict* (1851), a novel whose title page proudly announced that it was "Written from Prison," while a former chaplain of the New Hampshire State Prison, Eleazer Smith, marketed his sober account of ministering to inmates under the sensation-promising title *Nine Years Among the Convicts* (1856).[45]

Prisoner-poet Meadows and fellow contributors to *Voices from Prison* followed prisoner-poet Harry Hawser into the marketplace and were followed in turn by self-styled "prison bard" George Thompson (no relation to the novelist of the same name).[46] Thompson also published a prose volume called *Prison Life and Reflections* (1848), exposing conditions in the Missouri prison to which he was sentenced for attempting to help slaves escape to Illinois, joining other abolitionists who discovered a value in linking the prison reform and abolitionist movements.[47]

Competing camps of prison reformers took to the press to lobby on behalf of their chosen penitentiary schemes. *Prisoner's Friend* (1845–1857)—initially published weekly under the title *The Hangman* (an allusion to its concurrent interest in another important reform movement, the anti-gallows cause), later published monthly—became the chosen venue for supporters of the Auburn system of incarceration; supporters of the Pennsylvania system established the *Pennsylvania Journal of Prison Discipline and Philanthropy* (1845–1856) to defend it against attacks in *Prisoner's Friend* and elsewhere. While these specialized publications obviously constituted only a very small part of the publishing landscape, newspapers and magazines supplemented and amplified their discussions of penal reform theories. One finds major articles devoted to prison reform and reviews of books on the subject in the *North American Review* and the *United States Magazine, and Democratic Review* (among other magazines) during the 1840s.[48] Meanwhile, fiction writers contributed to the period's interest in criminal justice through their portraits of criminals, covering the characters' crimes, trials, incarcerations, and post-carceral lives in a range of formats reflective of an increasingly stratified market, including popular serials in newspapers, cheap city-mysteries novels published in parts, short stories in genteel monthlies, and full-dress literary novels issued by prestigious publishers and written by the nation's most celebrated authors.

This book is organized to roughly parallel the workings of the criminal justice system, beginning with the arrest of an alleged criminal as reported in the newspaper and following the process of trial, imprisonment, and discharge. In the 1830s, the urban penny paper defined as newsworthy the arrests and initial hearings of individual offenders, primarily drunks, thieves, and prostitutes—often African Americans and members of other minority groups. These arrest reports quickly acquired a generic form that involved mockery of the suspected criminal and condescending, racially inflected humor at his or her expense. Chapter 1 traces the responses to this form of two young journalists, Lippard and Whitman, who came to recognize the anti-egalitarian implications of the daily arrest report and experimented with it in ways that anticipated the sympathetic attitude toward criminals subsequently exhibited in their fiction and poetry.

During the 1840s and 1850s, criminal courts were widely criticized in the urban Northeast for biases and miscarriages of justice. Meanwhile, vigilante courts sprang up in the West as an alternative to the officially sanctioned criminal justice system. In chapter 2 I analyze three 1850s novels by Lippard and Hildreth that reflect on the implications of vigilantism as a response to ineffectual or corrupt courts, invoking an important contemporary context in the widely publicized actions of the San Francisco Vigilance Committee of 1851. Significantly, both Lippard and Hildreth dramatize African American participation in legislative and judicial roles, intuiting a connection between vigilantism's unpredictable diffusion of judicial authority and the prospect of African American civic agency, or, as Henry Clay provocatively phrased it on the floor of the U.S. Senate, "government by blacks."[49]

Next, I turn to the issue of penal reform. In chapter 3, an analysis of penal reform discourse identifies an archetypal narrative form that I call the carceral conversion story: the story of a recalcitrant criminal morally reformed through the process of incarceration. After demonstrating the ubiquity of the carceral conversion story in antebellum periodical culture, I discuss how Hale, Hawthorne, Thoreau, Southworth, and Rebecca Harding Davis endorse, adapt, or reject its premises in their prison-related works. Venturing into the American reception history of the transatlantic phenomenon known as the Newgate novel of the 1830s and 1840s, I also speculate that prison reform may have played an unappreciated role in the development of American fictional technique, nurturing the emergence of psychological interiority as a hallmark of successful characterization.

Chapter 4 identifies a second common narrative trope of prison reform discourse: the angel of the penitentiary, a virtuous middle-class woman who crosses the threshold of the prison and facilitates the conversion of hardened criminals. After establishing the wide use of this trope in periodical literature, I discuss the implications of its appearance in Judd's *Margaret: A Tale of the Real and Ideal, Blight and Bloom* (1845) and Southworth's *The Hidden Hand* (1859). Both Judd and Southworth transform the motif, manipulating generic convention in the direction of enhanced feminine agency. I also consider the extent to which prison matron Farnham leveraged the cultural capital she acquired as a real-life angel in the penitentiary to abet her own social reform ambitions.

Chapters 5 and 6 deal in different ways with the aftereffects of incarceration. Prison reformers circulated stories of formerly convicted criminals who "passed" quietly back into society after experiencing the moral rehabilitation that incarceration promised. In contrast, crime novelists such as Thompson and Buntline insisted that the discharged convict was "branded with infamy," permanently prevented by a racially coded stigma of incarceration from rejoining society on equal terms with fellow citizens.[50] These competing narrative strains contextualize an analysis of discharged convict characters in *The House of the Seven Gables* (1851) by Hawthorne and *The Empire City* (1850) by Lippard. While both novelists employ the figure of the discharged convict to challenge complacency regarding a penal system that was neither as just nor as humane as advertised, Lippard's discharged inmate Number Ninety-One offers the period's most unsettling portrait of the legacy of incarceration on its individual subjects.

In chapter 6 I analyze nonfictional first-person accounts of life inside antebellum penal institutions, including memoirs by prison chaplains, exposés of penitentiaries written by imprisoned abolitionists, and works by prisoner-poets attesting to the salvific opportunities of incarceration. The penal reform movement lent a special authenticity to the writings of those who had experienced or witnessed incarceration, a form of cultural capital that authors and editors attempted to turn to various individual and social agendas. This chapter tells the story of engraver Christian Meadows, an inmate in the Massachusetts State Prison who mastered the tropes of prison reform poetry to serve his successful bid for executive pardon—shortly before being convicted of counterfeiting and returning to prison. Looking at Meadows's writing career through the lens provided by Karen A. Weyler's analysis of "outsider authors," I gauge what was at stake for the prisoner-poets who contributed to the 1849 third edition of *Voices from Prison,* in the process restoring to such poets a degree of authorial agency that has been effaced by previous analyses of similar texts.[51]

Literary criticism on nineteenth-century American literature has sometimes posited a division between social reformers and literary authors in which the latter are seen to creatively appropriate the rhetoric of the former. In another variation, the well-meaning but deluded (or hypocritical) reformers are seen as having bought in to the period's most self-flattering assumptions, while the critic's author of choice is discovered through close reading to have penetrated the illusions the reformers peddled. While my own analyses in the chapters that follow sometimes conceptualize the literature–social reform dynamic along these lines, at other times these models of influence can seem insufficiently sensitive to historical contingency. For one thing, those writing in support of reform causes should be given more credit for rhetorical sophistication than they commonly receive. Reformers circulated sentimental stories about rehabilitated penitentiary inmates with the calculated purpose of softening public prejudice against the incarcerated, but experience among prisoners undoubtedly had its effect in complicating their perspective.[52] Furthermore, in the antebellum period no bright line can be drawn between reformer and literary author, in light of the number of authors now known primarily for literary work, including Whitman, Fuller, and Lydia Maria Child, who also wrote about prison reform as journalists.

Reformers such as Isaac Hopper, Farnham (herself the author of a well-received memoir about pioneer life in Illinois), and contributors to periodicals such as *Prisoner's Friend* surely participated in recognizable creative work when they composed (or simply recognized the value of and chose to circulate) stories about criminality that captured the public imagination and then became subject to the reprint practices of antebellum print culture. Russ Castronovo's account of memes moving through the eighteenth-century American printscape—in which he notes that memetic techniques "rely on scraps of catchy data as a sort of cultural DNA that evolves across different media"—also describes the process by which narratives about criminal justice migrated across different segments of antebellum print culture with a logic and momentum of their own.[53] Writers, editors, and publishers with complex agendas that cannot easily be pigeonholed (literary, social, commercial) were, in effect, unwitting collaborators in inventing and propagating these influential narrative patterns. Documenting this organic process of literary co-creation contributes to an ongoing scholarly project of demystifying a romantic view of individual authorship in favor of a more communal model that registers the "complex configurations of work, replication, revision, and attribution across media, including periodical and ephemeral forms such as the newspaper, magazine, and pamphlet" characteristic of nineteenth-century print culture.[54] This movement of popular narrative archetypes across a permeable boundary between social reform and literary discourses constitutes another site wherein the antebellum domains of literature and criminal justice overlapped.

A reconsideration of antebellum prison reformers seems especially timely given a charge about the racial implications of the prison reform movement that is on the verge of hardening, perhaps unfairly, into conventional wisdom. In *The Prison and the American Imagination*, Caleb Smith reminds readers of Thomas Jefferson's condescending analysis of African American character traits in *Notes on the State of Virginia* (1785) and then makes the provocative claim that prison reformers did not consider African Americans eligible for the process of rehabilitation through incarceration because they believed, following Jefferson, that people of African descent lacked the power of reflection.[55] The charge is picked up—and somewhat modified—by Jeannine Marie DeLombard in her book *In the Shadow of the Gallows*, where she suggests that only those black prisoners destined to be hanged were credited with the capacity for spiritual conversion.[56]

I readily concede the plausibility (and even the elegance) of applying Jefferson's notorious assessment of African American character to the prison reform movement, given the premium reformers undeniably placed on the capacity for solitary reflection. My reading in the literature of penal reform, however, including magazine accounts of prisoner conversions and chaplains' memoirs of their work within American penitentiaries, turned up case after case of preachers, wardens, and other officials hailing the conversions of African American prisoners who, having reflected on their guilt according to penal reform premises, had experienced a moment of conversion, repented of their crimes, and prepared themselves for reintegration with society. Chapter 6 makes reference to half a dozen cases (and more could be cited) of African American inmates credited with reform thanks to the workings of the penitentiary; in some instances, the race of the prisoners is highlighted in chapter titles announcing their successful rehabilitation. Whatever the flaws of the antebellum prison reform movement, this particular charge of racialist thinking depends on too monolithic a vision of the poetics of penal reform, one that fails to take account of the possibility of variations of belief on the part of individual reformers. Precisely because such a claim so conveniently matches critical preconceptions about hypocritical and/or misguided reformers, it must be carefully scrutinized in light of the available evidence.

Antebellum Americans cherished the idea that the administration of criminal justice was a critical indicator of a society's political and social health. In the words of Hildreth, "It might even be laid down as a general principle that the freedom or servitude of a people will mainly depend upon the sort of administration of justice which they have—especially of criminal justice." Or as the commonplace was phrased by Cooper in *The Ways of the Hour,* "Perhaps the most certain proof that any people can give of a high moral condition, is in the administration of justice."[57] Marking the point where the individual citizen encounters the coercive power of the state, the criminal justice system is an arena within American life where basic principles of governance are contested. Recognizing this area's importance as a measure of the nation's success in living up to its political ideals, American authors of the generation preceding the Civil War turned their attention to the criminal justice system at the very historical moment when its fundamental institutions were being developed or transformed and an expanding print culture stood ready to document these transformations. An investigation of the complex dynamics linking a wide variety of literary texts to this critical set of social institutions, therefore, promises to offer fresh insights into antebellum American culture.

1

"The Best Side of a Case of Crime"

George Lippard, Walt Whitman, and Antebellum Police Reports

The penny paper crime report represents a suitable starting point, insofar as it documents the moment when an individual offender comes into contact with the criminal justice system, beginning the cycle of arrest, trial, incarceration, and discharge on which this book is structured. Because the penny paper was a new feature of the publishing landscape of the 1830s, its crime reports also mark an early point of convergence between the criminal justice system and the rapidly expanding print culture of the antebellum United States. The editors of penny papers successfully sought to attract an unprecedentedly wide readership with a combination of low prices and sensationalized content, including coverage of street crime: the arrests and trials of prostitutes, thieves, and drunks. The success of penny papers gave young men with literary ambitions the chance for employment in the publishing industry as reporters and editors; the form's preoccupation with petty crime also meant that such writers often served an apprenticeship covering the local police station. In the cases of George Lippard and Walt Whitman, whose careers followed a similar trajectory from journalism to imaginative literature, this early immersion in the gritty underside of urban life was a formative experience that forced them to reflect on the social implications of representing criminality in print.

In the 1840s, both Lippard and Whitman were working journalists, Lippard writing for Philadelphia's *Spirit of the Times* and *Citizen Soldier* and Whitman for a number of publications, most notably as editor of the *Brooklyn Daily Eagle*. Both men by necessity tackled the staple commodity of the penny paper, the local police report. While critics praise both Lippard and Whitman for sympathizing in their literary work with outcast elements of society, this is a position that would have been particularly hard to reconcile with the demands of daily crime reporting. In this chapter I examine Lippard's and

Whitman's police reporting to see how they handled the form and where their journalism forecast the racially and socially progressive perspectives of their later work. Such an inquiry requires familiarity with the police report as it appeared in two of the pioneering penny papers of the period, the *New York Sun* and the *New York Herald,* since the content, purpose, and ideological import of such reporting had been firmly established by the time Lippard and Whitman came to the format.

A number of scholars have analyzed in broad terms newspaper crime reporting of the antebellum period. In Dan Schiller's account, news about crime was the arena in which penny papers staked their claim as defenders of the interests of the common man. Appropriating the rhetoric of the labor press that died out after the Panic of 1837, penny papers appealed to a wide audience of mechanics and laborers by exposing corruption in a criminal justice system weighted in favor of the social elite: "Modified and adapted, crime news in the penny press focused not only on the integrity of the state but also on the unequal effect of social class on the political nation and, specifically, in the law."[1] Schiller devotes sustained attention to coverage of the murder of the prostitute Helen Jewett. The *New York Sun* regretted the acquittal of Jewett's accused killer Richard Robinson, claiming that his wealth allowed him to purchase a favorable verdict, while *New York Herald* editor James Gordon Bennett saw revealed in the trial a conspiracy to cover up the misdeeds of the wealthy brothel patrons who set Robinson up as their fall guy. Either way, the editors wielded class-based rhetoric to impugn an anti-egalitarian legal system.[2]

Also focusing on the Jewett murder, among other cases, David Ray Papke hears in antebellum crime reporting a voice for the working and middle classes: "The crime journalism in *The Sun* and *The Herald* championed mechanics, artisans, clerks, and small merchants over the traditional landed and mercantile elites, which well into midcentury held power in the modernizing nation."[3] Adding to this consensus, Alexander Saxton observes that "crime and sex were not politically neutral" in the penny press, whose ideological origins he identifies in the urban workingmen's movement of the period.[4] Together, these commentators make a convincing case that certain kinds of sensationalized crime news allowed editors to deploy the language of artisan republicanism.[5] Alongside the occasional coverage of spectacular crimes and ensuing trials, however, the antebellum paper featured a more prosaic variety of crime news in its daily anecdotes about the activities of city police. Analyzing the daily police report, one finds a set of reportorial conventions with different ideological implications, and this was the format in which Lippard's and Whitman's commitments to defending society's least sympathetic elements would be shaped.

Penny Paper Crime Reports

When the penny paper first appeared in the United States, its coverage of local street crime distinguished it from the more expensive six-cent papers devoted to national and international events and items of commercial interest. The most important author of such reporting in the 1830s was George W. Wisner of the *New York Sun,* who (borrowing from reports of London's Bow Street Police Court in English newspapers) made police court reporting a central feature of that newspaper in 1833–34. Wisner is credited with inventing a style of police reporting in America, as described by James Stanford Bradshaw: "At times, he was sardonic; at times, facetious and, frequently, archly prurient."[6] Wisner treated readers to sensational cases of street violence, theft, public drunkenness, and other crimes, all narrated in his signature breezy and condescending tone. In one article, for instance, he notes that "Jane Dunn, an incorrigible old vagrant and rum head was ordered to the penitentiary for six months. . . . Sally Kip, a black Amazon of the Five Points was tried for petit larceny, stealing from Charles Welch, a silver watch and appendages and money, amounting to $23."[7] The humor in Wisner's reports usually came at the expense of his criminal subjects, as when he remarks that "Margaret Thomas was drunk in the street—said she never would get drunk again 'upon her honor.' Committed, 'upon honor.'"[8] One of Wisner's contemporaries, Isaac Pray, condemned the callous tone of police reporting in the *New York Transcript,* another of the penny papers that emerged in the 1830s. "The imitations of the Bow Street Reports are palatable to the public taste," he complains, "for the paper sells. Enough! That an innocent man, because he is poor and defenceless [*sic*], may be caricatured, and consigned to the infamy of a day, and even to the loss of employment, is of little consequence. The people must be amused."[9] Wisner had departed for the West by the mid-1830s, but the style of crime reporting he pioneered in the United States survived him in the pages of the *Sun*'s main competitor, Bennett's *New York Herald.*

In the early 1840s, when Lippard and Whitman both worked for daily newspapers, the *Herald* was one of the most widely read and influential penny papers in the nation. Surveying its treatment of petty crime in this period provides a benchmark by which to gauge Lippard's and Whitman's responses to established journalistic conventions. The *Herald* printed accounts of street crimes, including petty theft, assaults, prostitution, and passing of counterfeit notes, under the heading "City Intelligence," which usually appeared on the second page of the newspaper.[10] In their language and tone, the *Herald*'s "City Intelligence" columns of the early 1840s reflect Wisner's influence. The language describing criminal activity is usually direct and colloquial; the reporter operates under a presumption of guilt on the part of the perpetrators, who have for the most part been caught in the act by watchmen. Reporting on one crime, for example, the column remarks, "John Smith broke open the cellar door of Samuel Bradback, No. 55 Oliver street, by forcing off the padlock, and stole 20 pounds of butter, for which he will be tried and sent up among the others of his numerous and respectable family."[11] Mockery of individuals involved in criminal activity is common, as in this entry titled "A Lover Robbed": "A man named John McCarthy, while in the act of paying vows of love and adoration to one Mary Ann Ward, known as the Queen of Walnut street, commonly termed 'the Hook,' had his pockets relieved of $16,50. Officer King took the Queen in custody, and had her committed to answer."[12] The purported humor in this report derives from the humiliation of both parties involved, the hapless McCarthy and the prostitute who robs him, identified by their full names. The brevity and satirical tone of these reports offered little room for the editorial crusading on behalf of the mechanic class that commentators have noted in other facets of penny paper crime treatment.

The "City Intelligence" reports in the *Herald* reflect the racial and social hierarchies that structured antebellum life in the United States. As Hans Bergmann describes the reportorial persona that Wisner originated, "The police court reporter takes it upon himself to see what is going on among the immigrant classes and presents the results of his encounter with the (initially) inexplicable and unrecognizable 'other.'"[13] Stereotypes associated with particular immigrant communities provided reporters with obvious sources of race-based humor and offered ways of sorting ethnic others, diminishing their threat to a narrowly defined (and shifting) category of whiteness. The headline "A Jew Jewed" prefaces a story about a Jewish merchant on whom silver-plated merchandise is passed off as the real thing, with the reporter marveling at "the ingenious rogue who could cheat a Jew."[14] An anecdote involving P. T. Barnum sums up widespread suspicion of New York's immigrant Irish community. When Barnum observes "an Irish girl of suspicious character in his establishment," he arrests and searches her, finding that she is indeed a pickpocket preying on his patrons.[15] An underlying anxiety about the presence of immigrant servants in middle-class households is betrayed in two adjacent reports from a single day in 1842, when an Irish woman who had been employed as "a domestic" and a "German servant girl" are arrested in separate cases of theft.[16]

The *Herald* reserved its most condescending language for African American criminals. Himself an immigrant from Scotland, Bennett had no particular investment in antagonizing the Irish or German communities. As a supporter of slavery and purveyor of racist sentiment, however, he missed no opportunity to emphasize the supposed criminality of blacks. The race of African American perpetrators was not only identified in reports but also trumpeted in headlines such as "Colored Burglar Caught" or "Negro Gambling Cellar Broken Up."[17] Carol Stabile has noted how the *Herald* and its competitors differentially treated immigrant and black criminals: "While the penny papers often represented the Irish in broad stereotypical strokes . . . [they] were not singled out for the specific vitriol and hatred reserved for blacks."[18] Bennett railed against abolitionists, whom he described as "amalgamationists" whose ostensible goal was to promote interracial marriages. Indeed, among all the petty crimes the *Herald* covered, the failure to observe racial boundaries may have been the transgression that Bennett most aggressively policed.

The *Herald*'s "City Intelligence" reports publicly shamed whites, particularly immigrants, who crossed the color line in pursuit of sexual indulgence. These reports invariably inspired Bennett's most vicious racial invective. Under the sub-headline "Amalgamation," one report vilifies "Susan Thompson, one of the ugliest specimens of Africa's daughters extant," for picking an unnamed Irishman's pocket during a sexual encounter. Although "the Irishman got ashamed of his conduct at the police, and sloped away without making a complaint," the paper nonetheless found the violation of a taboo against interracial sex newsworthy.[19] In a similar case, "a well dressed and tight built sprig of Shillelah" was arrested for patronizing a black prostitute, "one of the flattest nosed, crooked legged, curly haired, blubber lipped, and aromatic wenches that the police has been honored with for ages past."[20] The next day's *Herald* finds another Irish immigrant, Armstrong Riley, "in the arms of one of Afric's descendants, whose perfume would have extinguished that of the musk in strength and vigor."[21] The venomous tone of these reports can be ascribed to a punitive impulse on Bennett's part: he seeks to punish the presumptuousness of African American women who consort with whites as well as the heedlessness of Irish immigrant men who would jeopardize their own (tenuous) whiteness through liaisons across the color line.[22]

The telling headline "Amalgamation Exposed" downplays prostitution and theft, staple crimes of "City Intelligence" reportage, in order to highlight the presumably more scandalous aspect of this encounter, once again its interracial sexuality: "A spruce, greasy looking, square sterned negro wench, named Josephine Emry, was summoned to attend at the police yesterday, to answer the charge of James Meehan, who had been hugging the dark Josephine to his longing arms, while she with fingers light was relieving his pockets of their content, amounting to $13,50 in specie. She was fully committed."[23] The *Herald* reports consistently aim to titillate and horrify readers with stories that combine criminal behavior with the spectacle of interracial sex. A black transvestite shares column space with Josephine Emry on New Year's Day 1842: "Pete was dressed about half male, the other female, and his voice, movements and action were most perfect imitations of a shy young she darkey." The report goes on to note that Pete had plied his trade for some years, inducing men "to test the peculiarity of amalgamation by his persuasive powers, and when the retaining fee was obtained, Pete would hoist petticoats, show his breeches, and run. He was committed." This piece appears under the subheading "A Cunning Darkey in the Dark." Pete Smalley (or Sewally) reappears in the *Herald* a couple of months later with the reporter cataloging his "waddling, mincing gait" and other feminine characteristics before condemning him as a "beast in the shape of a man."[24] The fixation of the *Herald* police reports on prostitution, racial mixing, and (in Smalley's case) nonconformity with traditional gender roles is consistent with what has been documented in the "flash press" of precisely the same era.[25] In dealing with the racial composition of the American urban scene, the police reports of the period tended toward either condescending humor or, in regard to African American subjects, undisguised contempt. These expectations for the format posed a challenge for any subsequent reporter inclined toward a more sensitive or less stereotypical portrayal of minority lawbreakers.

The *Herald* reporter announces each criminal's detention with a casual tone, often employing a terse "he (or she) was committed." This nonchalance obscures the squalid, inhumane conditions of the overnight jail. During his 1842 visit to the United States (which was widely covered in the penny press), Charles Dickens visited such a holding cell in New York, telling the jailer that "such indecent and disgusting dungeons as these cells, would bring disgrace upon the most despotic empire in the world!"[26] To the "City Intelligence" reporter, however, the condition of the overnight jail was irrelevant. It was the bracketing off of such conditions from the attention of readers that gave these reports their punchy tone; an analysis of the shortcomings of the criminal justice system would have spoiled the fun. With the offender's guilt ostensibly not in question, the implication of most reports is that the criminal got what was coming to him or her, however bleak a fate it might prove to be, as evident in this report: "A woman named Mary Brown alias Riley, was committed to the city prison on Thursday, charged with committing an aggravated assault and battery on a little girl named Mary Ann Webster. . . . Yesterday morning, Brown was attacked with delirium tremens, and died within a few hours. Such is the result of crime."[27] Though the moral of these capsule narratives was rarely stated so baldly, the message of moral turpitude justly punished would have been clear enough to readers.

The "City Intelligence" column in the *Herald* was distinguished from the less sensational court reporting, which was titled after the court in question (Court of Common Pleas or General Sessions) and usually included a recital of the facts in the case and the jury verdict, without much levity or comment. Regular newspaper readers saw perpetrators cycle through the criminal justice system as the individual initially described in a "City Intelligence" anecdote would be tried, convicted, and then sentenced a day or two later in a court session.[28] An understanding of criminality was implicit in the anecdotal format of the "City Intelligence" report: crimes are individual actions perpetrated by depraved and feckless people, often immigrants or people of color, whose misfortunes are a suitable subject for the reader's entertainment. "City Intelligence" reports abstracted crime from surrounding social conditions (such as urbanization, immigration, racism, and the transformation of the labor market), presenting the criminals—whose guilt was rarely in question—as meriting only the reporter's and reader's contempt. The title of the "City Intelligence" column conveys an aura of certitude about the extent of criminal behavior in the city, a message that was probably comforting, given the social unrest of the period. This reassuring narrative of criminality exposed and punished would be destabilized to some extent by the city-mysteries novels of the mid-1840s, of which *The Quaker City* (1845) by George Lippard was one of the earliest and most prominent examples. Before Lippard became a novelist, though, he put in his time on the police beat, where he alternately observed and subverted the conventions of the police report, opening a space for new ways to conceive and write about criminality in the United States.

Expanding the Definition of Crime:
Lippard and *Spirit of the Times*

Writing for Philadelphia's *Spirit of the Times* in the first quarter of 1842, Lippard authored that paper's column devoted to police reporting, titled "City News" or, more frequently, "City Police." The columns reflect a writer who understands the conventions of the genre but also strains to expand them. Lippard sometimes affects a Wisnerian pose of slangy, knowing condescension: "*Clarissa Williams* and *Matilda Anderson,* kicked up a row, and broke the peace into a number of pieces, on Friday night. Frail ones, they were sent down below," or "*Ann Jane Billing Augustus,* (one individual), a yellow gal, kicked up a breeze in Mary street, on Saturday evening. Did some swearing, and was otherwise eloquent. Bound over."[29]

Like his counterpart at the *Herald,* Lippard shows little interest in the post-arrest fate of those taken into custody; his reporting reaches its endpoint with the phrase "bound over" or "sent below." At times, Lippard indulges in the racial stereotyping and mockery that were characteristic of police reports. One story suggests that Lippard may have had his eye on the *New York Herald;* at least he shared its interest in the subject of interracial sex, singling out for notice the arrest of a black prostitute: "*Ann Haines,* an ebon beauty, was making love to ivory faces, in the neighborhood of Washington Square. Sent to the castle."[30] In another report, Lippard's persona attempts to create humor by applying the language of sentimental romance to African Americans: "As for my heroine, take Nancy Phillips, a stout female negro, composed of a tattered cloak, check handkerchief, headdress and copper kettle face. The villain of my story is Jo Robinson, a long bandy-legged mulatto, of refined manners and dashing appearance. He obtained the rich treasure of kind-hearted Nancy's affection, and deserted her for another sable goddess."[31] To modern admirers of Lippard's novels, one of whom has praised them as "distinguished among nineteenth-century American literature for their racial sympathy," such reports look like depressingly conventional exercises in racial stereotyping.[32] Criminals (especially racial minorities) are belittled; neither their motivations nor the social context in which their crimes take place is considered by the court reporter.

Lippard's crime reporting takes a dramatic turn in the March 19, 1842, issue of *Spirit of the Times,* under the unusually imperative subhead "You'd Better Read It." The offender, a homeless man named Jacob Achan, had illegally slept in a market stall belonging to the city. Instead of mocking Achan, Lippard sentimentalizes him, describing him as "an old man with tattered rags for clothes, a bald head, and grey hairs, as marks of age, and a heart wrung and withered by misery and distress." Lippard notes that Jacob (now referred to by his first name) had not eaten in twenty-four hours when he crept into the market stall to sleep. Then Lippard launches into an editorial on relative degrees of criminality in the urban setting:

> Had Jacob been director of a bank, had he beggared thousands, and ruined a whole community, had he been a hypocritical divine or a bargaining, buying, selling, and breaking merchant, these all might have been passed as "very forgive-able sins," but that he was poor, that he had slept on a market stall belonging to the corporation—these were sins not to be forgiven, and Jacob was arrested by a watchman—eager for his "quarter."[33]

This report may be regarded as an innovation in the genre of the police report, and even a self-reflective comment on its limitations. Lippard goes back in time, beyond the moment of the criminal's apprehension, where such reports usually begin, to Achan's preceding twenty-four hours of hunger and, by reference to the subject's age, poverty, and misery, to a much longer period of indigence and suffering that led to the crime. Without denying Achan's guilt, Lippard redirects readers' attention to the extenuating circumstances within which his actions should be understood. By contrasting Achan's crime with those of bank directors, "pettifoggers," office seekers, and ministers, Lippard reminds readers of the wider social context that was normally obscured by the anecdotal format of the police report. The soap-boxing here is consistent with the editorial outlook of *Spirit of the Times,* which Schiller describes as "a consistently radical journal."[34] Lippard's notable innovation is to see the potential for radical political commentary in a reportorial genre that normally embodied a reactionary outlook.

Lippard's reference to bank directors and other highly placed criminals seems designed to point readers toward a series of compositions that appeared simultaneously in *Spirit of the Times* with his police reports. In January and February 1842, Lippard penned a series titled "Our Talisman." The nine articles relate the adventures of a young reporter nicknamed "Flib" who discovers a ring (the talisman) that makes him invisible and permits him to read the thoughts of those around him. The second article in the series is the most interesting. The invisible Flib observes the Court of General Sessions, which seems an odd choice on Lippard's part since the proceedings were open to the public anyway. The first prisoner is a mixed-race ("mulatto") man convicted of petty larceny for stealing a toy box worth twenty-five cents (the insignificant amount is emphasized in the report). In contrast to the attitude toward African Americans normally displayed in police and court reporting, this article's narrator disapproves of the judge for making a joke at the defendant's expense: "Everybody seemed to think it the most pleasurable thing in the world, to make the most fun out of the fellow who could so atrociously commit so deliberate a crime." Flib goes on to condemn the severity of the judge's sentence: "With great lenity the Court . . . sentenced the prisoner to six months imprisonment in Moyamensing. . . . He will come out of prison with a good principle implanted in his head, viz.—never again to steal a paltry toy, but—following illustrious examples—to . . . abstract the funds of any particular bank, whether the property of widows, orphans, or any body else."[35]

Pointedly putting his invisible observer in a courtroom setting, Lippard establishes a relationship between his aims in the "Our Talisman" series and the "City Police" reports that appeared alongside them. Lippard removes the temporal brackets that normally attend the courtroom anecdote, looking forward to the impact of this unjust sentence on the defendant's future. The rest of the "Our Talisman" articles continue in this vein, exposing the crimes that by their nature escape the notice of police as Lippard shows the concept of criminality spilling over the boundaries in which the "City Police" report normally confined it. With its sympathetic treatment of a mixed-race criminal, this article looks forward to those moments in Lippard's city-mysteries novels where he envisions a cross-racial solidarity that "complicates the prevailing assumptions about the reactionary racial politics of the city-mystery genre."[36]

Through Flib's reports, Lippard offers a systematic inventory of Philadelphia's social institutions and the oppression visited upon the city's most vulnerable citizens. Subsequent articles in the "Our Talisman" series carry Lippard's activist journalism out of the courts into other areas of life where the talisman device is more logically employed. Flib watches a corrupt postmaster unjustly arrange the firing of a virtuous young clerk so that he can hire his own relations, as Lippard attacks abuses of political patronage.[37] At a theater, Flib observes the manager attempt to cheat musicians and carpenters out of their wages. The members of the orchestra threaten a strike, and the manager relents; in contrast, a poor young actress (with a child starving at home, for greater sentimental effect) has no such leverage upon the manager and is turned away with nothing.[38] In a dry goods store, the proprietors swindle customers with a misleading sign in the front window; one victim is an honest German farmer, whose dialect is recorded ("Tats de way dey cheated me") but not for the purposes of mockery, since the farmer is a justly aggrieved victim.[39] Lippard devotes three articles in the "Our Talisman" series to secret meetings of bank directors, who conspire to discount notes and defraud their customers.[40] The implicit message of these pieces is that socially responsible journalism does not limit exposure of moral turpitude to daily police and court reports. The series therefore shows *Spirit of the Times* engaging in the artisan republican critique of the criminal justice system that Schiller, Papke, and Saxton find characteristic of antebellum penny papers.

Writing police reports for *Spirit of the Times* gave Lippard a valuable opportunity to experiment with perspectives on the subject of criminality. A widened point of view that simultaneously exposed the corruption of the rich while impugning the criminal justice system for its treatment of the poor translated easily into the city-mysteries novel, which routinely traded in class-based animosity. In *The Quaker City*, the character Luke Harvey voices such sentiments quite explicitly: "Justice and in the Quaker City! . . . One moment it unbolts the doors of the prison, and bids the Bank-Director . . . go forth! The next moment it bolts and seals those very prison doors, upon the poor devil, who has stolen a loaf of bread to save himself from starvation!"[41] Lippard's later career reveals ongoing interest in the distortions and injustices promoted by the press in its sensationalized approach to crime reporting. At one point in his novel *The Empire City* (1850) Lippard pauses, not to castigate the criminal justice system itself but to fault the flash press for publicizing the name of an innocent man reputed to be a criminal: "The foulest sheets of the great cities, had made [the name] a word of loathing; the obscene libel of a Sunday, which is freshly coined and scattered ere it is dry, to the homes of the Empire City on the Sabbath Day, had coupled it with a dingy wood engraving."[42] Once an individual's identity as a criminal is fixed in the mind of the community by the press (the identification is made doubly powerful here by pairing a name with a face), the impression can be difficult to dislodge. Lippard's awareness of the complicity of the press in dehumanizing those accused (sometimes wrongly) of criminal behavior no doubt traces its roots to his newspaper work of the early 1840s.

The insight Lippard acquired as a crime reporter into the implications of representing criminality in the press also contributed to an innovative technique characteristic of his later literary writing. Lippard frequently introduces a character as a criminal, only to reveal later the figure's complicated history and remaining capacity for kindness, sympathy, or nobility. Whereas police and court reporting tended to define and fix a wrongdoer's identity as a criminal, Lippard insists in his fiction that criminal actions should not permanently define an individual and must be understood within a wider social context. The best-known example may be Devil-Bug from *The Quaker City*, who initially appears before readers as the depraved, physically grotesque, murderous doorkeeper of Philadelphia's den of crime, Monk Hall. Lippard waits several chapters before presenting Devil-Bug's backstory, which includes his birth in a brothel, and coming of age as an orphan there, an experience that deprived of him of conventional moral guidance. Still later in the novel, Devil-Bug performs selfless acts on behalf of his daughter and experiences a (temporary) religious conversion: "For a moment the soul of Devil-Bug was beautiful."[43] As David S. Reynolds describes Devil-Bug, "He at first appears to be thoroughly degraded but in the course of the novel becomes a remorseful figure who is actually capable of doing good."[44]

The pattern can also be observed in Lippard's 1846 novel *The Nazarene*, in which a minor character is initially introduced emphatically as a "DIS-CHARGED CONVICT" eager for employment in criminal activity.[45] But when given a chance to speak, the convict reveals that he was an orphan, driven to crime by starvation and sent to prison by the novel's villain, who also defrauded him of the education he was entitled to receive at philanthropist Stephen Girard's college. The characterization of John Hoffman / Number Ninety-One of Lippard's novel *The Empire City* also exemplifies this technique, insofar as he is initially introduced to readers as a discharged convict scheming to steal a valise full of money, but later recounts how he was framed for a crime he did not commit. His turn to a life of crime is explained by resentment against society born of the torture he experienced in prison as well as by the fact that no honest employment is available to discharged convicts.[46] The point is not merely that Lippard shows that criminals are human and deserve the reader's sympathy, but that his particular style of first introducing a criminal character and then complicating or humanizing him (or her) subverts the one-dimensional portrait of criminals that Lippard observed and came to deplore in his early career as a crime reporter.

Framing Crime in a Broader Social Context: Whitman and the *Daily Eagle*

Lippard was not the only thoughtful young newspaper reporter of the 1840s confronted with the problem of reconciling the genre of the daily police report with a socially responsible approach to writing about criminality. Editing the *Brooklyn Daily Eagle and Kings County Democrat* (hereafter *Brooklyn Daily Eagle,* or simply *Eagle*) in the period 1846–1848, Walt Whitman devoted a column to local news variously titled "City Intelligence" or "Local Intelligence." He included all kinds of local news in this column—accounts of lectures and sermons, lobbying for city parks, descriptions of picturesque locales in the city, weekly accounts of Sunday church services, and so on—while also tracking incidents of crime in Brooklyn on an almost daily basis. In the 1855 *Leaves of Grass,* Whitman's persona explicitly renounces the belittling mockery of the downtrodden characteristic of police reporting: "The prostitute draggles her shawl, her bonnet bobs on her tipsy and pimpled neck, / The crowd laugh at her blackguard oaths, the men jeer and wink to each other, / (Miserable! I do not laugh at your oaths nor jeer you)."[47]

But editing a daily newspaper did not nurture the compassion modeled by Whitman's later poetic voice, as suggested by the *Eagle*'s description of a prostitute removed by city authorities along with her child from a "den of filth and impurity at Red Hook Point near the old Powder House" and taken to the poorhouse; Whitman calls the woman "a most disgusting specimen of humanity."[48] According to Thomas Brasher, Whitman "frequently wrote in the accepted Wisner tradition when he prepared his daily report on what he had seen and heard during his morning visit to the Brooklyn police court."[49] Brasher cites as evidence Whitman's callous mockery of an elderly man picked up for public drunkenness: "Andrew Ryan, an aged subject of Alcoholic Rex . . . was last night taken in charge by a watchman. When brought to the police office he formed the most perfect specimen of perpetual motion ever seen in these demesnes, being afflicted with a shaking that would have done credit to a western ague."[50] Another example cited by Brasher shows Whitman, like his colleague Lippard, applying literary diction to the plight of a black woman, ostensibly finding humor in the imputation of chastity to her:

> The police office was darkened by a large assemblage of the Ethiopian race, who were attracted thither by an investigation into a charge of affiliation,

preferred against a young and "likely" mulatto, named Robert Brinkerhoff, by a wrinkled colored miss, aged about forty-five, named Martha Hicks—a widow, and the mother of just one dozen young black Hickses. She alleged that Robert had overcome her virgin purity, by virtue of a promise of marriage.[51]

This report conspicuously lacks the empathy characteristic of Whitman's poetic persona, even as it recalls similar attempts at humor at the expense of African American women in the *New York Herald* and *Spirit of the Times*.

Despite the occasional glaring example to the contrary, however, Whitman's police entries in his "City Intelligence" columns are noteworthy for their relative impartiality. Indeed, Whitman states explicitly in one column his philosophy on reportage of crime: "As a general thing, we are disposed to give the best side of a case of crime—and shall always hold that plan."[52] After reporting a litany of violent crime that includes a riot, dog fighting, and wife beating on a September Sunday, Whitman's tone is apologetic: "We regret for the credit of Brooklyn to be obliged to record such transactions." He goes on to defend such reporting, however, reasoning that "in order to be prevented, such scenes must be known, and we are convinced that if known and the public feeling excited generally against them, the authorities will guard against their recurrence."[53] Although this explanation was frequently employed by journalists whose true intent was titillation, Whitman appears to have been sincere. In his crime reports for the *Eagle*, Whitman often challenged readers' expectations for the lurid and the risible.

While the case of Martha Hicks shows Whitman crudely exploiting racial stereotypes for laughs, the preponderance of evidence suggests that he rarely engaged in the gratuitously racist commentary that was standard fare in other papers' police reports. Brasher's claim that Whitman's police reports depicted the free blacks of Brooklyn "as if they were performing in an eternal minstrel show" is at least unduly harsh, if not simply inaccurate.[54] Following conventions that were ubiquitous in the era's journalism, Whitman usually—but not always—noted the race of African American perpetrators. He customarily did so, however, without resort to the sensationalism or humiliation that characterized other papers, often merely noting, as he does here, "a black fellow": "A black fellow named Henry Moore was arrested on Saturday evening by officer Felt, while endeavoring to sell to a grocer in this city a number of hams, which, it was suspected, he had purloined in New York." In fact, in a follow-up report on the crimes of Moore two days later, Whitman omitted mention of his race altogether.[55]

Such occasional (and perhaps pointed) omissions were unusual for the period. Whitman reported that Benjamin Bailey was "colored," putting the word in parentheses, when the man was convicted of assault; the subsequent report on Bailey's sentencing omitted mention of his race altogether.[56] When police charged one John Sampson with burglary, Whitman avoided an ethnic or racial identifier while opining that "the proof against him is very slight." Readers of the *Eagle* learned that Sampson was African American only in the following day's edition, when Whitman noted that a "colored man named Sampson was examined upon and discharged from accusation of having committed a burglary at the carpenter shop of Mr. Herbert."[57] A rape committed by a black man against a white woman in New York garnered the sensational heading "Infernal Outrage!" in one edition of the *Eagle*. But in another instance, a fifty-year-old white perpetrator was arrested by police after having attempted, in Whitman's words, "one of the most disgraceful outrages that a man of his advanced age could be engaged in. The charge against him is an attempt to violate the person of his son's wife!"[58] In other words, Whitman's indignation in regard to rape was not predicated solely or primarily on the races of the perpetrator and victim. Unlike both the *Herald*'s police reporter and Lippard, Whitman betrayed no especially prurient interest in interracial sexual liaisons.[59] Whitman's apparent aversion to race-baiting may have been related to his growing support of free soil politics, a position that eventually cost him his job as the *Eagle*'s editor.[60]

Whitman's attempts at humor usually occurred in cases where the offense did not involve grave injury. Minor property crimes and cases of indecent exposure sometimes elicited a light touch. A fight between two couples commenced, according to Whitman, with "the malicious trespass on the part of some chickens, and ended in Charles getting his cranium considerably cracked, and the whole party bound over to the Oyer and Terminer."[61] Amused by one offender's alias, Whitman notes that a man "who rejoices in the very remarkable name of John Smith (!) yesterday fell into the toils of police, charged with having exposed himself and grossly insulted some ladies on Monday morning, at eight o'clock in Adams street."[62] The humor in one report arises from the perpetrator, "a derelict black fellow," who had stolen a gun and then repaired to the theater, being "greatly incensed because the officer insisted upon locking him up before he had time to finish his theatrical enjoyment!"[63] Whitman also favored readers with his account of a "decently dressed young Irish woman" arrested for stealing shoes, who "was seized with a sudden fit of lethean abstraction in regard to her cognomen, and stated to the magistrates that it was Donley; but, after some calm reflection on the matter, recollected that it was Quinn."[64] Whereas police reporting in other sources poked fun in a malicious spirit at the outcast and indigent, inviting readers to share an attitude of contempt, Whitman's humorous asides are usually better characterized as amused or gently ironic; he retains the purpose of entertainment without, for the most part, indulging in mockery.

The decently dressed young Irish shoplifter was not Whitman's only engagement with the intersection of crime and ethnicity in the *Eagle*. Though Irish and German perpetrators occasionally appear in the *Eagle* crime reports, Whitman usually chooses neither to emphasize nor to stereotype their ethnicity.[65] Whitman's Democratic political sympathies provide the explanatory context for his editorial restraint. Because Whitman associated nativist sentiment with his Whig political opponents, he defended and sentimentalized Brooklyn's immigrants, especially its Irish population, in "City Intelligence" reports. One "Local Intelligence" column laments the death of an Irish laborer who suffered an epileptic fit before dying of heat exposure. The headline is "Death of a Stranger," and Whitman describes the man, Richard Butler, as "a sober and industrious man."[66] For a few days, Whitman followed the case of an Irish immigrant who arrived in Brooklyn suffering from smallpox. His sister, who had immigrated previously, discovered him in the street and took care of him in what Whitman regarded as "a shining example of *real* affection."[67] Whitman also covered a labor dispute in which German workers replaced a group of Irish dockworkers who had struck for higher wages. In the midst of this dispute (which eventually inspired violent attacks by the Irish on their German replacements), Whitman defended workingmen's rights to a decent wage and the contributions of recent immigrants to American prosperity, including "the noble German, the warm-hearted Irish."[68]

The one cohort of criminals that Whitman's "City Intelligence" column consistently belittled were people arrested for public drunkenness. One column begins with Whitman's observation that the "police office this morning was filled with the scrapings of yesterday in the shape of drunken vagrants." He often used similarly contemptuous language for these lawbreakers, on one occasion referring to "that most loathsome of all human creatures—an inebriated woman."[69] Such women merited particular scorn:

> Two "speciments" [*sic*] of the drunken vagrant school of philosophy, named Catherine Cross . . . and Ellen Old . . . were yesterday placed in a position where they will be obliged for the next sixty days to forego their usual indulgences, unless they can devise some method of chemically coaxing their spiritual potations from the texture of the granite from which the Kings county jail is built.[70]

Even in this area, though, Whitman occasionally adopted a tone that shaded from neutral to sympathetic. The report mocking an elderly man suffering from the DTs might be countered with a report subheaded "Shocking Death":

> A [*sic*] Englishman named James Black died in the county jail yesterday afternoon of delirium tremens. He and his wife were committed to jail on

Tuesday for drunkenness for the last two months, and were confined in adjoining cells. When the man died she was not informed of the event; and remained within two feet of his corpse, totally unconscious of the fact. We can scarcely conceive of a more pitiable object.[71]

Whitman took a moderately pro-temperance stand in the *Eagle,* serializing an abridged version of his temperance novel *Franklin Evans* in November 1846.[72] He responded with particular enthusiasm to the Washingtonian version of temperance reform, attracted by its working-class affiliations.[73] To the extent that Whitman's support of the temperance movement was ideologically motivated (Washingtonian orators testified in detail to the ravages drunkenness wrought on working-class families in particular), his disdain for alcoholics is explicable, perhaps, because they failed to match his vision of a sober, and therefore empowered, laboring class. Similarly, Whitman in this period endorsed a comparatively progressive but still heavily idealized notion of femininity, which the intemperate women of Brooklyn, in his view, failed to exemplify.

In a notable departure from "City Intelligence" conventions, Whitman regularly used the column to educate readers about the plight of the unfortunate, including the incarcerated. Like Lippard, Whitman sometimes removed the brackets from the "City Intelligence" anecdotes, carrying the narrative of criminality beyond its normal temporal boundaries. Whereas Lippard had directed readers to consider the backstory of a man arrested for sleeping in the streets, Whitman encouraged readers to think about the situation of criminals after the moment of arrest. He reports, to cite one example, on the "melancholy suicide" of an inmate at Sing Sing who had been convicted in Kings County. The "young man named Pierce," according to Whitman, was so disturbed by a false report of his father's death that he hanged himself.[74] In a "City Intelligence" column from April 1846 (under the subheading "Poor Prisoners"), Whitman decries a recent act of the state legislature forbidding authorities from continuing to reimburse witnesses for the expense of testifying on behalf of poor prisoners, calling it "an act to proscribe the administration of justice."[75] In a brief article titled "Prisons" (which did not appear in the day's "City Intelligence" column but was on the same page, two columns over), Whitman labels as disgraceful "the cool-blooded cruelty of many of the prison regulations of the day," calls flogging a "method of torture," and complains, "Still is the remnant (little enough in some) of humanity left in the wretched convicts there, crushed out of them—systematically, as it seems!"[76] He objected frequently in the pages of the *Eagle* to capital punishment, calling it "a relic of barbarism which every civilized community should think it their duty to destroy."[77] The "City Intelligence" column of August 11, 1846 leads off with a story on "Prison Statistics," wherein Whitman details conditions in the Kings County Jail in anticipation of a state inspection: "The committee will have very little fault to find with the physical condition of the Kings county jail, for we do not think it can be surpassed in its incidents of cleanliness, ventilation, &c. by any prison in the country."[78] Whitman was hardly an advocate of coddling criminals—he believed that some transgressors were loafers who wanted to be supported by the state through the winter, and he advocated shooting home invaders—but he had little patience with editors who attacked prison reform as "mawkish sympathy."[79]

Whitman's concern for the well-being of prisoners was part of a larger cultural conversation regarding the methods and purposes of incarceration. In November 1846, Whitman approvingly noted U.S. publication of the book *Rationale of Crime,* written by the English journalist and phrenology popularizer Marmaduke B. Sampson. The assumption of phrenology that an individual's criminal behavior sprang from an inherited malformation of the brain (combined with the influence of an unwholesome environment) radically diminished wrongdoers' accountability for their actions. Sampson believed that the behavioral tendencies derived from these heritable traits could be overcome with appropriate treatment in a "moral hospital," thereby preparing the criminal for a return to society.[80] In his notice in the *Eagle,* Whitman "earnestly call[s] attention to this work," describing Sampson's "high, philosophic, *Christian* inquiry into the motives and ways of crime" as "worthy of the age!"[81] Shortly after taking over the *Eagle,* Whitman charged state prison officials with unnecessary brutality following the whipping death of a prisoner. He believed that too many prison guards were "persons of hardened and morose natures, disposed to judge harshly and punish severely—the last men in the world, it seems to us, for the position they hold."[82] Whitman repeatedly praised the efforts of Eliza W. Farnham, matron of the women's prison at Sing Sing in upstate New York and an advocate of improved prison conditions. (Farnham wrote an introduction and notes for the U.S. edition of *Rationale of Crime.*) After noting that he was "not surprised at the flippant opposition made to 'moral suasion'" when it came to convicted criminals, Whitman reflects, "It is indeed a difficult matter to exercise that forbearance which is due to [inmates], on account of their unhappy early training, their neglected moral nature, and perhaps many extenuating circumstances connected with their very guilt." Summarizing from a letter Farnham published in another newspaper, Whitman approvingly notes the cases of two convicts, a man and a young black woman, whose exposure to a gentler model of incarceration inspired emotional expressions of penitence.[83]

Whitman's concern for prisoners was not unique among New York journalists in the 1840s. In Horace Greeley's *Tribune,* Margaret Fuller wrote moving articles on the need for prison reform, describing prison conditions and arguing for the rehabilitative function of incarceration. But Fuller was not also responsible for a daily police report. Sharing prison reformers' belief in the potential for criminals to be rehabilitated, Whitman thoughtfully modulated the simplistic law-and-order perspective that "City Intelligence" columns normally purveyed. Though he sometimes jeered at criminals for the entertainment of readers, Whitman did not endorse the implication that an antisocial act entailed an irrevocable sacrifice of the perpetrator's claims to humanity.

The longer Whitman edited the *Eagle,* the less interest he showed in mocking the criminals on whom he continued to report. Perhaps, over time, Whitman came to doubt whether there was either public benefit or entertainment value in the exploits of petty criminals, as more than one column from late 1847 (nearly two years into Whitman's employment with the *Eagle*) includes a statement similar to this one: "There was nothing at the police or coroner's office yesterday to which the slightest degree of public interest could be attached."[84] Whereas the *Herald*'s reports started from a presumption of guilt, Whitman increasingly reported on court and police cases that belied this premise, finding that a prisoner's guilt "was very questionable on the merits of the case" or, in the case of a break-in at an unoccupied store, "It is supposed the prisoner had no criminal intent."[85] A man arrested for disorderly conduct, Whitman notes disapprovingly, was "severely treated by the watchman who took him from the sixth ward watch-house to the cells," the evidence for which was a bad cut on the head and bruises so painful that "he could hardly support himself."[86] When the Kings County Court discharged Charles Van Antwerp after having falsely implicated him in a forgery case in November 1847, Whitman called on other area newspapers to "do an act of justice to this young man by making a statement of his honorable acquittal."[87] While Whitman never entirely abandoned the condescension characteristic of the genre, the most cynical instances of this attitude tend to come from earlier in his editorial tenure, suggesting a gradual shift toward a compassionate view of even the city's least sympathetic residents.

The "City Intelligence" column as practiced by Whitman often outlined the importance of social institutions that dealt with the indigent. Whitman devoted columns of June 1 and 3, 1846, to describing conditions in the Kings County Poor House and Kings County Lunatic Asylum. He praises the almshouse as "a shining exception in its means of extending rational and Christian treatment to those who are obliged to quaff deeply of the bitter cup of sickness and poverty," assuring readers that it is maintained "at a comparatively moderate cost to the community."[88] Of the county's public lunatic asylum, Whitman approvingly notes that "every device which modern improvement can suggest has been employed to enhance the comfort and promote the health of these unfortunate persons."[89] Later in the month, he offered readers a history and description of Brooklyn's Orphan Asylum, adding that "this institution has, we regret to say, *no endowment,* and is entirely dependent upon annual subscriptions and donations."[90] Whitman called attention to a meeting of the Brooklyn Association for Aiding the Poor in one "City Intelligence" column, referring to "the good which this excellent and praiseworthy society has wrought" and hoping that it "would receive the aid which it merits" from benefactors.[91] Later in the same year, he supported an alderman's proposal for Free Night Schools in the belief that idleness among the city's young men was "the great source of vice, crime, and misery in great cities."[92]

The "City Intelligence" police anecdotes characteristically tracked the criminal actions of isolated individuals; Whitman included alongside these narratives a broader social vision. By promoting communal efforts to improve the quality of life in Brooklyn, even among the city's most destitute, he did not permit his readers the luxury of mere spectatorship when it came to social problems. After a rash of burglaries, Whitman used the "Local Intelligence" column to argue on behalf of a remodeling of the police system. Anticipating the objections of "our citizens who are already loud in their complaints of the large amount of taxes which they are at present obliged to pay," Whitman asserts that "we cannot have the services of an efficient number of watchmen unless they are well paid for it."[93] Readers of the *Brooklyn Daily Eagle* under Whitman's editorship may have been occasionally diverted with the misdeeds of rogues, but they were also asked to cultivate a sense of civic responsibility for dealing with problems of crime, poverty, and homelessness.

The 1855 edition of *Leaves of Grass,* published seven years after he left the *Eagle,* shows Whitman continuing to entertain questions that, as an editor, he had often faced: What is the significance of criminal behavior, and how should it be represented? Several poems in the volume feature images of exactly the varieties of crime most often represented in "City Intelligence" columns: thievery, prostitution, and drunkenness. The persona in *Leaves* endorses unconditional empathy with those who engage in these behaviors as the ultimate measure of his all-embracing love of humanity. From the poem later titled "Song of Myself" come these lines: "I become any presence or truth of humanity here / And see myself in prison shaped like another man, / And feel the dull unintermitted pain . . . / Not a youngster is taken for larceny, but I go up too and am tried and sentenced." Elsewhere in the poem the poet famously gives voice to the socially marginalized, including thieves and prostitutes: "Through me many long dumb voices, . . . / Voices of prostitutes and of deformed persons, / Voices of the diseased and despairing, and of thieves and dwarfs, . . . / Voices indecent by me clarified and transfigured." In the next poem the speaker asks, "Because you . . . was once drunk, or a thief, or diseased, or rheumatic, or a prostitute . . . do you give in that you are any less immortal?" Throughout the volume, the persona refrains from affixing a person's identity on the basis of criminal behavior. Instead, the poem envisions the formerly criminal in a redemptive light: "The insulter, the prostitute, the angry person, the beggar, / . . . They are not vile any more. . . . they hardly know themselves, they are so grown."[94] As he did in the *Eagle,* but more insistently, Whitman reminds readers to consider the humanity of those who commit crimes.

Bridging the presumed gulf between criminals and those who read about their actions in *Leaves of Grass,* Whitman removes the elements of sensationalism, voyeurism, and humiliation that often characterized narratives about crime in newspapers. Though Whitman's experience as a newspaper editor influenced the compassionate attitude toward criminals found in his poetry, his poetic persona differs significantly from his editorial voice. The speaker retains none of the amusement or irony of the editor. Moreover, the persona apparently rejects the editor's social vision: "What blurt is it about virtue and about vice? / Evil propels me, and reform of evil propels me. . . . I stand indifferent."[95] For the *Leaves of Grass* poetic voice of 1855, empathy with society's most despised elements is an individual act with spiritual implications, not the pretext for particular social reforms. Whereas the newspaper editor in Whitman's practice represents a sympathetic voice on behalf of the local community, including its transgressors, the poet (or bard) is a more mystical figure whose empathy for social outcasts transcends merely local concerns. In subsequent volumes of *Leaves,* as Paul Christian Jones has documented, Whitman would continue to portray prison inmates sympathetically and to "encourage readers to acknowledge the essential humanity they share" with criminals.[96]

Arrested in the act of committing crimes, the subjects of police reports in antebellum newspapers had seemingly forfeited their claims to sympathy even among otherwise humane observers. The same respect for the underlying principles of artisan republicanism that led editors to frame certain sensational criminal narratives in terms of the exploitation of the working class by their social superiors enabled a more ruthless dismissal of petty thieves, drunks, and prostitutes. By running afoul of republican regard for the value of private property and the dignity of labor (either by stealing or by rendering themselves incapable of work), or, in the case of prostitutes, by violating almost universally accepted norms regarding gender and sexuality, these particular social actors became easy targets for ridicule. The "City Intelligence" report provided the forum where their misfortunes were exhibited and mocked. These reports followed a set of narrative conventions that included humiliation of the arrested, racial stereotyping, and a lack of interest in causative social conditions. In their departures from these conventions, Lippard and Whitman led readers toward a more thoughtful consideration of the relationship between individual criminals and the broader social context.

Though modern readers familiar with Lippard's and Whitman's reputations for social radicalism might find certain insensitive elements of their police reporting distasteful, their attempts to impart basic human dignity to those involved in criminal behavior ultimately should stand out. Even if they sometimes descended to the form's demands, Lippard and Whitman nonetheless deserve credit for, at times, expanding the police report beyond its formulaic bounds. Giving the daily police report a socially ameliorative purpose served both writers as a rehearsal for expressing the enlightened attitudes toward the unfortunate that became characteristic of their later, more accomplished literary work.

2

Race, Vigilantism, and the Diffusion of Civic Authority

Measuring Justice in Novels by George Lippard and Richard Hildreth

In Nathaniel Hawthorne's fiction *The Blithedale Romance* (1852), Hollingsworth makes no concrete progress toward founding the institute for reforming criminals that is the object of his obsession. Instead, the single efficacious role relative to crime and punishment that Hawthorne assigns him is, ironically (given his presumed sympathy for criminals), as the judge of a vigilante court. In chapter 25, narrator Miles Coverdale comes upon Hollingsworth, Zenobia, and Priscilla in the aftermath of what he realizes has been an emotionally charged encounter. Although she has committed no crime that the legal system would recognize (having betrayed her half sister Priscilla into the hands of the sinister Professor Westervelt), Zenobia has nonetheless been on trial, as she dramatically puts it, for her life. Explaining to Coverdale what has just transpired, Zenobia exclaims: "It was too hard upon me . . . that judge, jury, and accuser, should all be comprehended in one man! I demur, as I think the lawyers say, to the jurisdiction." To demur to the jurisdiction is, in legal terms, to challenge the authority of the prosecuting tribunal. But her plea comes too late. Though Hollingsworth declines to sentence Zenobia for her actions, she perceives that before the "secret tribunals" of men, "any verdict short of acquittal is equivalent to a death sentence."[1] Zenobia's trial results in a de facto death sentence, in that Hollingsworth's exposure and renunciation drive her to suicide.

A fair number of Americans of the period could have identified with Zenobia's predicament: being put on trial for one's life before a court of dubious legitimacy. Although Hawthorne figures the proceedings with reference to a witchcraft trial, the vigilance committees of the frontier are at least as apt a comparison. Acting as adjuncts to a criminal justice system they claimed had broken down or been co-opted by criminal elements, vigilante courts proliferated in the American West and, particularly in the case of the San Francisco Vigilance Committee of 1851, generated substantial and not always unfavorable publicity.

Meanwhile, in the cities of the urban Northeast, courts faced a parallel crisis of accountability. Focusing on the conduct of criminal courts, radical writers had maintained since the 1830s that the justice system was biased in favor of social elites. In the eyes of critics, money bought access to favorable judicial treatment, insulating the wealthy from meaningful prosecution for their crimes. This charge found a receptive audience among readers of the nation's populist-oriented penny papers through the 1840s and 1850s, who avidly followed the details of widely publicized, sensational criminal trials. But in response to the egalitarian political developments of the 1840s, a competing conservative critique of the criminal courts also emerged. From this point of view, mobocracy made a fair trial impossible for the nation's "upper ten." Finally, following passage of the Fugitive Slave Law in 1850, abolitionists impugned judges' complicity with the morally indefensible institution of slavery. Weathering criticism from diverse directions, the judiciary's legitimacy was seriously undermined.

Searching analyses of these social problems—the flaws of the judiciary and the rise of vigilantism—were provided by George Lippard and Richard Hildreth in novels of the early 1850s. In *The Empire City* (1850), Lippard fantasizes a vigilante court, the Court of Ten Millions, which violently punishes criminals whose offenses escape the reach of the officially sanctioned (but corrupt and ineffective) judicial system. Yet three years later, in *New York: Its Upper Ten and Lower Million* (1853), a reprised version of the Court of Ten Millions models unexpected restraint, as Lippard apparently reconsiders his endorsement of vigilante violence as a remedy for social injustice. In *The White Slave; or, Memoirs of a Fugitive* (1852), lawyer, historian, polemicist, and pioneering antislavery novelist Hildreth invokes the lessons of American history to reject vigilantism in favor of official legal channels, even as he recognizes and deplores shortcomings of the American judiciary.

In all three of these novels, Lippard and Hildreth juxtapose commentary on the American judicial system with images of African American participation in a variety of legislative and judicial capacities. What led these two novelists working in very different subgenres (the sensational crime novel and the antislavery novel) to intuit a connection linking delegitimized courts, a recent wave of western vigilantism, and African American civic agency? In attempting to answer this question, the present chapter taps into debates ranging across the nation's print culture—in newspapers, pamphlets, magazines, and novels—about flaws in the nation's courts and the proper social response to their failures.

Faulty Criminal Justice in Antebellum Print Culture

By the early 1850s, Americans had been reading accounts of crime and punishment in their daily newspapers for almost two decades. Penny papers catered to readers' demands for true crime stories by providing detailed, sensationalized coverage of prominent criminal trials. The prosecutions of Richard Robinson (in 1836 for the murder of Helen Jewett in New York), John C. Colt (in 1842 for the murder of Samuel Adams, also in New York), Albert J. Tirrell (in 1845 for the murder of Mary Bickford in Boston), and John Webster (in 1850 for the murder of George Parkman in Boston) are some of the best known of the many criminal proceedings widely reported in newspapers. Meanwhile, pamphlet accounts of criminal trials proliferated in the early nineteenth century, "swamping all other forms of narrative." Trial reports, varying from pamphlets of eight or twelve pages to full-length books, "purported to be transcripts which recorded all trial testimony, the closings of counsel, the judge's instructions to the jury, the verdict, and, when the defendant was found guilty, the sentencing."[2] Taken together, such coverage invited public scrutiny of the criminal justice system.

One of the primary venues for such scrutiny was the *National Police Gazette*. Beginning publication in 1845, this New York–based weekly newspaper combined picaresque biographies of notorious criminals with a purported mission to protect the public through exposure of criminal activity, compiling arrest and trial accounts from Philadelphia, Boston, New York, and other cities. Reaching a national audience through a network of subscription agents and claiming circulation figures in the tens of thousands, the *Gazette* logged a litany of complaints against the nation's criminal justice institutions. It exposed corrupt New York City police officers who struck deals with criminals for personal emolument; denounced abuse of the pardoning power, by which convicted felons used ill-gotten gains to purchase access to sympathetic governors; and condemned judges for allowing criminals to receive lighter sentences in exchange for the return of stolen property.[3] One of the *Gazette*'s most outspoken editorials, from August 14, 1847, demonstrates its outraged, crusading tone: "The absolute and scandalous corruption which pervades every portion of the criminal departments of this city has arrived at a mark which has never been exceeded."[4] According to the *Gazette,* complicity among criminals, police officers, and judges meant that all profited together from criminal activity, leaving the average citizen unprotected.

The *Gazette* reserved some of its most aggressive criticism for the grand jury system. Convening in secret, and composed exclusively of wealthy members (owing to a property qualification), the grand jury epitomized a criminal justice system that proffered favorable treatment to people of wealth and social position. Describing a case in which a corrupt bank president evaded prosecution, a correspondent for the *Gazette* writing under the name "Probius" attacked grand juries for unequal enforcement of the law: "So long as secret tribunals, composed mostly of wealthy financiers, intervene between responsible and elective magistrates, so long may rich offenders rejoice in an impunity from the stern visitations of the law, and so long will poverty or social obscurity writhe under their most pitiless enforcement."[5] Dan Schiller traces the invocation of this rhetoric to the labor press of the 1830s, but contends it was widely parroted in the penny press during succeeding decades.[6]

The *National Police Gazette* was not alone in voicing class-oriented concern over the unequal dispensing of criminal justice. Surveying the journalistic career of *New York Herald* publisher James Gordon Bennett, who had helped to popularize sensational coverage of criminal trials, Isaac Pray summed up public opinion on criminal justice in the 1840s: "Law was becoming a mockery in the eyes of the people. The poor man was condemned, and executed—the rich man was found guilty, and ingenuity could invent means in quibbles to avert his legal doom."[7] Conditions in New York's famous jail and police court, known as the Tombs, bore out these perceptions. The Tombs was primarily occupied by prisoners awaiting trial, among whom material conditions varied widely according to personal wealth. (Recall the prison guard in Melville's "Bartleby, the Scrivener" who solicits money from the lawyer to provide better food for Bartleby.) Amid the poorly administered and overcrowded conditions of the Tombs, securing bail in a misdemeanor case virtually ensured an acquittal, since overwhelmed magistrates lacked the resources to summon defendants out on bail to trial. The *Gazette* crusaded against this system, noting that "the Devil himself would be discharged from custody if Mammon would 'go his bail,' while the angel Gabriel would be sent to the Tombs for want of wealthy friends."[8] Historian Timothy J. Gilfoyle concludes of the period, "In the end, the well-connected and well-financed criminal purchased his release, while the needy and friendless individual went to jail."[9] An 1855 article in the *New York Daily Times* cataloged various shortcomings in the city's administration of criminal justice, including court officials receiving kickbacks for directing cases toward particular lawyers and police officers shaking down houses of prostitution for payoffs. The author lamented, "Our whole municipal system is utterly rotten and corrupt."[10]

The situation was similar in Philadelphia, where the aldermen who presided over minor criminal trials came under scrutiny in the 1840s. According to criminal justice historian Allen Steinberg, the idea became widespread that "poverty and dependence, on the one hand, and widespread corruption, on the other, had turned the minor judiciary into just another mechanism of oppression."[11] Former Eastern State Penitentiary inmate Harry Hawser (the pseudonym of George Ryno) put dissatisfaction with Philadelphia's corrupt justice system in poetic form, lamenting that Justice was "not blind" in the courthouse, where the "light offence" was put in "galling fetters" if it came "clad in the garb of chilling poverty," while "murder, arson, incest, treason, rape, / Display the mighty dollar and escape."[12]

Another issue troubling public confidence in antebellum trial courts had to do with the relative powers of judges and juries. The conflict between "the people's aspiration for democratic government" and "the judiciary's desire for the orderly supervision of public affairs by judges," especially in regard to criminal cases, was a critical point of debate in legal circles throughout the nineteenth century.[13] According to legal historian Lawrence M. Friedman, the power wielded by juries in nineteenth-century America was "enormous" and "subject to few controls."[14] Early-nineteenth-century practice in various states gave juries the discretion to decide not only the facts of the case but also the applicable law. Juries uncomfortable with enforcing the death penalty, for example, asserted their supremacy by ignoring the judge's charge and convicting a defendant of a lesser crime, if they elected to convict at all. As the nineteenth century progressed and the bar became more professionalized, "criminal trial judges gradually eroded the jury's dominance, although their actions generated substantial controversy."[15] The movement to curtail jury independence began with Supreme Court Justice Joseph Story's influential opinion in *United States v. Battiste* in 1835 and continued throughout the century.[16] This legal development ran contrary to a traditional American belief investing independent criminal juries with the power to safeguard individual liberty against government tyranny, an idea grounded in English common law that held obvious appeal during the Revolutionary period.

Slavery-related cases intensified scrutiny of the American judiciary in the mid-nineteenth century. Positivist-minded federal judges such as Story and Lemuel Shaw maintained their obligation to uphold laws supporting the rights of slave owners even if they found slavery morally repugnant, while abolitionists endorsed a "higher law" position that natural rights superseded positive law.[17] After passage of the Fugitive Slave Law, abolitionists turned to sympathetic juries to nullify prosecution of northerners who aided and abetted fugitives in defiance of the new law, a development that one legal historian regards as "one of the most thorough jury revolts in history."[18] Lysander

Spooner asserted that juries had the right to decide "every part and parcel of the case," including the "existence of the law," the "exposition of the law," the "justice of the law," and the "admissibility and weight of all the evidence authored"; anything less would mean the "tyranny of the government."[19] Fellow abolitionist Hildreth championed the power of juries in the introduction to his American edition of an English legal history called *Atrocious Judges: Lives of Judges Infamous as Tools of Tyrants and Instruments of Oppression* (1856). "If the people of Great Britain and America are not at this moment slaves," he wrote, "it is not courts nor lawyers that they have to thank for it. How essential to liberty is the popular element in the administration of criminal law—how absolutely necessary is the restraint of a jury in criminal cases."[20] Hildreth's faith in juries as safeguards of liberty derived in part from his knowledge of Boston juries that declined to convict alleged rescuers of fugitive slaves, as detailed further later in this chapter.

The perceived failings of the criminal justice system migrated seamlessly into fiction of the late 1840s and 1850s. Ned Buntline, for example, used an appendix of his popular and influential sensational crime novel *The Mysteries and Miseries of New York* (1848) to call out that city's Court of Special Sessions for failing to prosecute gambling dens effectively, blaming "negligent and culpable magistrates" for letting proprietors off with minimal fines that were then written off as the cost of doing business.[21] In *The Convict* (1851), Buntline depicted himself (thinly disguised as heroic journalist and nativist political organizer Edward Cramer) as the victim of a corrupt trial court, where perjured testimony and a biased judge's prejudicial charge to the jury result in the protagonist's unjust conviction for helping to incite the Astor Place Riot.[22]

Dissatisfaction with a corrupt judicial system emerges as a major theme of James Fenimore Cooper's final novel, *The Ways of the Hour* (1850). The novel stages a murder mystery in which a rich young woman stands accused of murdering an elderly couple with whom she was a boarder. Taking place in the fictional locale of Biberry, Duke's County, New York, the trial attracts the attention of Manhattan attorney Thomas Dunscomb, who serves more or less as Cooper's mouthpiece on legal issues. Through the device of having the country lawyer Timms educate his Manhattan colleague on the way law is practiced in Duke's County, Cooper details the extraordinarily corrupt measures to which trial lawyers resort in the interests of their clients, a set of practices referred to by Timms as "out-door work" (in contrast to the "indoor work" of courtroom litigation). Outdoor work includes "horse-shedding," whereby lawyers plant agents in the public horse shed to malign the personality of a litigant in the presence of jurors, and "pillowing," which follows the same principle but takes place in country inns.[23] Reviewers devoted particular attention to these scenes of lawyerly misconduct.[24]

Whereas Cooper regards the ethically dubious practices of individual lawyers on behalf of their clients as deplorable, his larger target is the egalitarian trend of the antebellum period, which, in his view, rendered justice inaccessible to the social elite. This critique epitomizes Cooper's increasing alienation from the democratizing spirit of the 1840s, as symbolized for him in New York's anti-rent movement and revisions to the state constitution in 1846. In addition to expanding the roster of directly elected public officials, the new constitution provided for popular election of judges.[25] For Cooper, powerful judges appointed from the upper levels of society provided a needed bulwark against unpredictable juries. In *The Ways of the Hour,* Cooper charges that social elites, not the poor, are subject to courtroom injustice. Timms tells Dunscomb that "aristocracy, of late years, is a capital argument,"[26] and he can sway a jury against any party to a lawsuit perceived to be putting on airs. The novel characterizes juries as rogue agents within the criminal justice system, abusing their power and running roughshod over the discretion of judges and the facts of particular cases; in Cooper's eyes, as John P. McWilliams Jr. writes, the "jury . . . became associated with the legislature—a popular body, irresponsible by sheer weight of numbers, whose power and impunity Cooper wished to suppress."[27] The court fails spectacularly in the case of the novel's main character, Mary Monson; she is convicted of the murder of a man who later turns up alive, and it takes months for the court system to rectify its errors. In the meantime, the narrator laments that "few reflected on the defects of the system that condemned her to the gallows on insufficient testimony," ascribing the failure primarily to the weaknesses of the uneducated and biased jury.[28]

A populist indictment of the criminal justice system that had its roots in the radical press of the 1830s had, by the 1850s, spread far more widely into mainstream avenues of public opinion, acquiring new ideological overtones along the way. Favoritism toward moneyed interests, mobocracy's bias against the social elite, atrocious judges complicit with southern slave owners, and jury nullification of Fugitive Slave Law prosecutions contributed to skepticism regarding the American judiciary, exemplifying the "general loss of faith in the lawyer and in his republic of laws" that Robert Ferguson has identified as characteristic of mid-nineteenth-century America.[29] In regions removed from the urban Northeast where these complaints were centered, Americans' dissatisfaction with constituted courts often assumed a more violent form.

Vigilantism as a Response to Failed Courts

In the West, distrust of authorized courts sometimes resulted in the formation of extralegal tribunals, which claimed to fill urgent community needs for law and order.[30] The antebellum period's first significant outbreak of vigilantism occurred in the West in the mid-1830s. The execution of several alleged gamblers in Vicksburg, Mississippi, in 1835 was one of the earliest events to direct national attention to the question of extralegal justice, along with a nearly concurrent case of lynching in nearby Madison County, said to have been carried out to quell a conspiracy of insurrectionary slaves. In the same period, a number of anti-abolitionist mobs protested, with varying degrees of violence, the growing assertiveness of the antislavery movement, which had initiated its controversial national mailing campaign in 1835.[31] Responding to the rise of extralegal violence, Abraham Lincoln, then an Illinois state legislator, criticized in 1837 "the increasing disregard for law" pervading the country.[32] Anti-abolitionist mobs were particularly violent in the South, which seemed to possess a greater toleration for extralegal tribunals as a supplement to the criminal justice system: "In the South the legal and extralegal systems usually comfortably cooperated. Southern mobs took people they wanted to punish directly from courts and jails with no opposition."[33] Violence on the part of such groups risked inspiring a backlash of public opinion, especially after abolitionists recognized the propaganda value of publicizing the details of their brutality. The language of "lynching" was thereby discredited for a period in the wake of overzealous anti-abolitionist attacks, which sometimes had the effect of bringing converts to the abolitionist position.[34]

In the early 1850s, however, vigilantism acquired a newfound veneer of respectability in American culture. Writing in the pages of the *American Whig Review*, one author signing himself "P.P." expressed a widely held view defending the extralegal pursuit of justice, particularly in western communities where the criminal justice system was underdeveloped. P.P. listed the problems inhibiting pursuit of criminals in frontier territories: jails were insecure or had not yet been constructed, judges were bribed, and juries were intimidated. Over time, a criminal element gained in strength until lawlessness reigned in individual communities. In response to such conditions, he argued, "the only practicable mode is . . . that the whole body of settlers near should rise, arrest the criminal, try him impartially and justly, then mete out to him such punishment as their own common sense and correct ideas of right and wrong may dictate."[35] Nor was P.P. an outlier in his qualified acceptance of extralegal solutions to problems of crime. Richard Maxwell Brown emphasizes the surprising degree of official endorsement of vigilante movements throughout U.S. history: "Senators, congressmen, governors, judges, founders of state bar associations, legal philosophers, and even presidents have all endorsed, by word or deed, the taking of the law into one's own hands."[36]

No organization did more to legitimate extralegal violence in the early 1850s than the San Francisco Committee of Vigilance, founded in 1851 (and reconstituted in 1856). The organization arose in response to a perceived inability of the city's civil authorities to deal with the problem of crime, not a surprising state of affairs, given the sudden influx of population attracted by the Gold Rush. One historian of the committee notes that California courts in the early 1850s "quickly became notorious for their failure to convict and punish criminals, especially those who could pay for skillful defense." Poorly funded criminal courts put prosecutors at a disadvantage against generously compensated defense lawyers, while convicted defendants "had an excellent chance to escape because of the total lack of secure jails."[37]

Concern for public safety led a group of prominent citizens to found the committee of vigilance in June 1851, after which it commenced trials and, in a few cases, executions of suspected criminals. The San Francisco Committee of Vigilance published a constitution on June 9, 1851, in which members bound themselves "to perform every lawful act for the maintenance of law and order and to sustain the laws when properly administered" but also vowed that "no thief burglar incendiary or assassin shall escape punishment either by the quibbles of the law the insecurity of prisons or corruption of the Police or a laxity of those who pretend to administer justice."[38] The city's newspapers supported the actions of the committee, even after a grand jury found its members officially responsible for the hanging death of one of its victims.[39] When news of the actions of the San Francisco Committee of Vigilance reached the eastern seaboard, newspapers and other periodicals debated the legitimacy of its actions. While opinion was divided, Christopher Waldrep believes that the preponderance of coverage came out in support of the committee's actions: "The national debate over San Francisco set in the minds of many the notion that when the people judged their courts inadequate, they had a right, in the face of horrible crime, to act outside the law."[40] Given that courtroom justice was frequently discredited in the popular press of the urban Northeast, it was a short step from indictment of the criminal justice system to the fantasy of a more responsive and socially just (but extralegal) mechanism of punishing criminality, a step that George Lippard would take in fashioning his fictional Court of Ten Millions in *The Empire City.*

The vigilante committee of the antebellum period asserted its legitimacy by covering itself in the trappings and methods of legal authority. In San Francisco as well as other locales, criminals were given defense attorneys while members of the vigilante group served as prosecutors; a simulacrum of an adversarial justice system was created, although the proceedings were sometimes carried out behind closed doors.[41] The authors of a defense of the 1851 San Francisco Committee of Vigilance published in New York in 1854 noted of one prosecution, "Mr. Coleman was chosen public prosecutor, and Judge Shattuck and Hall McAllister were appointed counsel for the prisoners." The authors argued that the committee of vigilance was formed "not to supersede the legal authorities, but to strengthen them when weak; not to oppose the law, but to sanction and confirm it."[42] Extralegal tribunals endorsed the concept of courtroom-based justice even as they challenged its efficacy in particular regions or situations; that this recourse to impromptu courts over officially sanctioned ones was a recipe for social disorder did not escape observation.[43] An elemental conflict over the nature of legal authority played itself out with growing urgency in the early 1850s, posing questions about the legitimacy of extralegal justice that Lippard and Hildreth addressed in novels of the period. That these same novels dramatized—in radically differing ways—the possibility of African American civic agency suggests that these notions were somehow linked in the popular imagination.

Vigilantism, Civic Agency, and "Government by Blacks"

Radical pamphleteer David Walker noted and protested the absence of blacks from American courtrooms in 1829. Walker saw black participation on a jury as a small but crucial step toward full African American civic agency, demanding of his readers not "to show me a coloured President, a Governor, a Legislator, a Senator, a Mayor, or an Attorney at the Bar.—But to show me a man of colour . . . who sits in a Juror Box, even on a case of one of his wretched Brethren, throughout this great Republic!!"[44] Had he lived into the 1840s, Walker would have witnessed the appearance of the nation's first black attorneys in his adopted city of Boston. Macon Bolling Allen was admitted to the Suffolk County Bar in Massachusetts in 1845, an appointment that "was widely publicized in Boston and in other New England states." In 1847 Massachusetts governor George N. Briggs appointed Allen a justice of the peace. African American Robert Morris began to practice law in Boston in 1847 and was also subsequently named a justice of the peace, while in 1848 George Boyer Vashon became New York's first black lawyer.[45] As Jeannine Marie DeLombard has noted, the prospect of black lawyers evoked hostility from white colleagues, demonstrating "the reluctance, even inability, of many white Americans to conceive of African Americans in a legal capacity other than that of property, criminals, victims, or (most recently) witnesses."[46] In the wake of Allen's admission to the bar, J. Clay Smith Jr. reports, the following lyric appeared in a minstrel songbook:

> I wish de legislature would set dis *darkie free,*
> Oh! what a happy place den de *darkie* land would be.
> We'd have a *darkie* parliament,
> An' *darkie* codes of law,
> An' *darkie* judges on de bench,
> *Darkie* barristers and aw.[47]

African American civic agency was not unimaginable to antebellum white Americans, but to many the notion was deeply unsettling. In this minstrel song, the threat posed by the prospect of black civic agency is dissipated through exaggeration, as (white) readers are invited to contemplate the ludicrousness of black lawyers, judges, legislators, and codes of law.

But the recent emergence of black lawyers and justices of the peace, coupled with black (and white) abolitionists' boldness in challenging the Fugitive Slave Law, may have made African American civic agency seem suddenly a little less ludicrous in the early 1850s. In an incident that drew urgent national attention, fugitive slave Shadrach Minkins was arrested by a U.S. marshal and brought to the Boston courtroom of U.S. commissioner George Ticknor Curtis in 1851 to determine his status, in accordance with the requirements of the recently passed law. Robert Morris served on Minkins's defense team. After the commissioner adjourned the court to give defense counsel time to prepare their case, a crowd of men, many African American, broke into the courtroom and freed Minkins (who subsequently escaped to Montreal). Blacks also helped to liberate fugitive slaves from arresting officers in Christiana, Pennsylvania (a violent altercation in which several men, black and white, met their deaths), and Syracuse, New York, in 1851.[48] The role of African Americans in effecting Minkins's escape was a source of particular anxiety for white proslavery Americans, to judge by the reaction of Henry Clay. On the floor of the Senate, Clay reportedly reacted to news of the Minkins rescue by asking "whether our laws are to be enforced, or 'whether the government of white men is to be yielded to a government by blacks.' "[49] Clay's use of the phrase "government by blacks," however sarcastic or fear-mongering in intent, illustrates that black civic agency, imagined as leading inevitably toward a nightmarish scenario of white disempowerment, hovered within the horizon of possibilities in the minds of some Americans at the time.

The vigilante courts of the West distributed civic agency in unpredictable ways to previously unauthorized members of the community, who disputed the ability of officially recognized courts to meet communal needs. But the logic empowering vigilante courts potentially underwrote African American civic agency as well. If private, extralegal measures were justified in the face of absent, corrupt, or ineffective courts, could not African Americans— given almost total exclusion from meaningful participation in American courtrooms—claim authority to act outside the law on similar grounds? In the case of Minkins, blacks (and white abolitionist allies) seized extralegal authority to correct what they feared would be a grave miscarriage of justice by Commissioner Curtis remanding Minkins to the custody of his former owner. Let me hasten to clarify that I do not in any way propose moral equivalence between the dubious actions of western vigilante courts and the heroic rescues of Minkins and other fugitive slaves. Obviously, antebellum African Americans did not act through spurious extralegal courts, as western vigilantes did, much less carry out executions of presumed malefactors (although this is precisely what they do in Lippard's fiction, as will be seen). My argument is rather that some antebellum observers intuited a potential for black empowerment inherent within vigilantism's volatile diffusion of civic agency. Meanwhile, the emergence of a handful of black lawyers, justices of the peace, and fugitive slave rescuers made the prospect of "government by blacks," if hardly imminent, seem somewhat less remote (and significantly more anxiety provoking) than ever before for many white Americans. This suite of cultural and legal developments helps to explain why, in two vigilante-themed novels of the early 1850s, Lippard bestowed upon black characters the capacity to mete out justice in extralegal forums and imagined, in the distinctive idioms of sensational crime fiction, the forms such justice might take.

George Lippard's Court of Ten Millions

Sensational novels of the nineteenth century are usually, in an abstract sense, concerned with the notion of justice: virtuous characters tend to be rewarded and villains punished in accordance with their deserts by novel's end. Yet as Wai-Chee Dimock has provocatively observed, precisely calibrated justice persistently eludes the nineteenth-century novel: "The novel's narrative medium is not quite a neutralizing agency, not quite an all-purpose solvent."[50]

One finds confirmation of Dimock's analysis in Lippard's attempt to imagine an extralegal institution capable of achieving justice outside of sanctioned courts in his 1850 city-mysteries novel *The Empire City; or, New York by Night and Day.*[51] The novel follows a set of characters with claims to an immense fortune, the Van Huyden estate, to be distributed on Christmas Day 1844, twenty-one years after the death of eccentric merchant Gulian Van Huyden. In part three of *The Empire City,* one of the novel's principal villains, Harry Royalton, a wealthy plantation owner from South Carolina, is kidnapped and taken to a mysterious chamber. Speaking from the shadows, an unseen judge tells Harry that he is about to be tried in the Court of Ten Millions, so named because "it is backed by that amount of money, placed under the control of its Supreme Judge" (123). The judge explains that the court is necessary "to remedy the defective justice of those courts which, in the outer world, established by the wealthy and powerful, too often deny the commonest rights to the down-trodden and the poor, and too [often] make wealth, or the want of it, the sole test of innocence and crime" (123). The judge further informs Harry that the most infamous crime punished by the Court of Ten Millions is that of "*the thirst for Labor's fruits without Labor's works*" (123).

Taking the role of prosecutor is Harry's half brother Randolph, who tells the story of Harry's depravity. Violating his dying father's explicit wishes, Harry has attempted to dispossess Randolph and his (Harry's) half sister Esther from their share of the family fortune. (The family patriarch fathered Randolph and Esther by one of his slaves, Herodia, whom he regarded as a common-law wife. After her death, the patriarch married Herodia's white half sister and fathered Harry.) What Randolph particularly emphasizes in the trial scene is his having been whipped at Harry's behest, demanding redress in the form of Harry's enduring a commensurate punishment. When the court gives him the opportunity to defend himself, Harry is unable to answer Randolph's truthful charges and is convicted. To carry out the sentence, the judge calls upon the court's executioner—Old Royal, a former slave of the Royalton plantation. Spouting biblical references in slave dialect (*"Ehud I hab a message from God to dee!"* [130]), Old Royal applies thirty-nine lashes.

Lippard's debts to contemporary debates over courtroom justice are obvious. Echoing contemporary complaints, the vigilante judge charges sanctioned American courts with favoritism toward moneyed interests. A criminal justice system found inadequate to the needs of its society is replaced with a more responsive institution. Lippard's notable fictional innovation is to transplant the western institution of the vigilante court to the urban Northeast. Like the vigilante courts of the frontier, the Court of Ten Millions replicates, if imperfectly, the judicial trappings of the one it replaces: a judge presides over the trial, the criminal is given the opportunity to face his accuser and speak in his defense, and a carefully measured sentence is carried out. (The judge warns Old Royal neither to omit nor to add a single lash, at his peril [130].) The contradictions inherent in Lippard's conception of the Court of Ten Millions, however, bespeak his inability to imagine a way through the impasse of an ineffective criminal justice system. Correcting the influence of wealth over the court system with a competing pool of $10 million strains logic, even by the forgiving standards of the sensational novel. The omission of a jury from the Court of Ten Millions is even more telling. By empowering a "Supreme Judge" to punish criminals the official court system neglects to prosecute, Lippard conjures a figure whose power no jury exists to check; the Court of Ten Millions operates without the body that legal ideology of the period regarded as the critical safeguard against excessive authority. That the judge in question is humane, benevolent, and self-questioning, crying out, "Pity me, good Lord! Pity and forgive if I am wrong, in assuming thy attribute of Retribution!" (130), may suffice to ensure an approximation of justice within the conventions of the sensational novel, but it merely begs the question of civil liberties that mid-nineteenth-century vigilantism persistently raised.

Further paradoxes emerge from Lippard's handling of the subjects of race and slavery. While the court purportedly regards the appropriation of labor as the vilest of unpunished crimes, slave owner Harry Royalton is not put on trial for slavery. Although the novel represents slavery as unjust, Lippard diverts attention from its most oppressed victims, the plantation slaves, catering thereby to the affinities of his white working-class readership. For these readers, the mixed-race but white-appearing protagonists Randolph and Esther, whose condition of slavery is merely nominal, are more eligible repositories of identification. By investing Old Royal with the authority to carry out the court's mandate, the novel appears to sanction meaningful African American agency in dispensing (as opposed to merely suffering) legal punishment. Nevertheless, the relationship between judge and executioner in the scene is analogous to what Frederick Douglass ruefully observed of the period's abolitionist movement, in which white authority figures paternalistically regulated the participation of escaped slaves: Old Royal is merely the obedient instrument carrying out the court's decree.

If the 1850 incarnation of the Court of Ten Millions represents Lippard's initial reaction to the problem of prosecuting crime in antebellum America, he deepens and modifies this response with the court's resurrection in his 1853 novel *New York: Its Upper Ten and Lower Million,* which is a kind of sequel to *The Empire City,* returning to the story of the disbursement of the Van Huyden estate. (*New York* covers the same time period as *The Empire City,* revisiting the adventures of former characters, introducing new ones, and altering the story's ending.) Lippard's decision to bring back the Court of Ten Millions may represent his response to publicity regarding the San Francisco Committee of Vigilance of 1851, another extralegal body claiming to administer justice where the official courts failed. At first glance, the revivified Court of Ten Millions appears to verify Lippard's faith in vigilante justice. Given greater prominence in *New York* than in *The Empire City,* the Court of Ten Millions stages two trials, in the first of which the defendant is politician Gabriel Godlike (a gesture toward Daniel Webster, to whom the moniker "godlike Dan" was sometimes applied). The judge, now revealed to readers to be Martin Fulmer, executor of the Van Huyden estate, repeats the court's rationale from the first novel; it exists "to punish those crimes which, perchance, from their very magnitude, go unpunished by other courts of justice."[52] Godlike is abducted by the court's agents just as he threatens to rape Esther Royalton; the court coerces him into accepting its jurisdiction by threatening to expose him to a group of his influential acquaintances.

During the trial, the judge, doubling this time as prosecutor, emphasizes Godlike's misuse of political power. (He is compared unfavorably with the three lions of the antebellum Senate, Clay, Calhoun, and Webster.) Blessed with intellect and influence, Godlike has "mortgaged his official position, to those who enslave labor in workshop and factory, defraud it in banks, and rob the laborer" (164). Also central to the prosecution's case is Godlike's perversion of the law in his professional career as an attorney: "As a lawyer, having a profound knowledge of the technicalities of written law . . . he has used his knowledge of written law to gloss over and sanction the grossest wrongs" (164). Prosecuted not for any single crime but for neglecting to use his "Godlike" talents to defend the interests of the common man, Godlike is the novel's embodiment of both political and legal authority; dragging him before the Court of Ten Millions, Lippard puts American justice itself on trial. When the legal system is compromised by its own moral turpitude, vigilante justice, it would seem, is the only available recourse.

A closer look at this scene, however, suggests that the novel's embrace of vigilantism as a response to social injustice is carefully qualified. Godlike's sentence, to his astonishment and relief, requires him merely to sign two documents. In the first, Godlike admits to his attempted rape of Esther, "an outrage which, investigated before a court of law, would justly consign him to the State's Prison" (166). Signing the second document, Godlike renounces any claim to the Van Huyden estate. On the basis of his wickedness and venality, Godlike is (according to the moralistic requirements of the genre) justly excluded from partaking of the immense fortune, which will fall into more deserving hands at novel's end. The revelation that Godlike's crimes come within the jurisdiction of extant courts contradicts the stated rationale behind the Court of Ten Millions: that it prosecutes crimes unrecognized by the legal system. This revelation allows Lippard to endorse widespread claims that the legal system often fails in its mission even as he cautions against an inordinate extralegal response. The Court of Ten Millions in *New York* is a gentler institution than it was in *The Empire City;* instead of sentencing the defendant to lashes, it operates in a more abstract and legalistic realm. Conspicuously rejecting violence, the new Court of Ten Millions models restraint instead of retribution. Godlike signs the documents and goes on his way.

In its second prosecution in the novel, the Court of Ten Millions takes on additional nuances that complicate any apparent endorsement of extralegal tribunals. The defendant is Israel Yorke, who fakes his bank's failure in order to abscond with its funds, defrauding the poor laborers who hold its notes. Once again, the judge grounds the court's legitimacy in the premise that some social injustices fall outside the bounds of criminal prosecution; because the financier's crimes have been committed "within the letter of the law" (176), it has fallen on the Court of Ten Millions to punish him. Within two pages, however, Lippard reverses course. To manipulate Yorke into accepting the court's verdict, the judge puts before him "proofs of all [his] crimes, proofs

that would weigh [him] down in a convict's chains before any court of law"
(178). Faced with a criminal whose unpunished crimes expose the inadequacy
of the official justice system, the court would seem to have ample mandate to
execute a severe sentence. Nonetheless, in this scene the Court of Ten Millions again stops short of violence. Yorke, like Godlike, signs two documents:
one renounces his claim to the Van Huyden estate, while the other records
his promise to redeem his bank's notes dollar for dollar, saving their impoverished holders from destitution. A measure of social justice is achieved without
the resort to vigilante violence.

Lippard redirects his critique of American criminal justice in the unconventional additional sentence the judge imposes on Yorke: the banker is
forced to visit a tenement he owns, where one of his tenants, to spare his
family the gruesome suffering of poverty, has murdered his wife and children
and committed suicide after learning that all of the notes he had saved to
pay the family's rent had plunged in value when Yorke's bank failed. Yorke
"shrank back appalled from the bed" (206) where the victims lay, but the
court's agents force him—as Lippard does his readers—to confront the painful tableau. In Lippard's anticipation of "creative sentencing," the Court of
Ten Millions carries out the exposé function common to city-mysteries fiction: the court forces the novel's titular city, embodied by its namesake Yorke,
to look squarely at the victims of its unequal social arrangements. Nor do
voyeuristic readers escape the court's judgment, as the narrator ends this scene
with a lengthy indictment of their complicity with the excesses of industrial
capitalism. A passage that begins "Poverty! Did you ever think of the full
meaning of that word?" unspools into a ranting two-page litany of the many
victims of unfettered capitalism in the modern city to whose suffering readers
are usually inattentive. The narrator indicts the "proud lady" who sneers at a
newspaper story about a fallen seamstress, without considering the girl's abject
poverty, as well as the (white male) reader who rails against the slave market
while ignoring the plight of the city's desperate factory workers (206).[53]

Lippard undoubtedly had an eye on contemporary distrust of the courts in
creating the Court of Ten Millions, but his handling of the subject of extralegal tribunals evolved in the years between *The Empire City* and *New York*.
Whereas the earlier novel imagines a court that enforces its vision of social
justice through violence, the later one implicitly recognizes the futility and
danger of vesting an unofficial court with such power. The second incarnation of the Court of Ten Millions pulls back from violent sentences, con-
tenting itself with financial penalties and the defendants' recognition of their
own depravity; exposure trumps retribution as the court's main purpose. As
defendants, Godlike and Yorke stand in for the political and economic institutions that permit extremes of wealth and poverty to coexist in the modern

industrial city. But they also stand in for Lippard's readers, indicted by the code of justice of the sensational novel for complicity with the status quo, another crime that falls outside the jurisdiction of the justice system.

The Court of Ten Millions is not the sole extralegal tribunal of justice in *New York*. The novel's other vigilante court provocatively raises the possibility of African Americans arbitrating justice. DeLombard has written persuasively about how black criminality opened a path toward black civic agency through the confessional narratives that gave African American perpetrators a public voice and civic presence.[54] Lippard envisions a different intersection of criminal justice and African American agency in the form of the Black Senate, a group of thirty black men meeting in a subterranean room in New York's Five Points.

Lippard pointedly links the Court of Ten Millions with the Black Senate through the figure of Old Royal; the executioner of the Court of Ten Millions in *The Empire City* is the "speaker" of the Black Senate. Initially the scene stages a lecture in the manner of a minstrel performance (recall the "*darkie parliament*" in the minstrel song quoted earlier), as one of the assembled senators delivers a comical speech explaining the faux-philosophical reasoning by which he justified his escape from a Virginia plantation.[55] The Black Senate is disrupted when slave trader Bloodhound and villain Harry Royalton tumble unexpectedly into its chamber. Royalton dies in a confrontation with Randolph, leaving the Black Senate to deal with Bloodhound. At this point, the group transforms from a legislative into a judicial body. No longer relegated to the subordinate role he performed in *The Empire City*, Old Royal presides as judge over Bloodhound's trial, asking the assembled body, "Do you know de pris'ner?" (121). A chorus of voices responds affirmatively, identifying him as the man who kidnapped and sold their fathers, mothers, and children. The proximity of the Black Senate to New York's infamous site of official legal justice—it meets "near the Tombs" (116)—indicates its function as a parallel to the sanctioned criminal justice system. Whereas the Court of Ten Millions rejects violent sentences in *New York*, the Black Senate, at Old Royal's signal, descends on the cowering Bloodhound and stabs him to death in a scene whose language is calculated to terrify: "But every shriek only seemed to give new fire to the rage of the negroes; and gathering closer round the miserable man, they lifted their knives, dripping with his blood, and struck and struck and struck again, until his cries were stilled" (122).

Lippard in *New York* imagines African Americans acting in a variety of (extralegal) legislative and judicial capacities: as impromptu senators, jurymen, judge, and executioners. The plausibility in 1853 of a black judge (with two black justices of the peace active in Boston) may account for the terror with which the novel clothes black jurists, as opposed to its merely ridiculous figuration of black senators. Black activists' resort to violence in resisting enforcement of the Fugitive Slave Law also, one suspects, informs the scene. Because Bloodhound's crimes against the black community exactly fit the rationales offered in both *The Empire City* and *New York* justifying existence of the Court of Ten Millions—they fall within the letter of the law, thus preventing their adjudication within criminal courts, and they result from the thirst for labor's fruits without its work—the Black Senate's claim to vigilante-style jurisdiction over them seems justifiable on the novel's own terms. What separates the Black Senate from *New York*'s Court of Ten Millions, however, is its bloodthirstiness. The restraint modeled by the Court of Ten Millions is nowhere to be found in the Black Senate, where "every face was distorted with rage" (122). The novel invokes a racialist assumption that while a white vigilante court might be governed by reason and moderation, a black one, motivated by vengeance, would move swiftly toward uncontrolled, retributive violence. Absent a white judge governing his actions, Old Royal can no longer be counted on to limit punishment conscientiously to thirty-nine lashes.

While Lippard's readers presumably shed no tears over the execution of a cowardly slave trader, the danger of vesting nonwhites with any form of legal authority—Henry Clay's "government by blacks"—is nonetheless conveyed. The Black Senate's trial and execution of Bloodhound echo the activities of ad hoc groups on the western frontier claiming legitimacy to punish criminals. But whereas Lippard's white incarnation of these courts, the Court of Ten Millions, appears to enjoy the novel's qualified endorsement as a nonviolent adjunct to a chronically dysfunctional justice system, its black counterpart illustrates the peril (from the point of view of Lippard and his readership) of vigilantism's unpredictable distribution of civic agency: a society that condones vigilantism in response to a discredited judicial system hands African Americans a rationale for resorting to extralegal forms of justice that might give even a frontiersman pause.[56] Carefully predicating acceptance of extralegal judicial measures on the racial identity of the prosecuting tribunal, *New York* attempts to circumscribe the civic agency that the logic of vigilantism threatened to release.

Atrocious Judges and Empowered Juries in *The White Slave*

Resolving the conundrums associated with extralegal judicial institutions in *New York* required bestowing full civic agency on African Americans in an integrated legal system, as Hildreth appears to have recognized in his novel *The White Slave* (1852). First published in 1836 as *The Slave; or, Memoirs of Archy Moore,* the novel purports to recount the experiences of Archy Moore, son of a Virginia planter by one of the planter's favored female slaves. In *The*

Slave, Archy marries and fathers a child by his half sister, serves on a number of plantations, and eventually escapes to Great Britain by way of Boston, fighting on the side of the British in the War of 1812. The first edition of the novel met with a varied response (enthusiasm in abolitionist circles, hostility elsewhere) but little cultural impact, having been published when anti-abolitionist sentiment was running high and the public had little taste for antislavery fiction. Following the success of *Uncle Tom's Cabin,* however, Hildreth published *The White Slave,* adding chapters in which Archy returns to the United States in search of the wife and son he had left behind in slavery. A journalist, historian, pamphleteer, and member of the Massachusetts bar, Hildreth has lately enjoyed a modest level of interest from literary critics.[57] While one significant treatment of *The White Slave* from a legal perspective exists, the novel's deep investment in questions of legal and extralegal justice merits sustained examination.[58] Putting aside *The White Slave*'s provocative treatment of such matters as racial identity, sexuality, and incest, the following analysis of the novel's legal implications focuses in particular on its later chapters, published at a time when the northeastern press looked with measured sympathy on the actions of western vigilantes.

Hilredeth fascinates in part because of the apparent contradictions in his thought. Raised in a Federalist New England household, Hildreth was a staunch Whig who, in his newspaper writing, denounced Jacksonian demagoguery. The pro-Federalist bias is one of the most remarked-upon elements of his six-volume *History of the United States* (1856–1860). Yet Hildreth's writings also bear a strain of anti-elitism that runs counter to conservative respect for established authority. He attacked the native American political movement in the 1840s as a "monied, aristocratic faction" and published a pamphlet, *"Our First Men": A Calendar of Wealth, Fashion, and Gentility,* exposing the wealthy of Boston "to ridicule, scorn, or abuse," sentiments that could easily place him alongside a radical city-mysteries novelist like Lippard.[59] While Arthur Schlesigner Jr. persuasively accounts for these apparent contradictions by uniting them under the banner of utilitarianism, Hildreth's contradictions with respect to the law are no less intriguing.[60] Though he was a member of the Massachusetts bar, Hildreth did not establish a practice as a lawyer; his biographer Donald Emerson notes an early scrapbook entry in which Hildreth condemned the dubious ethics of the profession.[61] Contributing to the *Boston Atlas* newspaper in the 1830s, Hildreth supported the judiciary in Andrew Jackson's disputes with the Supreme Court. Later in his career, however, he condemned American judges for legal decisions in support of slavery, capturing his revised opinion of the judiciary in the title of the English pamphlet he edited and republished for an American audience in 1856: *Atrocious Judges.*

Hildreth wrote *The Slave* after witnessing slavery firsthand during a nineteen-month residence in Florida that began in September 1834. Published late in 1836, the novel was therefore composed against the backdrop of the mid-1830s peak in American mob activity. This edition of the novel depicts acts of quasi- or extralegal violence without coming to any consistent position on such actions. When an impromptu but nominally legal tribunal deals with slaves suspected of carrying out depredations on nearby plantations, Archy drily notes that five Carolina freeholders selected at random "constitute such a court as in most other countries, would hardly be trusted with the final adjudication of any matter above the value of forty shillings at the utmost. But in that part of the world, they . . . have the power of judging all charges against slaves, and sentencing the accused to death."[62] The court quickly reaches the wrong verdict, executing an innocent slave on the basis of faulty evidence. Twice in the novel escaped slaves avenge themselves on their former oppressors. With Archy's help, the escaped slave Thomas murders the overseer who was responsible for the death of his wife. Far from expressing remorse, Archy claims that they carried out the killing with a "lofty feeling of manhood vindicated, and tyranny visited with a just retribution" (206). In another key scene, Archy, fighting aboard a British privateer, encounters the captain, Osborne, who earlier had abandoned a group of slaves (including himself) helpless in a foundering ship during a storm. Captain Osborne asks for quarter, but Archy stabs him to death. Immediately afterward, though, he expresses reservations: "But justice ought never to be sullied with passion,— and if possible, should be unstained with blood. If in my feelings at that moment, there was something noble, there was far too much of savage fury and passionate revenge" (231). Although it is set in the first two decades of the nineteenth century, *The Slave* captures an atmosphere of pervasive violence reminiscent of the mid-1830s, when it was composed. In *The Slave,* the rule of law is tenuous, revenge killings take place outside of any legal framework, and moral judgments of extralegal actions are arbitrated case by case.

Hildreth arrives at a more coherent point of view on vigilantism, however, in *The White Slave.* What has been insufficiently emphasized in criticism on *The White Slave* is Hildreth's careful setting of the second half of the novel (that is, chapters 37 to the end of the book, simply added to the original work) in the mid-1830s, the period of the first half's composition.[63] Writing in the early 1850s, when extralegal tribunals flared up and garnered a certain amount of public approval, Hildreth claims the privilege of the historical novelist to comment on the present through re-creation of the past.[64] Although "lynching occupied a position of curious respectability" in much pre–Civil War American fiction, in the new chapters of *The White Slave* Hildreth foregrounds the dangers of punishing crime through extralegal tribunals.[65] In much of the landscape through which Archy travels in the later chapters of *The White Slave,* the rule of law is suspended. In Richmond, Virginia, a vigilance committee tries Archy on suspicion of his harboring abolitionist sentiments. Asking a lawyer whether Virginia is a country of laws and whether he is obliged to submit to the committee, he is advised that "in the present state of alarm, the law [is] suspended" (250). The vigilance committee's suspicions are heightened by Archy's possession of a letter from a Liverpool merchant named Tappan, whose name the committee members recognize as belonging to "one of the leaders in this nefarious conspiracy . . . to circulate these horrid incendiary tracts" (252). The committee mistakes the fictional Liverpool merchant for Arthur Tappan, the New York silk merchant and co-founder of the American Anti-Slavery Society, whose 1835 mailing campaign is hereby referenced. Archy is narrowly preserved from conviction in the case and suffered to continue his travels.

Moving on to the Carolinas, Archy witnesses the return of a successful slave hunt, which has captured his old friend Thomas, for twenty years the scourge of neighboring plantations; his capturers debate whether to "try and execute Thomas at once" or wait for his former owner to identify him definitively. When the opinion of the most drunken and violent of the party prevails, a "court of three freeholders" is immediately convened, which tries and convicts Thomas before sentencing him to burn at the stake (302–3). The same committee tries Archy but lets him go, on the grounds of his assumed English nationality, for fear of provoking hostilities with England.

As Archy travels west in pursuit of clues as to the fate of his wife, Cassy, Hildreth guides readers across a chaotic landscape, recovered from the historical record, where self-appointed courts have taken over the administration of justice. Entering Vicksburg, Mississippi, Archy sees five men hanging on an extempore gallows and is surprised to learn that their execution was not carried out by "process of law," but was instead "entirely an amateur performance, got up by a committee of citizens, headed by the cashier of the Planters' Bank" (352). Hildreth pairs this historic 1835 lynching with concurrent events taking place in Madison County, Mississippi, where Archy encounters the aftermath of a presumed conspiracy to incite slave rebellion, which has been checked by a "vigilance committee and volunteer courts" (355). After befriending an area planter (identifiable as the historical figure Patrick Sharkey) who expresses doubts as to the existence of such a plot, Archy is summoned to appear before the vigilance committee. The planter reminds the committee that he is "a justice of the peace" and refuses to surrender Archy except "on some lawful warrant" (357).[66] As the representative of the rule of law in this scene, the justice of the peace, if not quite powerless, does no more than buy time for Archy's escape from the marauding vigilance committee. Fleeing the region, Archy later learns that the committee returned to the planter's house and shot him, though his wealth and connections protected him from further prosecution.

Referencing multiple, more or less concurrent historical events (the added chapters of *The White Slave* also allude to Prudence Crandall's controversial Connecticut school for African American girls, established in 1833, English abolitionist George Thompson's 1834 lecture tour of the United States, and Richard Mentor Johnson's 1836 nomination as running mate to Martin Van Buren), *The White Slave* is much more concretely located within a historical period than *The Slave,* whose precise chronological setting remains somewhat vague until the intrusion of the War of 1812. This exceptionally specific historical grounding seems aimed, in part, at criticizing the 1850s embrace of vigilantism represented by positive newspaper coverage of the San Francisco Vigilance Committee of 1851 and other volunteer courts of its ilk. That the wave of extralegal violence of the 1830s made a lasting impression on Hildreth is evident from his referring to the "great excitement of 1834" in an article published in 1848 refuting the purported legality of slavery, in which he recalled southern villages "being regulated by the code of Lynch-law, the same parties acting in the four-fold capacity of accusers, witnesses, judges, and executioners."[67] While these chapters of *The White Slave* compellingly reflect the state of paranoia into which the South was driven by fear of abolitionists in the 1830s, they also issue a warning to those readers of the 1850s who regarded the newly empowered vigilance committees of the West as a pragmatic response to perceived breakdowns in the criminal justice system. As Archy appears before one vigilante court after another, saved from prosecution either by luck or by well-connected friends, Hildreth reminds readers that certain regions of the country have already experimented with vigilance committees as an alternative to legally constituted authorities, with disastrous results.

Readers familiar with Hildreth's biography might register a cogent objection to the idea that *The White Slave* condemns extralegal action, insofar as Hildreth himself was a member of a vigilance committee. According to Emerson, Hildreth belonged to a body formed in Boston in 1846 and designated "a Vigilance Committee of Forty" whose stated purpose was "to take means to secure the protection of the laws to all persons who may be in danger of abduction from the Commonwealth."[68] Distinctions must be made, however, between this organization and the vigilance committees depicted in *The White Slave.* The vigilance committee to which Hildreth belonged acted nonviolently and within the law. The Boston Vigilance Committee was a "relief organization for . . . refugees from slavery," "an organization for ensuring that fugitives who had been charged were given the best legal counsel possible" (the committee organized the legal defense of fugitive Minkins), and "an instrument of public opinion."[69] Hildreth's membership on this body is in no way inconsistent with the idea that *The White Slave* warns against the danger of private citizens assuming authority to prosecute social deviance.

In the novel's final chapters, Hildreth offers a detailed and carefully modulated defense of the American legal system, concluding *The White Slave* with two significant courtroom victories on behalf of former slaves. A compelling character from the second half of the novel is John Colter, a former slave trader and gambler whom Archy enlists in the search for Cassy and Montgomery, Archy's son. The villain of this section of the novel dealing with the second generation of Archy's family is Agrippa Curtis, brother to the deceased owner (and father) of Montgomery's beloved, Eliza. With the aid of his New Orleans attorney Mr. Gilmore, Curtis attempts to defraud Eliza of her rightful inheritance by contesting her father's will. (Though she is the stated beneficiary of the will, her legal status to receive the inheritance is in doubt because of her illegitimacy, as Hildreth explains in a lengthy aside on probate law in Louisiana and the rest of the United States.) Colter devotes himself to her interests, studies law, and, after a protracted five-year legal battle, "remitted to Eliza her half of the proceeds, having well earned the other half for himself" (403).

In the only work of criticism to deal with *The White Slave* from a legal perspective, Mark Gruner reads Colter's victory as a "malicious joke" on the grounds that "it is achieved by a decadent slavetrader–turned bankrupt gambler–turned probate lawyer," concluding that "a tormented laughter" informs Hildreth's apparent endorsement of legal solutions to slavery at the end of *The White Slave*.[70] Support for Gruner's position seems to come from the very end of the novel, when Hildreth takes readers to the present day and informs them that under the auspices of the Fugitive Slave Law, Mr. Gilmore and Agrippa Curtis work together as a slave-catching commissioner and a deputy marshal, respectively, with a judge as a secret third partner: "and of course, all three, commissioner, catchpole, and judge, play beautifully into each other's hands" (405). Hildreth hereby inserts into the narrative one of the "atrocious judges" against whom he would rail in his 1856 book for complicity with slaveholding interests. These details notwithstanding, in my view Gruner misreads the tone of Hildreth's novel, which expends extraordinary effort in sketching the complexities of American jurisprudence. Atrocious judges, it turns out, are not the novel's sole arbiters of courtroom justice.

The second courtroom victory from the novel's final chapter endorses the legal system by reference to that key tenet of antebellum American legal ideology, the power of juries to guard against injustice. The case stems from Montgomery's caning of Agrippa Curtis when the latter viciously insults him

on a Boston street (like his mother, Cassy, Montgomery has been manumit-
ted by a kind owner), calling Montgomery a "cursed runaway nigger, the son
of a ——" (387). Curtis makes a complaint before a police court, which fines
Montgomery $20. When Curtis initiates a private suit charging Montgomery
with assault and battery, retaining "three or four celebrated Boston lawyers"
and requesting damages of $10,000, the jury returns a verdict awarding him
twenty-five cents (404). Archy notes the composition of the jury, which "happened to be composed of very low people, mechanics and others; there was
only a single wholesale merchant upon it, and he not engaged in the southern
trade" (404). Courts conspicuously achieve just verdicts in this incident: the
police court punishes Montgomery for his act of personal violence (which,
given nineteenth-century codes of personal honor, many readers may have
regarded as justifiable), while the civil court essentially throws out a frivolous
suit. Moreover, the jury carries out the safeguarding function juries were traditionally assigned by American legal ideology: it protects an individual (in
this case, a mixed-race former slave) from unjust prosecution.[71]

Composing this scene, Hildreth undoubtedly recalled post–Fugitive Slave
Law prosecutions in which juries similarly acted across racial lines in refusing
to convict defendants of aiding and abetting escaped slaves. In the year preceding *The White Slave*'s publication, Hildreth's Boston Vigilance Committee
subsidized the legal representation of several defendants allegedly involved in
the Minkins rescue; in all four cases that made it to courtroom prosecution,
juries either returned acquittals or were unable to reach a verdict, leading to
dismissal of the remaining cases.[72] Hildreth had also written approvingly of
Massachusetts slaves suing for their freedom during the colonial era, noting
that, according to historical sources, the "juries invariably gave their verdict
in favor of liberty."[73] While the situations are not perfectly analogous, it is at
least clear that *The White Slave* dramatizes the principle Hildreth would later
express in *Atrocious Judges,* that juries provide a necessary check on the power
of judges and a safeguard against oppression. What Hildreth offers in *The
White Slave* is by no means a complete vindication of American jurisprudence
but rather a representation of a flawed yet functional legal system capable—
thanks mainly to the institution of the jury—of achieving justice even across
a racial divide, given a context of enlightened community sentiment, as manifested by Montgomery's working-class Boston jurors.[74]

Dramatizing courtroom victories for African Americans, the novel opti-
mistically suggests that U.S. courts have the potential to dispense justice in
favor of black litigants. Elsewhere, *The White Slave* endorses the notion that
African Americans possess the right and ability to participate fully in the legal
system. Discussing Frederick Douglass's conception of black civil recognition,
Gregg Crane notes "an important theme in American law that requires agency

as the prerequisite for the imposition of legal responsibilities and liabilities: each is premised on the other."[75] *The White Slave* includes a scene illustrating this principle, in which blacks both administer and subject themselves to a process of legal authority. Archy and Thomas meet a band of slaves who have organized a maroon community in a South Carolina swamp. When one member breaks the commonwealth's rules, he is subjected to punishment:

> Drinking whiskey away from home, according to the prudent laws of this swamp-encircled commonwealth, was a high misdemeanor, punishable with thirty-nine lashes, which were forthwith inflicted upon our guide with a good deal of emphasis. He took it in good part though, as being the execution of a law to which he had himself assented, and which he knew was enacted as much for his own benefit, as for the benefit of those who had just now carried it into execution. (209)

Although this judicial sentence takes place outside of a formal courtroom, it garners the legitimacy that vigilante courts lacked by virtue of its being enacted with the consent of the entire swamp commonwealth, including the defendant. In contrast to Lippard's depiction of the (first ridiculous, then violent) Black Senate, Hildreth evinces neither condescension nor terror in a scene that pointedly raises the possibilities of African American legal identity and civic agency: government by blacks, in Henry Clay's phrase, but without Clay's alarmist tone. This scene validates Alexander Saxton's judgment that Hildreth believed that African Americans, once fully liberated, "could become equal citizens in a republican society and ought to be so dealt with."[76]

Putting together this scene with the courtroom victories that occur at the end of *The White Slave,* one finds African Americans and mixed-race individuals occupying a variety of positions across the legal-juridical realm: making laws, administering criminal punishment to violators, submitting themselves to punishment in criminal courts, and defending their interests in civil courts. These scenes anticipate fictional accounts of black legal/civic agency that would follow in the 1850s, including an all-black plantation court in Harriet Beecher Stowe's *Dred* (1856) and the black and mulatto Grand Council that plots a Cuban slave insurrection in Martin R. Delany's *Blake* (1859), but neither of these novels shares Hildreth's vision of blacks and whites working together within the U.S. legal system.[77] Hildreth's confidence in the abilities of African Americans to assume legal and civic agency alongside whites may have derived in part from personal experience, insofar as one of his colleagues on the Boston Vigilance Committee was pioneering black attorney Robert Morris.[78] In a period when faith in American courts was ebbing, Hildreth portrayed them (if not without reservations) as an institution capable, under the right conditions, of moving the United States toward a future where justice would be handed down without regard to racial considerations.

Before the decade ended, the Supreme Court's infamous 1857 *Dred Scott* decision would belie Hildreth's vision of a racially objective court system even as it verified the applicability of his stinging epithet "atrocious judges." Hildreth's cautiously optimistic appraisal of the U.S. legal system in *The White Slave* arguably proved prescient only in the very long term, insofar as the legal victories of the civil rights era showed that courts could help achieve a measure of racial justice, although critical race theorists have pointed to national self-interest in the climate of the cold war—as opposed to disinterested pursuit of social justice—as an important factor in cases such as *Brown v. Board of Education*.[79] In any event, *The White Slave*'s qualified endorsement of the justice system is all the more notable when weighed against the era's widespread lack of confidence in courtroom justice. From charges of corruption and class-oriented bias to abolitionist critiques of judges complicit with slavocracy, antebellum Americans pointed to a persistent divergence between the claims of justice and the judgments of American courts.

Cognizant of this distrust, Hildreth sharply criticized the era's sometimes-championed alternative, vigilante justice, sketching the perils of extralegal courts at some length in *The White Slave*. Responding to the same social trends, Lippard fantasized the transposition of an ad hoc extralegal court from the frontier to the urban Northeast. In *The Empire City*, Lippard invests considerable faith in the Court of Ten Millions, apparently condoning the rough justice it administers to villain Harry Royalton. To judge by the court's subsequent incarnation in *New York*, however, Lippard walked back his earlier support for the notion that a corrupt criminal justice system justified vigilante violence. For Lippard, the first step to social justice was exposure of the morally indefensible status quo. As he did in his newspaper reporting on the subject of crime, Lippard lobbied for an expanded vision of what constitutes the criminal class, allowing for the prosecution of the bankers and politicians whose malfeasance nurtured the vast economic and social inequalities of the age. The Court of Ten Millions is transformed between *The Empire City* and *New York* from an arena of violent retribution into the site of surprisingly restrained prosecutions. As an extralegal institution, however, the Court of Ten Millions obviously offered no practical model for legal or social reform.

That both Lippard and Hildreth juxtaposed white vigilante courts with scenes of African American participation in various legislative and judicial contexts (from informal legislative bodies to official courtrooms) in novels of the early 1850s seems more than merely coincidental. Vigilantism's unpredictable distribution of judicial authority was one factor among others—including African American calls for expanded civil rights, the emergence of black lawyers, and the actions of black antislavery activists—leading antebellum Americans to think about the implications of black civic agency, particularly in a judicial context.[80] Lippard imagined African Americans arbitrating justice rather than merely being subjected to its punishments, but the uncontrolled violence he ascribes to his fictional Black Senate suggests that the idea of government by blacks remained threatening to him and his white working-class readers. Hildreth, in contrast, depicts African American and mixed-race characters rationally and responsibly inhabiting legal and judicial identities ranging from a swamp community's legislative council to courtrooms in New Orleans and Boston. If one of the burdens of the antislavery novel was to answer what social role African Americans might occupy in a post-emancipation world, Hildreth implicitly proffered the response that they possessed the intellectual and moral capacities to assume all the rights and responsibilities required of, and accorded to, full-fledged citizens.

3

Carceral Conversions

Redemption via Incarceration in Antebellum American Literature

In the early to mid-1830s, a minor literary controversy followed the publication of William Gilmore Simms's first novel, the now little-read *Martin Faber* (1833). Some reviewers questioned the moral tendency of the book, a judgment that Simms found, or affected to find, puzzling. In his advertisement to the second edition of the novel in 1837, Simms wrote that he was "incorrigible" enough to say that he "[did] not yet perceive where the moral fails."[1] The novel is told from the point of view of a murderer. Raised by overly indulgent parents who never check his behavior, Martin Faber grows to adulthood with no consideration for the wants and needs of others, becoming what twenty-first-century readers might identify as a sociopath. After Emily Andrews, the young woman he has seduced, threatens to reveal her pregnancy to his fiancée, Martin strangles her. Justice catches up with him at novel's end, however, when he is convicted of Emily's murder. The last few chapters of the novel take place in a prison cell, where Martin remains cunning to the last. He prevails upon his virtuous friend (the man who brought Martin to justice), William Harding, to bring him a dagger so he can foil the executioner. Then, out of sheer malignancy, he insists that his fiancée, Constance, curse Harding in the latter's presence; when she refuses to comply, he stabs her. The novel ends by dramatizing Faber's moment of death on the gallows, offering no unambiguous evidence that he feels remorse for his crimes. (He wishes at the last moment that he had believed in God, but "now, it is too late".)[2]

As Nina Baym has documented, the conventions governing the assessment of a novel's morality were well known to the period's authors, readers, and reviewers. A novel was considered immoral if it failed by the end to reward virtue and punish vice. Even a novel that punished vice could run afoul of critical standards if it glamorized vicious behavior in such a way as to appeal to unwary or impressionable readers. As Baym describes the principle, a novel "making bad people sympathetic confounded morality altogether."[3] Simms points out in his defense of the novel, however, that *Martin Faber* defies none of these conventions. Not only do the "virtuous triumph" (Constance survives her stabbing by Martin, thanks to Harding's intervention) while "the vicious are overthrown," but also the novel contains no single scene, in Simms's estimation, "calculated, by its voluptuousness, to offend a delicate sense, or to entice a weak one."[4] And indeed, Simms does not dwell with lubricious detail on the scene of Emily Andrews's seduction or otherwise make Martin Faber's criminality attractive. To what, then, did reviewers object?

In this chapter I provide a possible answer to this question by examining the prison reform movement of the first half of the nineteenth century and its influential literary offspring, the carceral conversion narrative. I reconstruct the features of this culturally resonant story and demonstrate its ubiquitous presence across antebellum print culture. Relying on readers' familiarity with the form, Henry David Thoreau, Nathaniel Hawthorne, E. D. E. N. Southworth, Edward Everett Hale, and Rebecca Harding Davis all creatively refashioned the carceral conversion story to suit a varied palette of literary and polemical ends. Venturing into the reception history of the transatlantic literary phenomenon known as the Newgate novel, I further suggest that as a consequence of the penal reform movement's significant presence in the period's print culture, a new criterion emerged for evaluating the moral tendencies of fiction, or at least that (not inconsiderable) subset of fiction concerned with criminality. Readers and reviewers looked for a criminal, particularly when exposed to the enforced solitude of the prison cell, to experience the awakening of the conscience and subsequent moral reformation upon which the new penal theories were predicated.

Penal Reform in the Antebellum United States

From the 1820s until the Civil War, Americans carried out a sustained discussion of various methods for incarcerating and, many of them hoped, reforming convicted criminals. Emerging from this debate, the discourse of penal reform, which sprawled across books, literary magazines, penal reform periodicals, institutional reports, newspaper editorials, and other printed media, represents an insufficiently appreciated influence over much of the period's imaginative literature. Discussion of imprisonment provided American authors with a vocabulary of narrative patterns and ideas about crime, punishment, and reformation that they subsequently endorsed, adapted, or challenged in stories, novels, and essays, ranging from the now obscure to the most securely canonical of texts. Of these patterns, the carceral conversion—the individual criminal reformed through the rehabilitative power of incarceration—was perhaps the most influential.

In the late eighteenth and early nineteenth centuries, Americans came to regard incarceration as a more humane method of dealing with crime than the colonial era's regime of public punishments and executions.[5] The desire to differentiate the newly independent republic from its British counterpart contributed to the reform of penal codes, and a first wave of prisons was constructed during the 1790s and 1800s. The term used for these institutions, *penitentiaries,* encapsulates the period's faith in the idea of rehabilitation. By the 1820s, the conception firmly took hold that penal institutions should not simply punish inmates but rehabilitate them as well. As David Rothman describes one of the essential features of the era's asylums and prisons: "These mechanisms promised to transform the inmate's character so that he would leave the institution a different person. The reformatory regimen would alter not only behavior but also personality."[6] While reformers agreed in conceiving of individual moral reform as a key component of incarceration, they differed on the specific methods by which to accomplish this goal.

Two rival systems emerged in the 1830s to compete for public approval and legislative funding throughout the United States. In the Pennsylvania (or separate) system, first instituted at the Eastern Penitentiary at Philadelphia (commonly known by its location, Cherry Hill), inmates were subjected to something very close to our modern notion of solitary confinement. Although the inmates were permitted to work in their cells during the day and to exercise alone either in a small adjoining outdoor yard (or, if on the second floor, a double-sized cell), their only human contact was with their jailers: prison administrators, extra-institutional inspectors, or members of the clergy. Hooded on their first entrance into the prison, convicts never saw another inmate, a measure designed to preserve their anonymity, thereby in theory easing their reintroduction into society after discharge. The Pennsylvania system was founded on the idea that intensive solitude would coerce prisoners into acknowledging and reflecting on their guilt. Over time, given the moral guidance of clergymen and appropriate religious literature, remorse would turn to penitence: their consciences newly awakened, the inmates would commit themselves to leading crime-free, socially productive lives upon release. In their report to the French government on American penal institutions, Gustave de Beaumont and Alexis de Tocqueville captured the essence of the separate system:

> Can there be a combination more powerful for reformation than that of a
> prison which hands over the prisoner to all the trials of solitude, leads him

through reflection to remorse, through religion to hope; makes him industrious by the burden of idleness, and which, while it inflicts the torment of
solitude, makes him find a charm in the converse of pious men, whom otherwise he would have seen with indifference, and heard without pleasure?[7]

The Auburn system, also referred to in the period as the congregate system
or the silent system, likewise stressed rehabilitation. In Rothman's description, "The Auburn school vigorously defended . . . the reformatory promise of the penitentiary, fully sharing the axioms and optimism of its rival."[8]
Initially implemented at Auburn Prison and then at Mount Pleasant Prison
(better known as Sing Sing) in New York, the Auburn system came to be
widely adopted in the United States. In contrast to the separate system, the
congregate system permitted convicts to work together silently during the
day in factory-like conditions; they retired to separate cells at night. Absolute
silence, which was to the Auburn system what solitude was to the Pennsylvania system—the condition necessary to ensure a prisoner's reflection on
his own moral culpability—was enforced by liberal employment of corporal
punishment. Proponents of the Auburn system argued that it gave inmates
the opportunity to learn or practice a trade, something that might not be possible given the more limited range of occupations that could be carried out
within an individual cell under the Pennsylvania system. Moral rehabilitation
was presumably achieved by the inculcation of steady work habits in addition
to the inmates' silent contemplation of their guilt. The other purported benefit of the Auburn system, as described by its promoters and quickly recognized by various state legislatures, was economic self-sufficiency, as the prison
could be operated on funds generated by sale of the convicts' labor: "The
Auburn system had . . . set the economics of imprisonment on a far firmer
footing than had previously been the case."[9] Supporters of the Pennsylvania
system piously charged that the Auburn model sacrificed moral reform on the
altar of economic expediency. Proponents of the Auburn model maintained
that the protracted solitary confinement imposed by the Pennsylvania system
was dangerous to inmates' mental and physical health. Although the Auburn
system was more widely adopted, proponents of the Pennsylvania system
continued to promote their regime; as a result, these two systems framed the
terms of debate over penology throughout the antebellum period.

Its competing systems of incarceration put the United States on the cutting
edge of an international penal reform movement, impelling observers such as
Beaumont and Tocqueville to visit U.S. prisons. By the 1830s and 1840s, an
indispensable stop on the itinerary of English literary figures traveling through
the United States included two penitentiaries, usually the Eastern Penitentiary and Mount Pleasant, allowing visitors to compare the Pennsylvania

and Auburn regimes. Three prominent English writers toured U.S. prisons within the span of a few years and published their observations in subsequent travel books: Harriet Martineau (*Society in America,* 1837), Frederick Marryat (*Diary in America,* 1839), and Charles Dickens (*American Notes,* 1842). Each writer interviewed prison officials and inmates, surveyed the physical conditions of imprisonment, and opined in favor of one of the two systems: Martineau and Marryat endorsed the Pennsylvania system, whereas Dickens favored Auburn.[10]

These travel books were carefully scrutinized by American readers, who were keenly sensitive to the opinions, and especially the perceived slights, of foreign travelers regarding American institutions.[11] The nation's commitment to reform of prisoners provided Americans with a significant source of patriotic sentiment, serving as one variety of proof, as Americans saw it, of the superiority of their political and social institutions over European models. The *United States Magazine, and Democratic Review* boasted in 1845, "The prisons of the United States are confessedly superior in their structure, economy, and reformatory influence, to those of any other nation on the globe."[12] Martineau appealed to Americans' self-regard in this respect when she wrote that the United States surpassed the rest of the world in its treatment of the incarcerated "exactly in proportion to the superiority of her political principles."[13] Dickens regarded prison discipline as a subject "of the highest importance to any community" and believed that Americans had shown "great wisdom, great benevolence, and exalted policy" in their championing of reforms, though he was not without skepticism about certain American innovations.[14] British adoption of the Pennsylvania system of incarceration for its Pentonville "model prison," which opened in 1842, seemed to confirm America's leadership on the subject. In 1846 an international congress devoted to penitentiaries, held in Frankfurt, Germany, endorsed the Pennsylvania system for implementation in various European countries.[15]

Interest in the project of rehabilitating criminals was not limited to government officials. Penal reform was widely discussed in the popular press, with interest peaking in the 1840s and 1850s. For example, Dorothea Dix, later to become famous as a supporter of humane treatment of the mentally ill, published her *Remarks on Prisons and Prison Discipline* in 1845. In 1847, Little & Brown of Boston issued Francis C. Gray's book *Prison Discipline in America,* which became the subject of a wide-ranging forty-six-page discussion of penal reform in the *North American Review.*[16] Three articles on prison reform appeared in the mid-1840s in the *United States Magazine, and Democratic Review,* whose editor, John L. O'Sullivan (best known among literary scholars for his patronage of Nathaniel Hawthorne), was an early supporter of the reform-minded New York Prison Association.[17] Margaret Fuller wrote numerous editorials and reports on the subject of prison discipline in Horace Greeley's *New York Tribune* in the 1840s, as did Walt Whitman during his editorship of the *Brooklyn Daily Eagle*. Journalists often excerpted sections from annual prison reports in their articles on the progress of prison reform, surveying the effects of minor deviations in a given institution's implementation of one of the two accepted carceral regimes (such as providing a library to the inmates or relaxing corporal punishment for minor disciplinary infractions).

Each version of prison reform inspired its own periodical. In Boston, *Prisoner's Friend: A Monthly Magazine Devoted to Criminal Reform, Philosophy, Science, Literature, and Art* supported the Auburn regime during its publication run from 1845 to 1857. In addition to lobbying against capital punishment, another significant reform movement of the period, this magazine became a forum for the annual reports of the Boston Prison Discipline Society. Louis Dwight, founder and guiding spirit of the BPDS, was an implacable and vigorous enemy of the separate system, which he attacked for the intolerable mental and physical burdens he believed it placed on inmates.[18] Meanwhile, the *Pennsylvania Journal of Prison Discipline and Philanthropy*, published quarterly from 1845 to 1856 in Philadelphia, touted the claims of the separate system, which it defended against Dwight's relentless attacks.

American tourists joined their European literary counterparts in surveying penal conditions at well-known institutions. The state prison at Auburn charged twenty-five cents each to the six to eight thousand people who visited the prison annually; warden Gershom Powers even wrote a guidebook for such tourists.[19] In one short story published in *Graham's* in 1841, a honeymoon tourist excursion to a prison is a significant plot element.[20] According to a history of the institution, the Eastern Penitentiary of Philadelphia "rivaled the Falls of Niagara and the United States Capitol as a tourist attraction." In the 1830s and 1840s the prison saw a few thousand visitors per year, and in 1858 almost ten thousand tourists observed its carceral regime firsthand.[21]

Carceral Conversion Narratives in Penal Reform Literature

The centerpiece of penal reform ideology was individual moral reformation. The idea of penitence by way of incarceration intersected with the discourse of sentimentalism to produce innumerable accounts of tearful jail cell conversions. The specifics of these narratives obviously varied, but in its archetypal form the tale included the following elements: a guilty criminal incarcerated; a period of recalcitrance against religious or moral instruction; an awakening of the conscience as a result of reflection and (often) pastoral guidance; an emotionally charged conversion to Christianity; and finally a successful reintegration into the community; or, alternatively, death in a state of grace. Carceral conversion stories traced their origins to the crime-related literature of previous eras. Daniel Cohen lists the execution sermon, criminal conversion narrative, broadside verses, and last speeches of condemned criminals as popular genres that flourished in New England in the seventeenth and eighteenth centuries. These genres all featured accounts of criminals who, in most (but by no means all) cases, confessed their guilt, expressed remorse and penitence, and admonished readers to avoid their misdeeds. Cohen notes that during the first half of the nineteenth century, "ministers rechanneled their fascination with crime and punishment into a vast polemical literature of penal reform."[22]

In its very first issue, the *Pennsylvania Journal of Prison Discipline and Philanthropy* published the notes of clergyman John Woolson, minister in the County Prison of Philadelphia, who reported numerous dramatic conversions: "G.W., was once a professed infidel. His conviction seemed deep; manifested by tears, sighs, and frequent prayers for about twelve days. He professed a change of heart: left on Saturday last. We prayed together at parting." Woolson saw the reformatory power of prison-administered religious training cross racial lines, reporting that "J.S., a coloured man, died triumphant. . . . I visited him daily, and had many happy scenes with him after his conversion, which was about six weeks before he died." In Woolson's telling, prisoners eagerly bought in to the rehabilitative purpose of incarceration. Several prisoners told him "they are glad they are here, as they now see their folly, and are determined to reform." Reflecting the optimism of this moment in the American penal reform movement, Woolson summed up his experience in the prison: "The prospect of a reformation among the prisoners at this time is more encouraging than at any time since I have been engaged among them. In my visits I find many who appear truly penitent: they manifest it by their tears, and inquiries to know what they shall do to be saved."[23] Editing the *Brooklyn Daily Eagle*, Walt Whitman retold the story of a convict, a native of London, bred to a life of crime. This inmate had suffered the hardship of transportation to Van Diemen's Land (Tasmania) but found no opportunity for self-examination until he came under the mild disciplinary auspices of the American penitentiary regime, specifically the Pennsylvania method of solitary confinement: "He protested that every incarceration only hardened and rendered him more desperate, and that it was reserved for the kind and gentle treatment of the American prison to disarm his passions and awaken his better feelings, so that now he was determined, when restored to liberty, to lead a different and better life."[24]

These elements of carceral conversion narratives transcended disciplinary regimes. *Prisoner's Friend* routinely traded in similar conversion stories. Reporting on recent attempts to improve conditions in the Massachusetts State Prison in Charlestown, an Auburn-style prison, an author for the periodical includes a poem written by a convict for whom incarceration works exactly as prescribed. The poet begins with recognition of guilt ("Oh! Reader may you never feel / Those pangs that sting a guilty breast"), proceeds to Christian-inspired penitence ("Now to that Father I will go, / And daily bow the humble knee; / And seek his aid to heal my woe"), and finally expresses a resolution to rejoin society a reformed man ("And if these erring feet should tread, / Once more upon this world's broad stage, / I'll strive to earn my daily bread, / From precepts in the sacred page").[25] The penitent criminal's anticipated reintroduction to society presumably stands as a testament to the efficacy of the Auburn regime. In the wake of reforms in New York's state prisons in the late 1840s (following the death of a convict by the lash), *Prisoner's Friend* ran extracts from the official reports of the state's prisons. The chaplain of the Clinton Prison reported several conversions he judged to be authentic during his short ministry. Among the as yet unconverted inmates, "several convicts are now on the track of serious reflection, perusing their Bible with earnestness, deploring their former habits, and avoiding, as far as possible, their old associates in sin." The journal argued that such results verified the positive effects of the humane reforms it had consistently promoted.[26]

With its appeal to the Christian ideals of penitence and individual redemption, the narrative of carceral conversion caught the imagination of the nation's influential religious press. For example, an article in the *New York Evangelist* told the story of a "colored woman" who found religion in prison and was baptized on the eve of her execution; according to the minister who conducted the ceremony, "Jesus honored the occasion with his presence, and for a brief period transformed the gloomy prison into a shiny palace."[27] Religious periodicals displayed an amusing combination of cynicism and sentimentality in using prison-based stories to promote their particular sectarian affiliation. In a March 1842 article from the *Christian Reflector,* religious instruction leads one prisoner, a Boston bank executive, to a painful recognition of his own guilt, which manifests in an "intolerable agony" that gives way to "relief at the foot of the cross." The man explicitly credits his extended period of incarceration with leading him toward penitence: "If I had staid here but five years, or even six, I should have been lost forever!" In an aside, the author tells readers that the prisoner traces his criminal behavior to an upbringing among an insufficiently conservative denomination: "Certain teachers of error should turn pale to hear him speak of that 'accursed Universalism' to which he attributes his career of infidelity and crime."[28]

A few months later, possibly in response, the *Trumpet and Universalist Magazine* told the story of Thomas Shuster, a convicted murderer who experiences conversion in prison. Eight months into his sentence, Shuster intends to resist religious instruction, telling his minister after the fact that "he had determined to receive no instructions at our hands." Shuster, however, finds himself "approached by influences which he had never before felt," after which he begins to study the Bible and read religious tracts. Shuster's conversion, as witnessed by prison inspectors, earns him executive pardon. Shuster asserts that if he "could have understood Universalism" in his youth, he never would have gone to prison, and the editors stress that eight months of "orthodox" religious instruction had had no effect on him.[29] The role of religious tracts, frequently provided to prison inmates in hopes of inspiring conversion, did not escape notice in the religious press. One article reported on the dramatic conversion of a woman imprisoned in Sing Sing, arising after she read a religious tract left in her cell. The article's title sums up the talismanic value ascribed to such printed materials: "Who, On Earth, Should Despair! Reading a Tract the Means of Hopeful Conversion."[30]

Literary authors would not have needed to scour the nation's prison reform and religious periodicals to be exposed to stories of criminals redeemed through incarceration. These narratives circulated through the popular literary press as well. In an 1847 issue of *Godey's*, the short story "The Jailer's Daughter" tells of a young woman, Kate Walden, whose father takes charge of a prison. On Kate's first visit to the institution, she is introduced to the inmates, including an Ohio riverboat gambler. The chaplain's wife explains of the gambler, "This time of quiet has done him much good, and he appears really sorry for what he has done." Eventually the chaplain tells Kate that as a result of her quiet sympathy, "he had never seen [the inmates] in a better state—in fact, there was not one among them he considered hopeless."[31] The story echoes Martineau's judgment that benevolent visits from members of the community were all most inmates needed in order to experience reform: "These friendly visitors could scarcely fail of restoring, more or less completely, the moral health of the objects of their benevolence."[32] Another piece that appeared in *Godey's*, "The Prisoner: A Sketch," tells of an indomitable criminal named Bradshaw who defies prison authorities, destroys machinery, and attempts to kill his keepers. Initially, the narrator of Bradshaw's travails, his prison physician, seems to doubt the efficacy of solitary confinement: "Rarely do men, when undergoing this punishment, resort to the Bible." Eventually, though, exposed to the harshest conditions prison officials can devise (including solitary confinement in a darkened cell and bread-and-water rations), a broken and dying Bradshaw succumbs to the reformatory impulse: "Neither menaces not entreaties, lenity nor harshness, had been able to subdue his sullen and vindictive pride, and he was now brought out from his solitary cell, to fill a convict's grave. . . . Humbled, and at the eleventh hour penitent, he survived his entrance into the hospital only three days."[33]

Accounts of prison conversions spread across fictional and (purportedly) nonfictional texts, serving as they did both polemical and dramatic agendas, depending on the circumstances of publication. In April 1847, the *National Police Gazette* availed itself of the narrative pattern for entertainment value in telling the story of legendary Tennessee criminal John A. Murrell, "The Great Western Land Pirate." Murrell proves hardened and cynical at first, approaching confinement with bravado and expecting members of his gang to free him. After extended confinement, however, he experiences conversion:

> Weakening continually under the vital drain, his mind became accessible to influences which it had before disdained, and by degrees the convict gave an increased attention to the gentle counsels of religious visitors, who by a generous devotion sought the redemption of his begrimed and blood-stained soul. At length the pertinaceous [*sic*] kindness won its reward: the dull patience of the convict changed to an intriguing interest which at length quickened to conversion, and the cruel-hearted and remorseless land-pirate of the west became a meek and sighing Methodist.

Murrell retains his penitent attitude even after securing a pardon, and the narrator regards his successful conversion as "a signal triumph for philanthropy."[34]

Counternarratives certainly existed to challenge the claims of reformers and sentimentalists. Marryat transcribed the results of interviews with about a dozen convicts, only one of whom, a young woman, seemed unambiguously reformed as a result of incarceration. Writing of an inmate who had murdered his wife, Marryat sees no hope for redemption: "Of course, in this instance, there was no repentance; and the Penitentiary was thrown away upon him."[35]

American writers, too, challenged the upbeat accounts of prison conversion peddled by interested parties. *Godey's* featured a story called "The Convict's Daughter," which told of a young woman, a presumed orphan, who discovers that her father is alive and about to be released from prison. She takes a house where she can care for him, but neither prison nor the ministering attentions of a dutiful daughter reform the man. He proves incorrigible, continuing his career of crime. After his death, the daughter finds herself making restitution to the bank he had robbed.[36] An 1846 poem titled "The Solitary Convict," also from *Godey's,* tells the story of an inmate suffering through solitary confinement for ten years. Hearing celebrations outside, the inmate gives way to terrible despair, but neither reflection on his (presumed) guilt nor a conversion experience is registered. The poem ends with his loss of sanity ("And the eye was gleaming with vacant glare / Around on the walls of stone— / But no more care had he to bear, / For reason had left its throne"), in what seems a pointed rebuke to the claims made on behalf of the solitary system.[37]

In the same year, a young sailor recently returned from adventures in the South Seas lodged an attack on prison reform ideology. Contrasting the supposed refinements of civilization with the lifestyle he discovered among the natives of the Marquesas Islands, Herman Melville scathingly denounces incarceration as a form of torture in *Typee* (1846):

> To destroy malefactors piece-meal, drying up in their veins, drop by drop, the blood we are too chicken-hearted to shed by a single blow which would at once put a period to their sufferings, is deemed to be infinitely preferable to the old-fashioned punishment of gibbeting—much less annoying to the victim, and more in accordance with the refined spirit of the age; and yet how feeble is all language to describe the horrors we inflict upon these wretches, whom we mason up in the cells of our prisons, and condemn to perpetual solitude in the very heart of our population.[38]

If such skepticism did not significantly undermine Americans' confidence in theories of penology, it nonetheless offered provocation for other literary authors interested in the subjects of crime, punishment, and incarceration. What follows are analyses of five appropriations of the carceral conversion story, chosen on varying grounds including contemporary popularity, subsequent canonical status, and/or depth of engagement with the discourse of prison reform. The authors register a variety of attitudes toward the premises of prison reform even as they creatively adapt the movement's most culturally powerful trope to suit their purposes.

Apotheosis of the Carceral Conversion Narrative: "The Man Without a Country"

In his alienation from the outside world, especially in the extreme solitude that characterized the Pennsylvania system, a prison inmate became a man without a country. A board of visitors associated with the Massachusetts State Prison stated its theory in support of isolation in an 1815 report: "It [prison discipline] should be as severe as the principles of humanity will possibly permit. . . . [The prisoner] should be cut off from the world, and know nothing of what is happening outside."[39] One warden of Sing Sing prison told inmates upon arrival, "You are to be literally buried from the world."[40]

Although later incarnations of the solitary system backed off from such overzealous interpretations of the theory of solitude, inmates suffering through separate confinement knew little about events outside the prison. A similarly alienated prisoner was the subject of one of the most popular short stories of the nineteenth century, Edward Everett Hale's "The Man Without a Country." Published in the *Atlantic Monthly* in December 1863, the now rarely read story promoted a message of patriotism that northern readers found irresistible in the midst of the Civil War.[41] The story was reprinted in "both authorized and pirated book editions that sold half a million copies" in the space of a year, with its lead character, Philip Nolan, becoming as iconic a figure, in the estimation of one biographer, as Rip Van Winkle or Ichabod Crane.[42] The story's success propelled Hale, a New England Unitarian minister, to national fame, fostering a literary reputation that persisted well into the twentieth century, mostly on the strength of this one wildly popular story.[43] While the story's patriotism (sometimes derided as jingoism) has rightly been noted in explanation of its wide appeal, Hale's indebtedness to the carceral conversion narrative has not been recognized as a key element of its extraordinary success.

Born to a Boston Brahmin family in 1822 and a member of liberal, reform-minded Unitarian circles, Hale came of age during the height of prison reform sentiment in the United States. As a writer for his father's *Boston Daily Advertiser* in the late 1830s, and later as a close friend of some of the region's most prominent reformers (including James Freeman Clarke and Thomas Wentworth Higginson), Hale was undoubtedly aware of the prison reform movement and the claims it made for individual moral reformation. The rehabilitative effect of extended incarceration on a prisoner's guilty conscience is arguably the principal subject of "The Man Without a Country." The story opens with news of the death of Philip Nolan, whose history is then unfolded. As a U.S. Army officer overly susceptible to romantic fantasies of military exploits, the naïve and youthful Nolan, more than fifty years earlier, had been easy prey for Aaron Burr, who recruited Nolan to join his southwestern expedition. Convicted of treason in a court-martial in 1807, Nolan cries out fatefully during his trial: "Damn the United States! I wish I may never hear of the United States again!" Nolan's shocked judges (among whom are Revolutionary War veterans) convene to decide his sentence, which is that he shall indeed "never hear the name of the United States again."[44] Nolan is placed on a naval vessel outward bound for a cruise, and subsequently spends the rest of his life being transferred from vessel to vessel, never returning to U.S. shores and forbidden to hear news of the country. Nolan serves this unusual sentence for over half a century, until his death.

Some of the story's appeal lies in Hale's careful evocation of the details of Nolan's carceral regime. The narrator, Frederic Ingham, recalls the initial instructions to Nolan's jailers, including the injunction that officers never provide him with any information about the United States. Under constant scrutiny aboard ship, Nolan is "not permitted to talk with the men unless an officer was by" (33). Conversation is strictly monitored during messes to maintain this cloud of secrecy; an awkward moment occurs at a captain's table when Nolan innocently asks about Texas, not knowing of its annexation (84). In this curious arrangement in which Nolan lives and works among a community of sailors, yet carefully scripted conversation never strays outside of authorized bounds, one hears an echo of the silent (Auburn) system of incarceration. Nolan's reading material is carefully censored by authorities; before books and newspapers can be given to him, "somebody must go over them first, and cut out any advertisement or stray paragraph that alluded to America" (37). Nolan develops a strictly regimented routine to help him pass the time, which includes reading, making scrapbooks, and naturalist studies. Ingham recalls hearing him say "that no man in the world lived so methodical a life as he" (65). Supporters of both prison reform camps expressed confidence that achieving an inmate's moral rehabilitation was simply a matter of the correct engineering of his carceral regime. Reformers obsessed over details related to isolation, communication, labor, reading material, diet, clothing, and so on in order to discover the optimal formula for inspiring penitence. The story suggests that Hale implicitly subscribes to this line of thinking, as the impulsive young Nolan, as years of confinement wear on, evolves into a model inmate: a "gentle, uncomplaining, silent sufferer" (85).

Nolan's initial conversion experience transpires relatively early in his incarceration. Before it, he treats his imprisonment as "a mere farce" (44), and affects to enjoy the voyage, resembling the hardened criminals of various prison-related stories, such as Bradshaw from "The Prisoner, A Sketch" or Murrell the Western Land Pirate. Nolan's conversion occurs when he joins the sailors in passing the time by reading aloud from Walter Scott's *Lay of the Last Minstrel.* The poem's paean to love of country evokes an emotionally charged breakdown. Turning "a little pale" at the poem's celebration of "my own, my native land," Nolan gags, turns red, chokes, and finally throws the book into the sea (42–43). According to the narrator, this event "shows about the time when Nolan's braggadocio must have broken down." He disappears into his stateroom for two months, after which, says Ingham, "he never was the same man again" (44–45). In the wake of this episode, Nolan "repented of his folly, and then, like a man, submitted to the fate he had asked for" (81). Nolan's conversion is not explicitly religious; it is rather an initiation into the civic religion of patriotism that developed in the North in response to secession and Civil War. As the story continues, though, Hale colors Nolan's conversion with appropriately Christian elements. Ingham recalls Nolan as having been "always ready to read prayers" (69), and his last words are "Look in my Bible, Danforth, when I am gone" (98). The popularity of prison reform narratives stemmed in part from their adaptability to various literary and social ends; here Hale expertly braided strands of Christian piety, sentimentalism, and patriotism into the carceral conversion story.

Drawing attention to Hale's shrewd adaptation of the tropes of prison reform narratives does not fully account for the complexity of the story's portrait of imprisonment. What lends the story a weirdness that verges on absurdist or existentialist literature is the idea that Nolan has fallen into a bureaucratic black hole. He occupies a legal limbo; the government "had failed to renew the order of 1807 regarding him," which means that individual commanders are on their own in deciding how to handle him (86). The narrator tells of trying to effect Nolan's official liberation on the grounds that his incarceration may be legally actionable as false imprisonment, but the secretary of war refuses to issue an order one way or another, which Ingham interprets as "If you succeed, you will be sustained; if you fail, you will be disavowed" (87). Ingham complains, "It was like getting a ghost out of prison" (79). Elsewhere in the story, Ingham explains that once "they began to ignore the whole transaction at Washington," Nolan's imprisonment "began to carry itself on because there was nobody to stop it without any new orders from home" (63).

Antebellum prison reformers placed a lot of confidence in the administrative competency and basic decency of prison officials; they trusted to record keeping, inspectors' visits, and an unexamined assumption of official transparency to ensure the humane treatment and timely release of individual convicts. Perhaps needless to say, this confidence was often misplaced, as exposés occasionally revealed.[45] Nolan suffers what looks at times like a grimmer version of the convict's fate than reformers accounted for; he is completely forgotten by the outside world, his very existence unacknowledged by the institution charged with his care. Nolan does not have a name among the common sailors; they refer to him as "Plain-Buttons," since even his uniform buttons have been stripped of the insignia of the United States (34). Some antebellum prisons effected a similar deprivation by assigning convicts numbers in place of names. Stripping Nolan of an identity as well as a country, leaving him stuck in a Guantánamo-like legal impasse in which releasing him could implicate the imprisoning authority in its own transgression of the law, Hale unwittingly exposes the underside of Americans' unbounded confidence in penal rehabilitation. This frisson of horror, while obviously at odds with Hale's overtly patriotic intentions, surely helps to account for the story's popularity. "The Man Without a Country" allowed American readers, collectively fascinated by the notion of imprisonment but also, perhaps, obscurely cognizant of the threat it posed to individual liberty and the inordinate power it invested in authority, to flirt with—but then safely renounce—a dystopic vision of perpetual incarceration.[46]

Nolan's story ends with an emotional climax that sweeps away any doubts about the legality or efficacy of incarceration. As Nolan lies on his deathbed, he implores an officer named Danforth to break the code of silence to which he has been subject for fifty-six years. Readers discover that Nolan's stateroom has become a shrine to the nation he once impulsively disowned: "The stars and stripes were triced up above and around a picture of Washington, and he had painted a majestic eagle, with lightnings blazing from his beak, and his foot just clasping the whole globe, which his wings overshadowed" (88). Nolan has drawn a map of the United States from memory at the foot of his bed, filling in the states he surmises have been added during his long imprisonment, exclaiming, "Here, you see, I have a country!" (88). Danforth tells of having filled Nolan in on half a century of American history, with one very significant omission: he cannot bring himself to tell Nolan of the South's secession and the ensuing war. This passage allows Hale to sketch a thumbnail narrative of American triumphalism, with accounts of the War of 1812, the Mexican-American War, inventions such as the steamboat and the telegraph, and so on. One of Nolan's final acts is to ask Danforth to read with him a Presbyterian Book of Public Prayer, which includes the following petition to God: "Most heartily we beseech Thee with Thy favor to behold and bless Thy servant, the President of the United States, and all others in authority" (98).

Though the Civil War and its aftermath would soon turn Americans' attention away from prison reform, Hale's story was perfectly timed in 1863 to unite interest in both subjects, shrewdly grafting the still influential carceral conversion narrative onto an emergent ideology of national unity. Ardent patriotism stands as a crucial but not wholly sufficient explanation for the story's extraordinary popularity; after all, northern newspapers and magazines were filled with stories appealing to patriotic sentiment.[47] Hale's achievement in "The Man Without a Country" was to embed his encomium to nationalism within an already popular narrative form involving transgression, imprisonment, and redemption. "The Man Without a Country" appealed to nineteenth-century readers by indulging a fantasy that had occupied writers and reformers for more than a generation: the creation of the perfect carceral regime.

The Skeptics: Comedy, Tragedy, and Contrariety in Carceral Conversions

The carceral conversion narrative could also be parodied for comic purposes, as in E. D. E. N. Southworth's immensely popular novel *The Hidden Hand; or, Capitola the Madcap* (first serialized in the *New York Ledger* in 1859). Following the journey of its appealing main character, Capitola Le Noir, from the streets of New York to the Virginia plantation aristocracy, the novel is centrally concerned with issues of criminal justice. In addition to numerous scenes transpiring in courts and a denouement involving the liberation of a condemned criminal (discussed in chapter 4), the middle of the novel includes a wittily rendered jail scene indebted to the formulas of prison reform literature. At this point in the story, a trio of criminals charged with kidnapping Capitola and bringing her to their leader, Black Donald, find themselves in a county jail awaiting sentencing after having been foiled by the resourceful heroine. Having dressed the wounds the trio suffered during the failed kidnapping, one of the novel's minor characters, Mrs. Condiment, develops sympathy for the men and concern about their spiritual state. Their incarceration coincides with the annual revivalist camp meeting held in the region, inspiring Mrs. Condiment to undertake their reformation.

Southworth leaves little doubt that she is consciously invoking the tropes of prison reform literature. For example, she offers a description of the jail the men occupy, "a simple structure of gray stone, containing within its walls the apartments occupied by the warden."[48] The term "warden" seems grandly inappropriate for a small county jail unless the scene is understood as a parody of the stories of prison reform normally associated with the penitentiary. Elsewhere in the novel a beleaguered minister exclaims, "Good angels! I am fated to hear more great sins than if I were a prison chaplain" (184), suggesting that the language of prison cell conversions was familiar enough by 1859 to be regarded as a cliché. A few details of incarceration are provided for readers, including the information that the "three imprisoned burglars languished in jail, each in a separate cell" (212). Isolated as prescribed by approved theories of incarceration, the prisoners seem perfectly situated to experience a penitence that would satisfy readers' expectations for conversion. Southworth's efficient deployment of these narrative patterns deftly sets up the reversals to follow.

Although Mrs. Condiment's intentions are noble, the novel portrays her as ridiculously naïve when it comes to criminality. The novel's narrator warns readers that there can be "neither honor, confidence, nor safety among men whose profession is crime" (212). In contrast, Mrs. Condiment subscribes to the notion that a concerned preacher's care is all the criminals require to experience saving grace. Therefore, although she is aware that the area's ministers "have all been to see them, and talked to them, [and] not one of the number can make the least impression on them," she nonetheless implores a newly arrived camp meeting preacher, Father Gray, to try his powers of persuasion on the three: "Now I thought if *you* [Father Gray] would only visit them, you could surely bring them to reason" (215). Since Father Gray is in fact the gang's leader, Black Donald, in disguise, Southworth ensures that Mrs. Condiment will be disabused of her confidence in criminal rehabilitation.

The scene that unfolds in jail swiftly undercuts the assumptions on which prison reform was based. For example, the men immediately resent the intrusion of a group of visitors to observe their incarceration. "You go along out of this! the *whole* on you. I'm not a wild beast in a cage to be stared at!" says one of the prisoners (217). During a decade when the Eastern Penitentiary of Philadelphia allowed nearly ten thousand visitors per year to tour its site, inmates might well resent being put on display. Nor do the inmates respond favorably to the prospect of religiously motivated intervention in their affairs, though they are used to ministerial visits. One prisoner, Hal, exclaims on the appearance of the new preacher: "Here's another! There's three comes reg'lar! here's the fourth! . . . It's getting' to be entertainin'! It's the only diversion we have in this blamed hole!" (216). Perhaps most striking is the way that Black Donald's plan for liberating his crew from prison depends on the community's belief in narratives of carceral reform. Too well known in the region to adopt a conventional disguise, Black Donald emaciates himself by way of a month-long regime of reduced diet, and then establishes himself as a newly arrived preacher with the onset of the annual camp meeting. Insinuating himself among the religious authorities of the town, Black Donald takes it for granted that this identity will ensure him access to the county jail. He never broaches the subject of visiting until Mrs. Condiment makes her request. Instead of converting the inmates, Black Donald smuggles guns and files into their cells, allowing them to make their escape. While Southworth's not-so-hidden hand brings this far-fetched plan to a successful conclusion, she relies no less than Black Donald on the assumption that her audience will be quite familiar with the ideology and narrative tropes characteristic of antebellum prison reform.

For Rebecca Harding Davis, rejection of the carceral conversion story signaled commitment to a nascent doctrine of literary realism. Appearing in 1861 in the *Atlantic Monthly* (the periodical in which Hale's "Man Without a Country" would appear two years later), "Life in the Iron-Mills" militantly resisted prison reform pieties.

Welsh iron puddler Hugh Wolfe sits in a county jail, awaiting transportation to the state penitentiary to serve a harsh sentence of nineteen years' hard labor for theft. Though weakened by consumption, Wolfe has made two desperate escape attempts already. Wolfe's jailer Haley takes his desperation philosophically: "Fightin' for life, you see; for he can't live long, shut up in the stone crib down yonder."[49] Speaking through Haley, Davis does not share the culture's confidence in the possibilities of penal rehabilitation: it's clear to readers that nineteen years in a penitentiary is the equivalent of a life sentence for someone in Wolfe's compromised physical condition. Haley says of other inmates he's observed: "It acts different on 'em, bein' sentenced. Most of 'em gets reckless, devilish-like. Some prays awful, and sings them vile songs of the mills, all in a breath" (446). Inmate prayer is neither more nor less significant than a millworker's bawdy work song in Davis's vision. The tracts on which reformers hung such high hopes are nowhere to be seen, nor would they have much efficacy among a population that is presumably illiterate; Wolfe, after all, stands out from his fellow workers on the basis of "a quarter or so in the free-school" (435).

Davis punctuates her bleak prison scene with the chilling sound of Wolfe slowly sharpening the scrap of tin with which he will commit suicide. Dwelling on the people and animals that he can see from his cell walking freely through the marketplace, Wolfe anticipates the effects of incarceration at some length: "He knew what it was to be in the penitentiary,—how it went with men there. He knew how in these long years he should slowly die, but not until soul and body had become corrupt and rotten,—how, when he came out, if he lived to come, even the lowest of the mill-hands would jeer him,—how his hands would be weak, and his brain senseless and stupid" (447).

Davis's story is framed by the device of ushering a middle-class reader into the depths of a normally invisible social stratum. If jail cells were anything but invisible within the prison-saturated literary culture Davis confronted, she might have depended on readers' familiarity with carceral conversion narratives to effectively overturn their expectations. Presumably unread in the hopeful conversion stories circulated in penal reform periodicals and popular magazines, Wolfe can have acquired his knowledge of the penitentiary's punishing regime only from personal acquaintance with discharged inmates whom the system has broken. Davis therefore counters readers' expectations by privileging Wolfe's experiential knowledge of the debilitating effects of incarceration over the sentimentalized narratives of carceral conversions common in periodicals.

Davis refuses to say whether Wolfe becomes eligible for salvation during his time in jail. Moreover, whatever redemption he experiences is presumed to come not because of, but rather despite, imprisonment: "Whether, as the pure light crept up the stretched-out figure, it brought with it calm and peace, who shall say? His dumb soul was alone with God in judgment. A Voice may have spoken for it from far-off Calvary, 'Father, forgive them, for they know not what they do!' Who dare say?" (449). If anyone is in need of conversion, it is judicial authorities, Davis implies, who knew not what they did when they unjustly condemned Wolfe to a nineteen-year sentence.

In this scene, Davis premises her pioneering strain of realism on rejection of the sentimental assumptions implicit in carceral conversion stories. To portray Wolfe's gruesome suicide as a fate less onerous than extended incarceration seems ample evidence of Davis's skepticism regarding prison reform ideology. The ubiquity of the literature of prison reform, however, made its tropes difficult to avoid. While Hugh is beyond earthly salvation, his cousin Deb, also sentenced to imprisonment, is not. As I document in chapter 4, narratives of women in prison partook of a separate set of literary conventions, from which Davis found it harder to break free.

Involving a process of several discrete steps unfolding over time, the carceral conversion narrative typically covered a period spanning months to years: recall the prisoner in the *Christian Reflector* who rejoiced that a seven-year sentence had proven just sufficient to facilitate his redemption. In contrast, Henry David Thoreau experienced a prison conversion in a single night. Harnessing carceral conversion to an urgent antislavery polemic, Thoreau's adaptation of the form is characteristically caustic. A glance at the "Economy" chapter of *Walden* confirms Thoreau's disenchantment with his culture's investment in prison reform. Three paragraphs into his diatribe against philanthropy, Thoreau focuses on the English prison reformer John Howard: "Howard was no doubt an exceedingly kind and worthy man in his way, and has his reward; but comparatively speaking, what are a hundred Howards to *us,* if their philanthropy do not help *us* in our best estate, when we are most worthy to be helped?" Thoreau also scorns a minister who ventured to praise England's Christian heroes, among whom he numbered (along with William Penn) two prominent prison reformers, Howard and Elizabeth Fry. Thoreau complains, "Every one must feel the falsehood and cant of this."[50] Thoreau singles out prison reform as the cause that best symbolizes Americans' excessive regard for philanthropic projects.[51] This disdainful treatment of the premises of penal reform carries the augmented moral authority of a writer who has experienced incarceration not as an inspector or journalist but—however briefly—as an inmate.

Seized by constable Sam Staples for nonpayment of a poll tax as part of his principled opposition to slavery, Thoreau in 1846 spent a night in the Middlesex County Jail in Concord. In "Resistance to Civil Government," Thoreau turns his night in jail into a set piece within the essay, providing the kinds of inside details of prison life that prison reform discourse often dwelled on: the "walls of solid stone, two or three feet thick," the "door of wood and iron, a foot thick," the breakfast of "a pint of chocolate, with brown bread," and the verses (graffiti?) composed by former inmates. Whereas morally uplifting pamphlets were sometimes credited with sparking a criminal's repentance (as in "Reading a Tract the Means of Hopeful Conversion"), Thoreau dryly mentions that he "had soon read all the tracts that were left there," without comment upon their quality or impact.[52]

Although his experience lacks the trappings of Christian piety normally present in such narratives, Thoreau undergoes an immediate and irrevocable conversion: "It was like traveling into a far country, such as I had never expected to behold, to lie there for one night. . . . When I came out of prison . . . a change had to my eyes come over the scene,—the town, and State, and country,—greater than any that mere time could effect." In a reversal of the expected pattern, the prisoner's conversion entails neither recognition of his guilt nor a resolve to reform; instead, he is struck with the moral turpitude of the people of New England: "I saw yet more distinctly the State in which I lived. I saw to what extent the people among whom I lived could be trusted as good neighbors and friends; that their friendship was for summer weather only; that they did not greatly purpose to do right; that they were a distinct race from me by their prejudices and superstitions, as the Chinamen and Malays are."[53] A lengthy and blistering indictment of the ethics of his fellow citizens follows. Jason Haslam astutely notes that Thoreau's night in jail "details a specific moment of transcendence which ironically duplicates the reformative rhetoric of the nineteenth-century prison system."[54]

In Thoreau's bracingly contrarian twist on prison reform stories, the inmate's awakening takes the shape of a newly jaundiced view of his fellow citizens: they are the ones who must recognize their morally crippling complicity with the institution of slavery. Upending the assumptions on which prison reform ideology was based, the convert in Thoreau's essay occupies the privileged moral position, carrying a message of reform to a morally compromised (but presumably educable) community. Thoreau's vision of a society in need of the prisoner's reforming insight anticipates Hawthorne's own complex retelling of the penal reform narrative.

Prison Reform Ideology and *The Scarlet Letter*

Perhaps no antebellum novel is more concerned with issues of crime and punishment than *The Scarlet Letter* (1850). Structured around a disciplinary mechanism, the novel mentions close to a dozen methods, in addition to its signature scaffold, by which communities through time have punished crime: the guillotine, the gallows, the dungeon, the prison, the stocks, the pillory, branding, whipping, scourging, and, of course, sartorial injunction. In its extended meditation on the aftermath of a criminal act, the novel asks questions that also occupied Hawthorne's contemporaries in the prison reform movement: What could a society do to inspire penitence in a criminal? What effect did extended isolation from one's community have on the offender? Is the purpose of criminal punishment deterrence, retribution, rehabilitation, or some combination of these and other motives? The answers found in Hawthorne's novel implicitly respond to, and sometimes deviate from, his culture's orthodoxies on the subject of criminal reformation.

Whereas Hawthorne's devotion to historical accuracy in *The Scarlet Letter* is sometimes taken for granted, his depiction of the prison in the novel's opening chapter shades toward the anachronistic. The most dubious statement is the narrator's confident assertion regarding utopias and prisons: "The founders of a new colony, whatever Utopia of human virtue and happiness they might originally project, have invariably recognized it among their earliest practical necessities to allot a portion of the virgin soil as a cemetery, and another portion as the site of a prison."[55] Beyond its ironic suggestion that naïve social reformers are chagrined by the accommodations they have to make for the human inevitabilities of death and crime, the statement implies that a prison has from ancient times existed as a primary method for punishing criminals; it naturalizes incarceration as civilization's invariable response to crime.

This claim simply does not accord with the fact that the prison, as Hawthorne's audience would have understood the term, was largely an invention of the Enlightenment. Before the widespread acceptance in Europe and the United States of incarceration as a presumably humane alternative to other forms of punishment, prisons certainly existed. They were, however, mainly conceived of as a stopgap measure to confine a criminal until judicial sentence was passed or as an expedient to coerce debtors into meeting their obligations. In the early years of Massachusetts, for example, the "most notable" purpose of imprisonment was for debt, while in other cases incarceration served a segregative function, "prevent[ing] persons from causing political or moral harm to the community rather than punishing them for doing so."[56] To go back further in history, prisons existed in the ancient world as just one among many commonly employed methods of punishing social deviants. One possible explanation for Hawthorne's misrepresentation is that by the middle of the nineteenth century, in part as a result of the public relations efforts of penitentiary advocates, the prison had become such a ubiquitous social institution that it was difficult even for a knowledgeable student of history to conceive of criminal punishment without it.[57]

An explanation more consistent with the depth of Hawthorne's research into colonial history is that he knowingly capitalized on the availability of the historical novel as a site for examining present-day complacencies. Without claiming that Hawthorne polemically inserts *The Scarlet Letter* into contemporary debates about prison reform, it is nonetheless possible to argue that the novel's occasional imposition of nineteenth-century ideas about crime and punishment onto seventeenth-century Boston society results from Hawthorne's awareness of prevailing criminal reform theories and constitutes, on one level, his thoughtful response to them.

Others have noted the anachronism of the novel's opening chapter, "The Prison Door." Robert Shulman writes that the first paragraph of the novel "is dominated by the image of a nineteenth-century prison, not a seventeenth-century jail, which was like an ordinary house."[58] While Shulman's pointed observation is correct, it is worth noting that the general idea of a Puritan prison was available in Hawthorne's historical sources. Hawthorne evidently borrowed his fictional prison and the name of its keeper from one of his more important sources, Caleb H. Snow's *History of Boston*. Writing about the property of a prominent colonist, Snow includes this description: "His next neighbor on the south was Richard Parker or Brackett, whose name we find on the colony records as prison keeper so early as 1638. He had '*the market stead*' on the east, the prison yard west, and the meeting house on the south."[59] Published in 1825, Snow's *History of Boston* is itself the product of the age of prison reform, whose terminology it uncritically adopts. (Surely a "prison yard" has more to do with emergent nineteenth-century penitentiaries than with the ad hoc structures that served as jails in the seventeenth century.)

Even Snow's history did not tell Hawthorne when this prison had been erected; its actual physical existence as a free-standing structure in 1640s Boston could not be inferred from his sources, which accounts for the guardedness of Hawthorne's cagey remark that "it may be safely assumed that the forefathers of Boston had built the first prison-house, somewhere in the vicinity of Cornhill, almost as seasonably as they marked out the first burial ground" (47).[60] In another of Hawthorne's known sources, Thomas Hutchinson writes of Quakers being confined in a prison awaiting trial in Boston in the 1650s.[61] The salient point is not that some form of prison did not exist in Puritan Boston, but that Hawthorne's foregrounding of the prison as the centerpiece of a society's criminal justice system (the "black flower of civilized society," as Hawthorne euphemizes it in the opening chapter [48]) owes a considerable debt to nineteenth-century discussions of penal reform, as do subsequent depictions of the effects of Hester Prynne's sentence.[62]

During his reading in colonial history, Hawthorne may have noticed a telling correspondence between seventeenth-century New England Puritan and nineteenth-century American theories of criminal justice. Like their descendants, Puritans put faith in a malefactor's capacity to reform. As George Lee Haskins notes in his legal history of colonial Massachusetts, "The evidence of the court records provides notable illustrations of the extent to which the magistrates directed the criminal law of the colony away from traditional concepts of retribution which permeated English criminal law, toward practices which emphasized moral persuasion in order to reform the offender."[63] Haskins emphasizes the legal process of admonition, whereby social authorities such as ministers or magistrates admonished offenders to acknowledge their sinfulness and demonstrate repentance; signs of sincere penitence were rewarded with a reduction in sentence. This belief in the possibility of individual criminal reform was present in John Winthrop's journal, another of Hawthorne's sources. In an entry dated January 27, 1642, Winthrop writes of William Aspenwall, formerly a member of the antinomian faction. Returning from Rhode Island, "Mr. William Aspenwall . . . made a very free and full acknowledgement of his error and seducement, and that with much detestation of his sin," after which "his sentence of banishment was released." Similarly, a woman named Anne Hett, who had been excommunicated from the church for "wicked and blasphemous courses and speeches," after a few weeks "came to see her sin and lay it to heart . . . and so was brought to such manifestation of repentance and a sound mind, as the church received her in again."[64]

The magistrates' insistence that Hester Prynne publicly name the father of her child during the first scaffold scene may be regarded as an admonishment to her to acknowledge her sinfulness and the justice of the sentence passed upon her, after which she could hope in time to rejoin the community, a trajectory much like the one that reformed convicts in antebellum jails were expected to follow. The rest of the novel traces Hester's path toward penitence in language that sometimes overlays nineteenth-century theories of individual criminal reform onto the not perfectly identical (and yet, to Hawthorne's readers, strangely familiar) seventeenth-century Puritan notions of sin, confession, and repentance.[65]

The tension between seventeenth- and nineteenth-century concepts of criminal punishment is evident throughout the novel, whenever the purpose or effect of Hester's sentence is broached. Whereas the penitentiary of the nineteenth century had taken the criminal's suffering out of the public eye (if only to reframe it to a large extent within the period's abundant print culture), the purpose of various seventeenth-century types of punishment, including the spectacle Hester embodies on the scaffold, had a crucial public component: to remind the community of its shared values and of the price of disobedience. This deterrent model of punishment is invoked not only in the first scaffold scene but also later in the novel, when, for example, the narrator tells how Hester sometimes became the subject of an impromptu sermon delivered on Boston streets: "Clergymen paused in the street to address words of exhortation, that brought a crowd, with mingled grin and frown, around the poor, sinful woman" (85). The point of affixing letters to a criminal's garment was not to reform the offender who was thereby humiliated but to deter others from the same transgression. Another seventeenth-century punishment would simply remove the transgressor from the community. After all, Anne Hutchinson was neither incarcerated nor forced to wear an ignominious symbol; she and her followers were banished, preventing the widespread adoption of her dangerous heresies. The novel raises this model of punishment in its offhanded reference to "an Antinomian, a Quaker, or other heterodox religionist" about to be "scourged out of town" (49).

Again and again, however, the novel returns to the idea that the primary purpose of criminal punishment is the individual moral reformation of the malefactor in accordance with the antebellum model. Hester is said to hold this view of her sentence in chapter 5, "Hester at Her Needle," when she tells herself that "the torture of her daily shame would at length purge her soul, and work out another purity than that which she had lost; more saint-like, because the result of martyrdom" (80). The narrator, too, subscribes to this view in the much-discussed chapter 13, "Another View of Hester," where the fact of Hester's impenitence and wide-ranging speculation about injustices toward women are taken as evidence that "the scarlet letter had not done its office" (166). If the office of the scarlet letter had been to signal to the community that Puritan Boston does not condone adultery, then Hester's inward response to the judicial sentence would be beside the point. Hawthorne avails himself of Puritan notions of sin and repentance in order to dramatize what was for nineteenth-century readers a very contemporary kind of story: the individual criminal's journey toward penitence.

It would not be going too far to claim that Hester Prynne is figuratively the subject of a carceral regime, and that Hawthorne uses *The Scarlet Letter*, as Caleb Smith argues, "to explore the pressing issues of the penitentiary age."[66] On a literal level, of course, Hester is no longer an inmate from the moment she defiantly issues out from Hawthorne's vaguely anachronistic prison door. Without delving too deeply into the evidence, however, Shulman asserts that "Hester's situation is . . . similar to that of a prisoner in one of the institutions designed to reform the deviant through isolation."[67] A number of elements of the characterization mark her as the subject of a penal regime, starting with Hawthorne's ruminations on imprisonment in the novel's first chapter, the title of which, "The Prison Door," so pointedly foregrounds the idea of incarceration. Hawthorne's memorable portrait of Hester's brazenness on the scaffold—that "haughty smile" and "glance that would not be abashed" (52–53)—calls to mind the criminals in popular literature whose initial bravado eventually withers in response to the painful self-scrutiny that incarceration supposedly entailed. Clothing designed to mark out and humiliate the criminal was not unknown in the nineteenth-century prison, as in Massachusetts's experiment with particolored clothing (which carried the benefit of making escapees easily identifiable).[68] An administrator of the Massachusetts State Prison noted in 1815 that even the prisoner's clothes "ought to be a means of punishment."[69]

Ultimately the way Hester lives and works in a community, and yet remains ineluctably separate from it, is the most significant resemblance between her position and that of a nineteenth-century prison inmate. Hawthorne emphasizes Hester's alienation:

> In all her intercourse with society, however, there was nothing that made her feel as if she belonged to it. Every gesture, every word, and even the silence of those with whom she came in contact, implied, and often expressed, that she was banished, and as much alone as if she inhabited another sphere, or communicated with the common nature by other organs and senses than the rest of human kind. She stood apart from mortal interests, yet close beside them. (84)

Whether her radical isolation calls to mind the Pennsylvania model's ideal of separate confinement in an individual cell or the Auburn system's brutal enforcement of absolute silence even in the midst of a factory-like work space, Hester indeed finds herself, as Melville had expressed the situation of the prison inmate, "condemn[ed] to perpetual solitude in the very heart of our population."

The idea that solitude was not inherently reformatory is one of two major challenges to prison reform orthodoxy posed by *The Scarlet Letter*. It is a critical commonplace of the literature on Hawthorne that severing the magnetic chain of humanity binding people together is perhaps the greatest misfortune an individual in a Hawthorne story can experience. Well-known Hawthorne characters such as Ethan Brand and Parson Hooper exhibit the dreadful psychological consequences of (in their cases self-imposed) alienation. Prison reform ideology was premised on the rehabilitative effect of just such a severance. Rothman quotes a partisan of the Pennsylvania system who boasted that the inmate was "perfectly secluded from the world . . . hopelessly separated from one's family, and from all communication with and knowledge of them for the whole term of imprisonment."[70] That such isolation could result in any redemptive outcome runs contrary to the spirit of much of Hawthorne's fiction. In *The Scarlet Letter*, Puritan authorities, modeling antebellum prison reformers, expect Hester's isolation to make her penitent; instead it makes her rebellious. Isolated from society and given plenty of time to think, Hester "cast away the fragments of a broken chain. The world's law was no law for her mind" (164). Hester's neo-carceral solitude encourages the "latitude of speculation" in which she wanders "without rule or guidance, in a moral wilderness" (199). In his most direct statement regarding the effect of isolation on Hester, the narrator has this to say: "Shame, Despair, Solitude! These had been her teachers,—stern and wild ones,—and they had made her strong, but taught her much amiss" (199–200). Hester's isolation from the community does not have the expected effect of causing her to reflect on and recognize her guilt; in fact, she apparently renounces any acknowledgment of guilt when she famously reminds Arthur that their initial act of sin, whatever society's interpretation of it, had "a consecration of its own" (195).

The portrait of a character fundamentally changed during an extended period of solitude in prison was a compelling fictional narrative adopted by literary authors and reformers alike. What most supporters of prison reform ideology did not anticipate or express, however, was that the inmate's change could be in the direction of increased alienation from society rather than reintegration with its basic values.[71] Solitude leads Hester toward resentment of authority and confirmation of the rightness of her initial criminal conduct; the Puritan exercise of criminal justice (with its overtones of the antebellum carceral regime) takes Hester away from penitence, not toward it.

Hawthorne's second major challenge to penal reform ideology is perhaps even more radical than the first. Hester achieves penitence not during her painful isolation from the community but during her residence in New England after Pearl's (presumed) marriage: "Here had been her sin; here, her sorrow; and here was yet to be her penitence" (263). Credited by the people of Boston with a distinctive wisdom born of her experiences, Hester becomes an informal social worker for the city's disaffected women: "Women, more especially, . . . came to Hester's cottage, demanding why they were so wretched, and what the remedy! Hester comforted and counselled them, as best she might" (263). The implication seems to be that Hester's penitence is somehow coupled with this ministry to alienated women. Hester's reformation is premised upon her sharing what she has learned about the conflict between individual desires and social responsibilities with other people struggling with similar moral dilemmas. Mere service to the community is not the issue; Hester's almsgiving effected no personality change during the initial years of her sentence. Instead, Hester imparts to the women of Boston the unique insight she has gained from having transgressed its laws related to gender and sexuality and suffered the officially imposed consequences.

Penal reformers aimed to rehabilitate the fallen criminal through incarceration, as if to lift him or her up magnanimously to a normative relationship with citizens who had never transgressed. Not unlike Thoreau, Hawthorne endows the transgressor with a higher wisdom unavailable to those who have not been through a process of judicially imposed punishment: the reformed criminal then passes on this hard-earned wisdom to others in a process that is both socially beneficial and morally ameliorative for the offender. This insight is consistent with the view proposed by Brook Thomas, who identifies Hester's return to Boston and counseling of wayward women as a key to the novel's politics. For Thomas, *The Scarlet Letter* "tells the tale of a how a 'fallen woman' finds redemption by helping to generate within a repressive Puritan community the beginnings of an independent civil society."[72] Instead of passively and anonymously rejoining society, the rehabilitated criminal in *The Scarlet Letter* actively contributes to a healthy civic order; this engagement with the community reflects and finalizes the transgressor's individual moral reformation. Hawthorne pointedly exposes the condescension implicit in the writings of penal reformers, who seem rarely to have considered that the vectors of social utility between convicts and citizens could run in both directions.

Interiority and Assessments of Morality in Reviews of American Fiction

Reading backward from the carceral conversion narratives of the 1840s and 1850s may help explain the problematic reception William Gilmore Simms's *Martin Faber* received in the 1830s. The conflicting reviews of *Martin Faber* and the author's own bemused response to them—I take Simms more or less at his word that the specific nature of the backlash against the novel surprised him, though he may have intuited (and hoped) that its bleak subject matter and depraved central character would cause a sensation—expose a culture on the verge of transition, in which the criteria for evaluating fiction's moral tendencies were shifting in concert with the spread of prison reform ideology. (At the time of *Martin Faber*'s publication in the fall of 1833, the celebrated Eastern Penitentiary at Philadelphia had received its first prisoner in 1829, the Auburn Prison had released influential reports on its operations in 1829 and 1830, and Tocqueville and Beaumont's *On the Penitentiary System in the United States and Its Application in France* had been published and reviewed that summer.) An early reviewer in *The Knickerbocker* adhered to the traditional standard of evaluation in stating unequivocally of *Martin Faber*, "This [novel] contains a broad and good moral, the reward of virtue, and the agony and punishment of guilt, brought about by their own natural tendency." A reviewer in the *Southern Literary Journal* agreed: "Morality and virtue were vindicated, and the laws of God, and the laws of man, enforced. What more was necessary?"[73] Under the paradigm requiring that virtue be rewarded and vice punished by the story's end (assuming vice was not painted in too attractive colors), *Martin Faber* passed critical scrutiny.

An alternative, emergent standard of judgment demanded instead, however, that a criminal given the opportunity to reflect on his crimes experience guilt and penitence in accordance with the tenets of prison reform. Simms had Faber subscribe to a philosophical determinism in which his life was part of, in the character's words, the "necessary sequence in the progress of time" and he was "but an instrument in the hands of a power with which [he] could not contend."[74] The reviewer in *Atkinson's Saturday Evening Post* pinpointed the "very philosophy inculcated in the excuses of the hero" as objectionable because of its challenge to "human accountability." But after making the protagonist's philosophical defense of his behavior (which Simms suggested in his advertisement readers should easily recognize and discount as self-serving) the grounds of the novel's supposed immoral tendencies, the reviewer went on to speculate about the effects such a philosophy would have on the criminal justice system: "Look at all offences in such a light, and . . . [w]hat is the use of law? and what are its penalties, but cruel inflictions, for misfortunes that could not be averted?"[75] This reviewer's leap from a philosophical to a juridical (or, perhaps more accurately, a penological) rationale for questioning the morality of *Martin Faber* appears to betray the influence of prison reform ideology. Reformers insisted that the United States had left behind an era of "cruel inflictions" when it embraced the moral rehabilitation of criminals in modern penitentiaries, where prisoners reflected on their guilt and experienced contrition. But Faber's philosophical determinism both absolves him of guilt and precludes repentance. Conceiving an imprisoned murderer who remained unrepentant even as he evinced the disposition and intellectual capacity to reflect in solitude on the meaning of his crimes, Simms unwittingly challenged the premises of a potent ideology to which Americans increasingly subscribed.

Further evidence of the shifting criteria by which crime-related fiction was evaluated in the 1830s emerges from American reviewers' responses to the short-lived phenomenon of the Newgate novel, especially as practiced by (as he was then known) Edward Bulwer. Regarded as the premier British novelist after the death of Walter Scott (until the ascendancy of Dickens), Bulwer wrote several so-called Newgate novels, which entailed a focus on a criminal protagonist whose life resembled (or was drawn from) the criminal biographies collectively known as the *Newgate Calendars*.[76] Disagreements similar to the ones following publication of *Martin Faber* were present in American reviews of Bulwer, whom Simms's reviewers readily identified as an influence.[77] Conflicting criteria surfaced, for example, in assessment of the moral tendency of Bulwer's *Eugene Aram* (1832), the story of a real-life eighteenth-century criminal. In Bulwer's telling, Aram is an intellectual who murders a wealthy miscreant after weighing the morality of the deed in light of the good that he might do for the world if possessed of the man's wealth; thirteen years later, the murder is exposed and Aram is brought to justice. Writing in *The Ariel,* one reviewer succinctly expressed the view that depicting Aram's death on the gallows satisfied the novelist's moral duty. Aware of the possibility that the novel might have "a decided tendency to weaken the cause of morality" in light of Aram's positive character traits, the *Ariel* reviewer asks, "If all the high attributes given to the character to impart this interest, cannot save him from an ignominious death, consequent and flowing from his crime, how by that interest is the cause of morality injured?"[78] The *New-York Commercial Advertiser* took the same line, noting: "It is said that to make a murderer interesting, is to prejudice the cause of morality. Does it do so, if the murderer is hanged, like a common felon?" Answering negatively, the reviewer concluded that Bulwer's handling of the plot sufficiently indicated the author's disapprobation of Aram, rendering the novel's moral "unexceptionable."[79]

But other American reviewers objected to *Eugene Aram,* not on the hitherto conventional grounds that it aroused sympathy for a criminal (which continued to preoccupy British reviewers),[80] but because Aram was insufficiently penitent. The reviewer for the *Philadelphia Album and Ladies' Literary Portfolio* complained that Eugene Aram's regret for his crime stemmed from "fear of detection" instead of "sincere penitence": "If, for example, Eugene Aram, instead of being held up to the reader as perpetually haunted by the fear of his guilt being discovered and punishment ensuing, had been stung to the soul by an inward and constant pang of remorse, . . . then the moral would have been perfect and salutary."[81] Social reformer Robert Dale Owen (no cultural conservative) lodged the same objection: "Had Bulwer painted Eugene's punishment as entailed on him by recollection, reflection, and self-accusation alone, uninfluenced by just cause to fear detection and rational grounds to anticipate legal vengeance, then the moral, though common-place enough, would have been supported." Owen regarded feelings of remorse as the "natural and necessary" consequences of criminal behavior, which Bulwer had failed to depict.[82] Similar principles appear in American reviews of other Bulwer novels; for example, one reviewer opined that *The Disowned* was "free from all censure" on the grounds of morality because it depicted "the corroding sting" and "the continued thrusts of conscience" accompanying crime, while a reviewer of *Falkland* condemned that novel because a reader "naturally expects such a criminal to become either a conscience-struck penitent, or the victim of some extraordinary punishment," neither of which happened to a villain "who, even in his last thought, indicates no compunction for his crimes."[83]

Owen was not alone in regarding feelings of remorse as the natural and inevitable consequence of crime. Americans tutored in the philosophy of prison reform came to believe that the eventual awakening of a criminal's guilty conscience was an inviolable law of human psychology. An outraged reviewer of Bulwer's *Paul Clifford* blasted the novel for failing to depict this awakening in the main character (a principled highwayman whose final end is not the gallows but transportation to America). The reviewer objected to the novel's moral tendency because it portrayed the life of highwaymen "in brilliant colors," giving "the charm of energy, courage, and heroism" to their conduct "by throwing into the shade whatever penalty remorse might inflict." But the reviewer went further, criticizing the novelist's failure to understand the psychology of the criminal: "Providence, in its kindness, has connected suffering with crime; not only remotely and feebly, but directly and acutely. . . . [W]henever the heart is displayed to us, we find it to be so, without one solitary exception. . . . And we know it so to be by the melancholy story, which remorse has again and again drawn in agony from [the felon's] lips." What is the melancholy story drawn in agony from the felon's lips if not a carceral conversion narrative? A novelist who did not depict what the reviewer reiterated was the "necessary and inseparable connexion of suffering and sin" either failed to understand or disregarded widely held assumptions about human psychology.[84] Severing the link that prison reformers had been at pains to establish between transgression and the punishments of conscience was deemed morally irresponsible because it robbed crime-centered fiction of any deterrent effect on impressionable readers.

These reviews suggest a subtler way reformers influenced American fiction, beyond supplying literary authors with the adaptable template of the carceral conversion narrative. The underlying assumptions of the prison reform movement, among other cultural developments, helped point novelists toward the privileging of psychological interiority. In the British context, a similar argument has been made by Sean Grass, whose examination of novels with scenes set in Victorian prisons leads him to assert that "the prison . . . provided both the impetus and the model for increasingly interior fictions of the psychological self."[85]

Admittedly, various factors led novelists to explore the form's potential for revealing characters' inner lives, among which the ideology of romantic individualism and the focus of sentimentalism on the affective life of characters seem especially pertinent. But the attention antebellum Americans directed toward understanding the psychological state of the incarcerated criminal in both fictional and nonfictional discourses was also at work. Nothing was more critical to the ideology of prison reform than assessing the effects of incarceration on the prisoner's state of mind. Reformers' confidence that solitude inspired penitence bled over into literary reviews, where assessments of characterization and morality became inextricably linked: crime-centered fiction that failed to depict an awakening of the criminal's conscience misrepresented human psychology in a socially irresponsible way. For their part, successful crime novelists provided a glimpse into the criminal's mind which validated assumptions that remorse invariably followed wrongdoing. Discussing reviewers' assessments of characterization in the antebellum novel, Nina

Baym dates a new emphasis on interiority to about 1850, when "the inner life increasingly takes precedence," a development she attributes primarily to the literary influence of Charlotte Brontë.[86] An alternate account of the origins of interiority as an evaluative criterion pushes back the date of its emergence by a decade or two and, more important, places some credit for this development on the influence of penal reform ideology. This account is consistent with Christopher Castiglia's provocative idea that Americans conceived a new model of interiority in the antebellum years that was intimately linked with the rise of social reform institutions (such as prison reform) and that limited the possibilities for democratic agency.[87]

Once again, reviews of the Newgate novel offer supporting evidence. It became a commonplace for critics to observe that Bulwer, in contrast to Walter Scott, excelled in the depiction of the interior life. Thomas Augustus Worrall wrote in the *North American Magazine* in 1833: "Bulwer differs from Scott greatly. Scott paints the external world, and . . . is deservedly celebrated; but Bulwer analyzes the heart—penetrates and explores its hidden recesses, examines each thrilling cord, each quivering fibre, from the diapason to the highest and lowest note of feeling."[88] This judgment was seconded in the *American Monthly Magazine,* which suggested that "Scott was the more vivid painter, Bulwer the deeper and freer thinker; Scott superior in delineating the external effects of passion, Bulwer in tracing out its inner workings." The author went on to praise *Eugene Aram* because it was there that Bulwer displayed "his acquaintance with the human mind."[89]

The accolades accorded to Bulwer for his insight into the psychology of the criminal would soon be transferred to Dickens on the strength of his portraits of Sikes and Fagin in *Oliver Twist* (1839). Writing in the *Christian Examiner and General Review* (which a decade earlier had attacked Bulwer's *Paul Clifford* for failing to recognize the burden of crime on a wrongdoer's conscience), J.S.D. applauded the "moral power" of *Oliver Twist*: "The old Greek 'Furies' of Orestes were not more tragic, than the terrors of conscience which here hunt down the desperate murderer."[90] *Atkinson's Saturday Evening Post* averred that "[Dickens] possesses the most intimate knowledge of the human heart, of any man of the age."[91] The notion that it is the inner life of the *criminal* that gives Dickens his special claim on readers' attention, however, is best expressed by the reviewer in the *Yale Literary Magazine:*

> And here, we think, [Dickens] shows his knowledge of human nature, and appears not only the attentive student of the outer world, but also a profound scholar in that deeper study, the concealed movements of the heart. There has seldom been a more masterly delineation of a mind, racked by fear, remorse, and despair, and overwhelmed with the prospect of inevitable death, than the chapter in *Oliver Twist,* describing the Jew's

trial and imprisonment, before execution. . . . We feel, we know that every thought which flashes across [Fagin's] burning brain, is such as nature would suggest.[92]

Clearly, American reviewers came to value interiority in fiction as early as the 1830s. But insight into the mind's inner workings was not prized equally across every character type; it was the portrait of the criminal character in particular whose interiority reviewers most urgently demanded to see.

Hawthorne has long been credited as a pioneer for introducing psychological complexity into American fiction; in his history of the nineteenth-century American novel, for example, Philip Gura pinpoints *The Scarlet Letter*'s innovation as residing "in its psychological dissection of the emotional lives of its three central characters."[93] As he crafted his depiction of his characters' inner lives in *The Scarlet Letter*, Hawthorne could not have been uninfluenced by assumptions about character and morality expressed consistently across reviews of novels by his predecessors and contemporaries. These assumptions undoubtedly guided *The Scarlet Letter*'s reception.

The related ideas that the measure of a novelist's skill is his insight into the inner life of a criminal and that a novel's moral tendency hinges on its depiction of the criminal's penitence (as opposed to punishment) are readily discerned in reviews. Multiple reviewers focused on and applauded *The Scarlet Letter*'s portrait of characters experiencing remorse for their transgressions; the *Portland Transcript* noted approvingly the "ever gnawing remorse and anguish of the minister," while *The Athenaeum* singled out for praise Hester's "slow and painful purification through repentance."[94] Evert A. Duyckinck described the novel as a "psychological romance" and "a tale of remorse, a study of character in which the human heart is anatomized, carefully, elaborately, and with striking poetic and dramatic power," language one finds repeated in other reviews, and which is strikingly similar to the praise bestowed on Bulwer and Dickens in the 1830s.[95] In a lengthy, ambivalent response to the novel in the *North American Review* (which had published an extensive review of the penal reform debate two years earlier, in January 1848), Anne W. Abbot cited similar criteria by way of objecting to the characterization of Dimmesdale. That the minister endured a seven-year period during which his need for social approval trumped his impulse to confess violated Abbot's understanding of the natural order of things: "Mere suffering, aimless and without effect for purification or blessing to the soul, we do not find in God's moral world."[96] In these reviews, the criterion for successful characterization was the characters' modeling of psychological truths about guilt and penitence that reviewers assumed were universal. Nonconformity with these purported truths compromised a novel's claims to moral soundness, as Abbot's reference to "God's moral world" makes clear.

To the extent that the morality of *The Scarlet Letter* was called into question, it was primarily the issue of penitence that was at stake. One of the
novel's most sympathetic early reviewers, E. P. Whipple, credited Hawthorne
with rehabilitating the subject matter of French novels, adultery, because "his
guilty parties end . . . as the spiritual laws, lying back of all persons, dictated
to him," that is, feeling contrition for their crimes.[97] In his (now) notoriously unfavorable review of *The Scarlet Letter,* however, Orestes Brownson
charged that the novel was morally flawed precisely because neither Hester
nor Arthur experiences penitence. Brownson thought that Hester suffers "not
from remorse, but from regret, and from the disgrace to which her crime has
exposed her," and charged that in the final scaffold scene Arthur "shows no
sign of repentance, or that he regarded his deed as criminal." Brownson felt
obliged to "condemn" the novel for misunderstanding the nature of guilt,
repentance, and confession—unwittingly echoing the disapproving reviews
of Bulwer's *Eugene Aram* almost two decades earlier.[98] Reviewers of *The Scarlet
Letter* subscribed to the notion that solitary dwelling on one's guilt would
inevitably lead a criminal to penitence, merely disagreeing as to whether or
not the novel dramatized this process. Translating the concept into the terminology of "spiritual laws," Whipple expressed the belief that this process
was an inherent part of human nature, as penal reformers had been propagan-
dizing for decades. The review criterion that first emerged in the mid-1830s,
when William Gilmore Simms unexpectedly ran afoul of critical opinion,
had become entrenched by the 1850s.

Another way to illuminate the link antebellum reviewers forged between
criminality and interiority is to look at reviews of a popular contemporary
book concerned with the interior life of a non-criminal character, Donald
G. Mitchell's *Reveries of a Bachelor* (1850). Although the very premise of the
book was its presentation of the bachelor's extended interior monologue (his
reveries), reviewers' acclaim was not couched primarily in the language of
psychology. The admiring reviewer in the *Yale Literary Magazine* praised the
book for inspiring readers' feelings of sympathy with the rest of humanity
while also noting "our author's skill in painting" (a decidedly exterior-focused
criterion) and "the pathos and the vein of religious feeling that runs through
the book" among its principal charms.[99] Similarly, *The Albion* praised *Reveries
of a Bachelor* for "some lively fancies, . . . scraps of humour, and . . . ram-
bling reminiscences," while the *American Whig Review* commended "the very
ingenious form into which it is thrown, the beautiful thoughts and sentiments with which it abounds, and the charming pictures of character and
scenery that adorn it."[100] The reviewer who comes closest to crediting Mitchell
with psychological acuity, while allowing that the book discloses "the fine
feelings of a heart in sorrow" with "quiet precision," also complains by way

of comparing Mitchell unfavorably with Hawthorne: "But we look upon it rather as a curious operation, than the exposition of a terrible interior."[101]

For antebellum readers primed in the conventions of the carceral conversion narrative and its underlying ideology, exposure of the "terrible interior" of a criminal mind spoke to cultural preoccupations that portraits of the inner life unrelated to criminality did not address. Over time, and under the influence of differing cultural conditions, novelists explored and reviewers learned to appreciate the quality of psychological interiority in non-criminal character types, with the technique finding fullest expression, of course, in the stream of consciousness experimentation of modernist writers. The opening wedge of interiority as a hallmark of successful characterization, however, can be traced in part to the influence of early-nineteenth-century penal reform ideology, specifically its interest in the conscience of the criminal.

The popularity of carceral conversion stories in antebellum literature is not difficult to explain. American leadership in an international penal reform movement was a significant source of civic pride, insofar as the nation's penitentiaries were taken to embody a progressive and humane commitment to dispensing criminal justice in ways consistent with republican ideals. Meanwhile, the religious revivals of the Second Great Awakening lent appeal to stories of sin and redemption, while the emotional tone of reputed prisoner conversions fed into the era's embrace of literary sentimentalism. Combining elements of patriotism, piety, and sentimentality, carceral conversion narratives proved irresistible to the authors, editors, and readers who together shaped the contours of the period's rapidly expanding print culture. Prisoner conversion stories migrated from nonfiction sources explicitly supporting the penal reform movement into more literary venues, where they took on increasingly complex and varied shades of meaning. Thoreau turned the carceral conversion story inside out to register moral outrage over his community's complacency with regard to slavery, while Hale retained the form's traditional outlines to promote a vision of national civic unity during the Civil War. Whereas Southworth deftly played on readers' expectations to give the form a comic turn, Davis recognized that invoking and then rejecting the premises of carceral conversion in the tragic story of Hugh Wolfe best promoted her realist agenda.

Because the incarcerated criminal's state of mind was so important to assessing the success of the new penal regimes, carceral conversion narratives turned cultural attention to the interior life of the criminal. This emphasis on interiority found expression in the way American novels dealing with crime were evaluated. From an earlier model in which a novel merely needed to reward virtue and punish vice in order to suit the moral standards of the day, now fictional accounts of criminals were judged on their fidelity to a theory of human nature in which solitary contemplation of one's guilt inspired penitence. When the criminal in question was a murderer, as in many Newgate novels and Simms's *Martin Faber,* the requirement that he exhibit penitence evidently took on additional urgency (whereas when Thoreau, Southworth, and Davis tweaked the form in contravention of readers' expectations, none of their criminal figures was accused of so grave a crime). The review criterion that chagrined Simms in the 1830s appeared commonplace in 1850, when it was invoked either to condemn (in a few cases) or validate (more widely) Hawthorne's achievement in *The Scarlet Letter.* By this point, the premises of the penal reform movement had rippled outward to shape, alongside other important cultural factors, the development of American fiction. Hawthorne's engagement with the carceral conversion story combined sustained attention to the inner lives of his morally flawed characters with a recognition of the rehabilitated criminal's value to society, extending the familiar story in an unanticipated direction.

Critics regard Hawthorne's creation of Hester Prynne, especially in its deviation from the stereotypes of womanhood associated with sentimental domesticity, as one of his most impressive accomplishments. This achievement becomes more marked if Hester's experiences are regarded as partaking to some extent of the discourse of penal reform. Although the majority of American prisoners in the antebellum era were men, women, too, routinely cycled through the criminal justice system and ended up in prison. Prison reformers often addressed the experience of women inmates, projecting onto the female prisoner the same assumptions that pervaded Victorian American culture with regard to womanhood. In the next chapter I examine women in prison, as both inmates and caretakers, in prison reform discourse and novels of the antebellum period. The predictable patterns into which such writing often lapsed further showcases, in retrospect, the sensitivity and originality Hawthorne employed when venturing into this subject matter.

4

The Angel in the Penitentiary
Women and Incarceration

The prison cell as envisioned by antebellum reformers was an implicitly feminized space: it was devoted to values that the culture tended to assign to womanhood, including silence, order, cleanliness, moral reflection, and spiritual renewal. These qualities characterized prisons regardless of carceral regime: both the Auburn and Pennsylvania systems depended on the inmate's opportunity to reflect on his or her crimes in silence as the centerpiece of the reform program. When observers entered the prison cells of women, therefore, it is not surprising that they often perceived the cultivation or restoration of feminine virtues: the jail cell was a place in which women seemed naturally at home. Frederick Marryat captures this way of thinking about incarcerated women in *Diary in America* (1839), recounting a visit to the Eastern Penitentiary at Philadelphia in the late 1830s. Marryat writes of inmate number nine, imprisoned for larceny:

> She was very quiet and subdued, and said that she infinitely preferred the solitude of the penitentiary to the company with which she must have associated had she been confined in a common gaol. She did not appear at all anxious for the expiration of her term. Her cell was very neat, and ornamented with her own hands in a variety of ways. . . . When I visited this girl a second time, her term was nearly expired; she told me that she had not the least wish to leave her cell, and that, if they confined her for two years more, she was content to stay. "I am quite peaceful and happy here," she said, and I believe she really spoke the truth.[1]

Marryat approved of the solitary system as the more effective and less cruel of America's competing carceral regimes, and the male inmates in his interviews at times voice complacency with regard to their fate: inmate number two, for example, says of his confinement "that it could do no harm, and might do much good."[2] Nonetheless, only inmate number nine experiences this deep contentment.

The presumed effect of confinement on women comes across with greater force in Charles Dickens's *American Notes* (1842), published a few years after Marryat's account. Dickens fiercely criticized the separate system as he witnessed it in Philadelphia, regarding it as a cruel and dangerous experiment with the inmates' mental health: "I hold this slow and daily tampering with the mysteries of the brain, to be immeasurably worse than any torture of the body."[3] Nonetheless, Dickens observed salutary effects on the women prisoners who endured the regime. Writing of three women he met in the Eastern Penitentiary of Philadelphia, Dickens notes, "In the silence and solitude of their lives they had grown to be quite beautiful." He offers this description of one of the three:

> One was a young girl; not twenty, as I recollect; whose snow-white room was hung with the work of some former prisoner, and upon whose downcast face the sun in all its splendour shone down through the high chink in the wall, where one narrow strip of bright blue sky was visible. She was very penitent and quiet; had come to be resigned, she said (and I believe her); and had a mind at peace.[4]

Like Marryat, Dickens pointedly affirms his belief in the woman's sincerity; both writers imagine—and then immediately dismiss—the possibility of a woman dissembling about the contentment that confinement bestows.

Dickens goes on to describe the young woman's longing to be free and his belief that the Pennsylvania system was "as cruel and as wrong" in the case of women as in the case of men, yet he could not shake the notion that its effects on women were inherently different than on men: "The faces of the women, as I have said, [the solitary system] humanises and refines. Whether this be because of their better nature, which is elicited in solitude, or because of their being gentler creatures, of greater patience and longer suffering, I do not know; but so it is."[5] When antebellum journalists and prison reformers approached the subject of women and incarceration, they often followed the culturally approved script that Marryat and Dickens intuited; a penitentiary regime in which male prisoners recovered their humanity restored to female inmates the more gender-specific gift of femininity.

The literature of penology in the antebellum period often tells another, parallel story about the relationship between women and imprisonment. Much as the home provided a sanctified space where the antebellum middle-class husband rehabilitated himself from the moral corruption that attended his forays into the competitive world of laissez-faire capitalism, the prison offered the subject of carceral experimentation an opportunity to rediscover the moral purity that he had sacrificed by taking up a life of crime. But if the idealized household of the period had a morally pure wife to reawaken a husband's moral sense, who would perform that ideologically crucial function in the penitentiary? To some extent, as discussed in chapter 2, a chaplain or confessor sometimes facilitated the criminal's moral conversion. Prison reformers and popular authors alike, however, often delegated the task to the same figure whose beneficent moral purity was indispensable to the period's sentimental literature: the middle-class woman. Antebellum writers discovered a potent narrative formula in the story of a virtuous woman who ventures into the penitentiary, dispensing care and effecting conversions among the prisoners whose lives she touches. For her services, this figure, whom I will refer to as the angel in the penitentiary, often reaps the rewards conventionally bestowed upon the heroines of the period's sentimental literature: marriage and domestic bliss.

The present chapter traces the migration of these two narratives—the woman who recovers her femininity in the prison cell and the angel of the penitentiary who miraculously transforms the lives of prison inmates—from prison reform discourse into imaginative literature. As a middle-class heroine who proves her virtue through the extension of sympathy to the socially disadvantaged, in the process awakening readers' own emotional responsiveness, the angel in the penitentiary is, of course, a quintessentially sentimental figure. Analysis of the figure's appearance in two popular antebellum novels supports recent reevaluations, however, crediting nineteenth-century sentimentalism with previously unrecognized complexity; in Cindy Weinstein's words, individual texts in the sentimental mode make "surprisingly diverse ideological and aesthetic contributions" to nineteenth-century American literature.[6] In Sylvester Judd's *Margaret* (1845) and E. D. E. N. Southworth's *The Hidden Hand* (1859), variations on conventional ways of representing women in prison take sentimental tropes in unexpected directions, aiding larger projects of rethinking social and gender norms. This chapter also affords a glance at the career of real-life prison matron Eliza Farnham, who traded on the status journalists accorded her as an angel in the penitentiary to facilitate her brief rise to prominence in penal reform circles.

The Transformation of Ann Carson: Sentimentalizing the Female Prisoner

The emergence of sentimentalism as the primary vocabulary for depicting women in prison during the antebellum period can be glimpsed in two books chronicling the life of Ann Carson, a figure of considerable scandal in Philadelphia during the 1810s and 1820s. Carson first came to public attention

when her estranged and presumed-dead husband, John Carson, returned
to Philadelphia from a years-long absence at sea and found Ann living with
another man, Richard Smyth. Carson attacked the armed Smyth, who shot
him; when Carson died from his wounds, Smyth was tried and convicted of
murder in 1816. Coming to the remarkable resolution to kidnap the governor
of Pennsylvania to coerce him into signing a pardon for her beloved Smyth,
Ann Carson was arrested and charged with conspiracy—a charge she beat,
apparently thanks to the influence of the governor's political enemies. She was
later convicted, however, of being an accomplice to a robbery and spent eleven
months in Philadelphia's Walnut Street Prison in 1820–21. After release, she
lived an eventful life that included drifting into the criminal underworld in
various cities on the eastern seaboard and publishing a ghostwritten account
of her life. Continuing to associate with a circle of professional criminals, she
was convicted of counterfeiting and died during another incarceration in the
Walnut Street Prison in 1824.

With the assistance of ghostwriter Mary Clarke, Carson attempted to capitalize on her notoriety through publication of *The History of the Celebrated
Mrs. Ann Carson* in 1822. The scenes in this book detailing conditions in
the Walnut Street Prison during Carson's almost yearlong incarceration are
decidedly unsentimental. Once considered a model prison, Walnut Street had
become the scene of overcrowding and riots by the early 1820s.[7] Mocking the
institution's reputation for wise and humane treatment of inmates, Carson
paints the Walnut Street Prison as an "abode of vice, misery, and tyranny." As
a consequence of her desire to preserve before readers an air of middle-class
respectability despite her checkered history, Carson refers with the utmost
condescension to fellow female inmates, whom she describes as "generally the
lowest grades of society, scarce one removed from the Hottentots."[8] (She is
also deeply offended by the racial mixing of prisoners.) Whereas the spiritual
benefits of incarceration would by the 1830s and 1840s become a staple of
literature about the prison, Carson refuses to attend Sunday services on the
grounds of liberty of conscience. (Raised a Presbyterian, she considers the
Methodist preacher socially beneath her.) Her intractableness puts Carson in
conflict with one of the prison inspectors and lands her in solitary confinement on limited rations. Carson exposes the religious professions of her fellow
inmates as pure hypocrisy, faked in hopes of being recommended for pardon.
In Ann Carson's 1822 *History*, female inmates are vulgar lowlifes beyond the
reach of reformatory measures, while Carson herself defies prison authorities
at virtually every turn.[9]

A distinctly, even startlingly different tone characterizes the second edition
of Carson's memoirs, published after her death under the explicit authorship
of Carson's former ghostwriter, Mary Clarke. Clarke's 1838 book *The Memoirs*

of the Celebrated and Beautiful Mrs. Ann Carson reprints the original 1822 version (which Clarke had silently co-written) but also adds Clarke's account of the last few years of Ann Carson's life. For the most part, Clarke is at pains to distance herself from the disreputable Carson, describing herself as a charitable soul exploited by Carson's scheming. (Carson defrauded Clarke of the proceeds of the *History* and stole her furniture.) But when Clarke touches on Carson's 1820–21 term of incarceration in Walnut Street Prison, the language is notably at odds with Carson's account published sixteen years earlier, as Carson becomes a ministering angel within the prison. Whereas Carson describes herself as mostly aloof from the inmates whom she held in contempt, Clarke claims that the other women prisoners lamented Carson's departure from prison, since she had become a nurturing, maternal presence: "Even the female prisoners who loved her, increased her regret at leaving them by their clamorous expressions of sorrow at parting from her, she who had been to them as a mother, was now to leave them perhaps forever."[10] The language of sentiment could not be further from Carson's own description of the "fifty miserable wretches, of all colours and ages," whose appearance shocked and mortified her upon her entering the institution.[11] After Ann is convicted and sentenced to seven years' hard labor for counterfeiting in 1824, Clarke describes her demeanor as penitent, a note that is never struck in the 1822 *History:* "She said she was contented, that she merited her present punishment, and took it as a salubrious medicine." At the very end of the book, Carson's son tells Mary Clarke that Ann Carson "died, as I would wish, a sincere penitent, with a sweet gleam of hope warming her heart, and a trust that the blood of Christ had washed her clean of sin."[12]

According to Susan Branson's illuminating dual biography of Carson and Clarke, Clarke was a professional writer who aimed to make a living by her pen: she edited a short-lived women's magazine before going on to write sensational trial pamphlets, a play about a notorious murder case, and a biography of a (married) theater manager accused of promoting his lovers to stardom.[13] A writer who banked on satisfying popular tastes to make a living, Clarke opportunistically adapted the story of Ann Carson's death in prison to fit with emerging sentimental trends: the egotism and defiance of the 1822 book are replaced sixteen years later with submissiveness, penitence, and Christian piety. The prison reform movement achieved its greatest visibility and political influence in the United States at a moment when conventions of sentimentalism increasingly governed the literary depiction of women. Both ideologies, meanwhile, were fueled by the rapid expansion and commercialization of the American publishing industry between the 1820s and 1850s. The result of this convergence was the dissemination and amplification of prison reform tropes by a variety of writers and publishers with varying agendas: these included prison reformers who published books, pamphlets, and periodicals to broadcast their message, as well as popular writers like Mary Clarke who had no particular interest in prison reform ideology but found that certain ways of writing about women in prison struck a chord with readers. The prisoner served as the ultimate test case of womanhood's claims to powers of moral rehabilitation, and the virtuous woman's influence over criminality became a widespread (and underappreciated) staple narrative of antebellum literature. If, as Joanne Dobson argues, nineteenth-century sentimentalism is primarily concerned with affective connections between people, with primary emphases on "family . . . intimacy, community, and social responsibility," then the woman working altruistically in a jail, forging emotional ties to society's least sympathetic members, is a perfect embodiment of its core values.[14]

Female Prisoners and Reformers in *Prisoner's Friend*

Prisoner's Friend, a periodical dedicated to both the anti-gallows and prison reform causes, offers a rich archive for exploring antebellum representations of women in prison. One common mode of writing about imprisoned women featured dramatic restitution of inmates' femininity after exposure to the carceral regime. Writers often emphasized the women's violent temperament upon entrance into prison, supporting the commonplace notion that a woman's fall from virtue was more vertiginous and comprehensive than a man's. James B. Finley, a prison chaplain in Ohio, took this approach in describing his work among female inmates to readers of *Prisoner's Friend.* Finley reported having observed "the great and incomparable stubbornness and depravity" of the "violent and ungovernable" female convicts. He feared that his description might sound strange to readers who did not know "how utterly woman falls, when she falls at all."[15] Readers were probably unsurprised, however, in a culture that often figured a woman's initial deviation from rectitude as the first step down a nearly inevitable, though not irreversible, trajectory toward ruin. One well-known prison reformer described imprisoned women— before reformatory measures had taken effect—in decidedly masculine, if not animalistic, terms: "Thus trained, aggression and resistance are the spontaneous and continued fruits of their minds. They come to the prison, therefore, prepared to war against physical measures, and the supremacy of animal courage, and to derive their highest enjoyment from such contest."[16]

Scenes of women's extreme degeneracy in prison served multiple ideological and literary purposes: they buttressed the culture's investment in an all-or-nothing standard of womanly deportment, and they set the stage for dramatically satisfying narratives of femininity rediscovered, thereby confirming reformers' theories about the effects of incarceration. Chaplain Finley witnessed such a scene, thanks to the ministering efforts of the institution's kindly warden and his wife. To the minister's surprise, the warden proposes taking the female convicts outdoors on a Sabbath afternoon. Almost immediately, "the stubbornness, the violence, the jealousy of these women were soon very nearly vanquished." The prisoners unexpectedly recover a key element of their feminine identity: susceptibility to natural beauty. As the chaplain describes the scene:

> Not one of them had beheld a tree, or a flower, or a skipping animal, since their commitment to these gloomy halls. I watched their countenances with deep curiosity. No language can describe how they acted and appeared. . . . A leaf, a plant, was a greater wonder to them than a rolling world had been in their better days. Some gazed on the trees, others on the water, others on the green, soft grass; others looked upward, with perfect ecstacy [*sic*], to the blue heavens above; while from every eye the tears were trickling down.

The chaplain notes with satisfaction that the effect has been lasting: "From that memorable hour a new spirit has reigned among them. They are completely subdued and softened."[17] Their tears mark the Ohio inmates' telescoped passage from irreclaimable criminality to redeemed womanhood.

A similar transformation was recorded by the celebrated and controversial matron of the Female Department at Mount Pleasant State Prison (better known as Sing Sing), Eliza Farnham. In an 1845 letter to the *New York Tribune* reprinted in *Prisoner's Friend,* Farnham recounted a visit to the department from the famous Hutchinson Family Singers. Music proves as serviceable as nature in reawakening the prisoners' emotional sensibilities: "Tears coursed down many a furrowed and soiled cheek . . . as the exquisite strains died away within the rude walls." Farnham notes that the song "My Mother's Bible" inspired the strongest emotional response among the prisoners: "The exquisite beauty of the words, with the touching character of the music . . . seemed to conjure before each unfortunate creature a picture of domestic peace, holiness and virtue such as she might have participated in long years ago, but to which her heart was now a stranger."[18] Farnham's observation economically aggregates the qualities to which the female inmates could suddenly become responsive: aesthetic sensibility, piety, maternity, and domesticity.

If a woman inmate did not respond positively to imprisonment, then perhaps her very claim to femininity, and even to humanity, was in doubt. Such at least is suggested by the peculiar story of an incorrigible and apparently insane female inmate of Sing Sing identified as "J.S., a colored girl." This eighteen-year-old prisoner defiantly shrieks through the night from her cell for a period of months, keeping other inmates awake, even after extraordinary disciplinary measures (straitjacket, gag, bread and water rations, and extended solitary confinement). As Farnham describes:

> It appeared that she was no sooner left than she commenced a series of *serpent-like* contortions, and continued them until she had wound herself quite out of the ropes, and released herself from the gag and jacket. I was the more struck with this statement, as I myself had noticed in all her movements, actions or [*sic*] marked resemblance to those of that reptile. Her skin was also spotted like a common species of snake, and her pulse, even in health, was so small as scarcely to be perceptible, and her flesh cold.

Farnham concludes that the woman embodies "nothing human . . . but her form—an idiosyncrasy of her race."[19] While a modern reader can only assume that J.S. suffered from schizophrenia or a similarly serious mental illness, the need to identify a criminal unsusceptible to the usual reform measures as something other than human marks the confidence with which reformers assumed that virtually any woman would eventually become compliant under a carceral regime. J.S.'s status as a "colored" woman probably factors into Farnham's perception of her as less than human, but as I discuss in chapter 6, it can be dangerous to reflexively attribute racist attitudes to antebellum prison reformers. If J.S.'s bizarre behavior marks her as an "idiosyncrasy," then whether "race" is understood to mean "black" or "human," the implication remains that other members of the grouping retain their full human identity.

The most prominent angel in the penitentiary in antebellum periodicals was an English Quaker named Elizabeth Fry, best known for reforming conditions among the women inmates in London's infamous Newgate Prison in the 1810s and for founding an Association for the Reformation of Female Prisoners. *Prisoner's Friend* featured biographical sketches of Fry several times in the 1840s, in response, it seems likely, to news of her death in 1845. The editor of *Prisoner's Friend*, Charles Spear, used an image of Fry as the frontispiece to his volume of poetry written by prison inmates, *Voices from Prison*, published in 1847.[20] Though set in early-nineteenth-century London, narratives about Fry foregrounded the same elements of women's prison life that characterized contemporary American accounts. According to a short 1849 version of her life, when Fry entered Newgate, she "found the prison a place of begging, swearing, gaming, dancing, fighting, obscenity, dressing in men's clothes, &c." This description of women's ungovernable behavior in the prison setting includes the not-at-all veiled implication, embedded in the account of cross-dressing, that an essential part of the inmates' femininity has been temporarily sacrificed. Echoing Farnham, the passage figures imprisoned women as something akin to animals: "We look with wonder and astonishment at the man who enters the cage of the lion and tiger, and by his presence calms the ferocity of the wild beast. But how much more wonderful is it to see a poor lone female enter amidst the ferocity of human beings, and calm and regulate human passion!"[21]

A cornerstone of the Fry narratives is that prison officials warn her of the danger she courts by going into the jail, but Fry refuses to be accompanied, as in an 1845 article: " 'I am fully aware of the danger,' meekly replied Mrs. Fry. 'I do not go in my own strength. God will protect me.' " In accordance with the codes of sentimental women's literature, Fry carries with her the irresistible moral sanctity of middle-class womanhood. It proves to be all the protection she needs. The prisoners respond miraculously to Fry's intervention: "The astonished inmates of the prison gazed on her, as though she were indeed an angel. The pure and tranquil expression of her beautiful countenance soon softened their ferocity."[22] Fry secures the prisoners' consent to read to them from the Bible and continues her visits until she is able to impose order and tranquillity at Newgate, eventually educating the women's children, bringing the inmates clothes, and tutoring them in the tenets of Christianity. *Prisoner's Friend* occasionally printed poems devoted to the memory of Elizabeth Fry, including one that consecrates her "A priestess of heaven on the threshold of hell."[23] A similarly lionizing account appeared in the rival *Pennsylvania Journal of Prison Discipline and Philanthropy;* the bitterly divided partisans of America's two competing carceral regimes found common cause in celebrating Fry's efforts.[24]

Women in Prison: Popular Periodical Literature of the 1840s

Veneration of Elizabeth Fry transcended prison reform literature and moved into the pages of popular magazines, suggesting deep cultural investment in the image of the female prison reformer. Lydia H. Sigourney published "On Seeing Mrs. Fry at Newgate Prison" in *Godey's Lady's Book,* memorializing a scene in which the Quaker reformer takes leave of the convicts she has tutored as they embark for transportation to Australia. Rehearsing the now familiar story of Fry's heroism, Sigourney notes: "She has a Bible in her hand, / And on her lip the spell / Of loving and melodious speech, / Those lion hearts to quell." The departing women shed tears of grief, penitence, and gratitude in a "strange and plenteous shower."[25] This poem predated Fry's death, though that event in 1845 intensified the outpouring of Fry-related literature. A few years later, in 1847, *Godey's* invoked Fry in an article titled "A True Heroine." The article celebrates Fry only incidentally; the author goes on to praise a lesser-known prison reformer, Sarah Martin, an Englishwoman who labored among prisoners of both sexes imparting religious instruction, arranging for labor within the prison, and helping inmates upon discharge. Over time, nonfictional figures like Fry and Martin spawned fictional avatars in popular magazines, where the willingness to carry her moral influence into the midst of criminality became a shorthand way for popular authors to establish a female character's worthiness.

A paradigmatic fictional treatment of this subject was published in *Godey's* in 1847. "The Jailer's Daughter," attributed to Mrs. C. Latham, tells the story of Kate Walden, whose intemperate father, on the verge of poverty, decides as a last resort to accept a newly opened position as keeper of a county jail. Kate, a model of dutifulness in her attentions to her family's needs, presses him to take the job: "Father, do go! I will help you; I will take dear mother's place while she is unable to assist you, and I will do all you ask of me." The family auctions off its possessions, and Mr. Walden takes charge of the jail. Upon her first entrance into the jail, attended by the wife of a staff member, Kate has a talismanic effect on the prisoners: "And how broke this vision of innocent beauty upon the long-dimmed sight of these unhappy men? They looked at her, indeed, as at an angel." Cheerleading the girl's efforts, the story's intrusive narrator solicits readers' approval of Kate's ministry: "Read on and see what a young girl can do in a county jail." As the story unfolds, Kate brings her innocence and piety into the lives of the imprisoned, including a climactic moment when she reads to the prisoners from the Bible. Her presence has a transformative effect on the men in jail. The prison's chaplain tells Kate "that he had never seen them in a better state—in fact, there was not one among them he considered hopeless. They looked happier, though without liberty, and they had a ministering angel among them who directed them all aright."[26] Though Kate briefly fears she will sacrifice her preferred suitor during her seclusion among the prison inmates, she need not worry: the author has marriage in store for her all along. At the story's close, Kate has been married for ten years to the sweetheart of her youth, a kindly doctor whose assessment of her virtue is based on the success of her efforts in the prison.

Within the period's magazine literature, wives and daughters often demonstrated their virtue by attending to their loved ones in prison. Like the women observed by Dickens and Marryat, these characters find their femininity expressed and deepened by their presence in a jail. A poem titled "Alethe" that appeared in *Graham's Lady's and Gentleman's Magazine* offers three separate tableaux of the title character. The first covers her innocent childhood, while the second finds her in a prison, "Where prison-walls enclos'd a parent dear; / And like an angel, she had come to keep / Watch while he slept—to comfort him—to pray." The third stanza rewards Alethe for her tenderness with the gift of maternity: "at her breast / Hung a sweet infant, and the radiant smile / That revell'd round its lips while calm at rest, / Was like the smile of cherubs."[27] A poem from *Godey's* titled "For Better, for Worse" is set in a prison cell, where the persona addresses her wrongly imprisoned husband, whom she refuses to abandon. The faithful wife's presence converts the cell into a home: "I will not leave thee! Though this cell / Be all the home thou call'st thine own."[28]

Graham's featured another wife faithful to her incarcerated husband in an 1843 story, "The Wife," by the popular author Ann S. Stephens. Lucy Sprague, a wealthy London heiress and orphan, marries a profligate man against her guardian's wishes. Her naïve confidence in her husband's moral rectitude (the husband, named Burke, was something of a rake in his bachelorhood) is challenged after the marriage, as he dissipates her fortune, resumes drinking, and lands in debtor's prison. Lucy visits Burke there, learns from the penitent man that her guardian prudently reserved some of her money from him, and successfully petitions to receive it. Lucy redeems Burke from prison, and the two of them head to America—where she eventually dies of tuberculosis. Lucy's premature death may seem to exempt the story from the typical pattern in which a heroine's behavior within a prison is rewarded by story's end, but it is worth noting that her reformation of the husband is successful, as confirmed by his tears. Seeing the thousand-pound note she brings to his cell, Burke "did not pick it up then, for a dearer burden lay against his heart—his wife— his own true wife—who wept upon his bosom as she had never wept before in her whole existence."[29] Burke persists in his good behavior, and the couple enjoys a brief period of renewed marital bliss before Lucy expires.

E. D. E. N. Southworth was one of the most prominent writers of the period to recognize the fictional power of an angel in the penitentiary. Southworth's short story "The Thunderbolt to the Hearth," published in *The National Era* in 1847, has been discussed as an example of the author's anti–capital punishment fiction, on the grounds that it "implores readers to consider murderers not as monstrous objects of fear but as individuals led to tragedy by unfortunate circumstances, as they themselves might be."[30] This conclusion is sound insofar as it analyzes the situation of the murderer in the story but does not completely account for the depiction of his wife. The story concerns the Reed family: husband William, wife Emily, their two children, and William's father. Conspicuous in the family's parlor is a portrait of William's cousin, who was seduced and abandoned by a famous actor. William, having sworn to avenge the crime if the opportunity arises, encounters the seducer in the street and fatally shoots him. The story follows William's trial and conviction, as well as an unsuccessful petition to pardon him.

As the execution nears, Southworth's narrator increasingly directs attention toward William's young and self-sacrificing wife. Two months into his incarceration, readers find Emily in his cell, "sitting on the edge of the mattress . . . kneeling beside him, an open Bible on the bed before her." The narrator emphasizes the suffering Emily endures in concealing her pain for the sake of her husband, who refers to her as "my angel wife"; though she senses her own impending death, "yet her words were always comforting, and her smile was always sweet." Awakened in the jail cell she inhabits with William by the sound of workers erecting his gallows, Emily prays: "Oh! God . . . Spare and strengthen thy handmaid a few hours longer, that the stricken and doomed one before thee may not see the death of his wife, may not know the depth of her suffering." Though readers are led to expect Emily's death concurrently with her husband's, Southworth's narrative takes a different turn: "Emily Reed . . . called on God, bore up, and lived. Nor was her life passed in vain regret or unavailing gloom. . . . She lived, and her life was rich—rich in the affection of her children; rich in the esteem of her friends; rich in good deeds; and rich in the hope of a blessed re-union in heaven."[31] Another of the period's heroines whose claims to virtue are confirmed by her behavior within a prison, Emily Reed learns that faithful ministry to the incarcerated is duly rewarded with domestic happiness. Even marital bliss remains within reach, in Emily's confidently anticipated afterlife.

Marriage Reform, Utopianism, and the Angel in the Penitentiary in *Margaret*

Though she arose out of reform discourse and sentimental popular texts in which the functions she performed were predictable and circumscribed, the angel in the penitentiary, like sentimentalism more generally, proved adaptable to serve more diverse ends. This adaptability may be traceable in part to the antebellum prison's dual identity as both a private and a public space. Individual inmates may have been expected to reflect on their crimes and awaken their consciences in privacy, but the prison's visibility in the public sphere of print (where the theory and practice of penal reform were extensively documented and debated) meant that their experiences, and the efforts of their caretakers, had a crucial public component.

Novelist Sylvester Judd recognized the potential for a wider public role implicit within the angel-in-the-penitentiary character, offering an ambitious transformation of the trope in his 1845 female coming-of-age story, *Margaret: A Tale of the Real and Ideal, Blight and Bloom*. Judd was a graduate of the Harvard Divinity School and a Unitarian minister who, at a formative age, fell under the spell of New England Transcendentalism. Judd's remarkable first novel—which was admired by leading literary figures including Margaret Fuller, Nathaniel Hawthorne, and James Russell Lowell—is variously a record of the folkways of early-nineteenth-century New England, an attempt to translate Transcendentalist philosophy into fictional form, and, in its final section, a utopian fantasy envisioning the successful implementation of many of the era's social reforms, including prison reform.

Throughout its length, *Margaret* is centrally concerned with matters related to criminal justice. Sympathetic to the claims of the penal reform movement, Judd believed that prisons "should be primarily places of regeneration, not primarily places of punishment."[32] The novel's earliest prison scenes predate the heroine's birth, in flashbacks to the previous generation. Margaret's adoptive father, Didymus Hart, begins a friendship that will shape his unborn daughter's life when he is jailed for defying town authorities in the early days of the American Revolution. In Judd's portrait, Hart is motivated not so much by Loyalist sympathies as by drunken bravado and a contrarian opposition to being bullied into compliance with the prevailing mood. Hart is joined in this sentiment by the town's schoolmaster, Master Elliman, who impatiently dismisses the committee of safety and refuses to sign an oath of loyalty to the Patriot cause. During an imprisonment of a few months, the two men "became very good friends," as a result of which Elliman eventually tutors Hart's precocious daughter in classical literature.[33] Judd registers the way that incarceration in a time of political turmoil can be abused to enforce ideological conformity, an insight that opens the door for sympathetic treatment of criminals and prison reform later in the novel.

Though Margaret grows up in rural poverty with her hardscrabble adoptive family, her actual origins are more romantic. The story of Margaret's biological parents relies on the formula of an angel in the penitentiary. As readers learn from a chapter interpolated into the account of Margaret's childhood, her father was a poor and sensitive German immigrant, Gottfried Bruckmann, a conscript among Hessians enlisted to fight for the British during the Revolutionary War. Margaret's mother was Jane Girardeau, the daughter of a wealthy Boston merchant. After hearing Gottfried play the flute, Jane develops an interest in him that is both compassionate and romantic. Undaunted by Gottfried's poverty, Jane spends time with him against her father's wishes until Mr. Girardeau vindictively has the immigrant imprisoned for debt. Incarceration proves no barrier to the couple's union: "[Jane] undid the fastenings of her room, she escaped into the street. Going to the Jail, she obtained access to the cell and was locked in with Bruckmann. Through his drooping heart and wasting frame he received her with a bland, welcome smile. She fell at his feet, and poured herself out in a torrent of tears, her swollen heart broke in sighs, sobs, and convulsions" (84). The account of Margaret's birth parents resembles Stephens's story "The Wife," in which the heroine uses her own money to redeem her husband from prison and the two share a brief but happy married life. Jane follows her sickly husband to the grave shortly after giving birth to his daughter; one legacy she passes on to Margaret is an impulse to sympathize with the imprisoned.

Margaret's interest in the incarcerated arises early and spontaneously. When her brother Hash is imprisoned for brawling during the town's military exercises, Margaret visits him in jail. She encounters Hash's cellmate, identified by Judd as a murderer, whose suffering so moves her that she impulsively offers consolation: "She went to him, he took her in his lap, pressed her hard to his breast, and stroked her hair" (99). As she leaves, Margaret promises to return with flowers to brighten the man's squalid life. On her next foray into town, to attend church, Margaret stops at the jail to deliver flowers to the man as promised. She places them outside the grated window and hears other inmates crying out for flowers. Driven off by the town jailer, Margaret devises a way to satisfy all of the prisoners: "She retreated into the street, and gaining a point where she could see the upper cell-windows, she displayed her flowers in sight of the prisoners, holding them up to the extent of her arm, and heard the prisoners shout with joy" (110). Judd stages a scene in and around a prison that collects and emphasizes the markers of his heroine's feminine virtue: Christian piety, love of nature, and compassion for the imprisoned, who respond to flowers here with the same enthusiasm as the Ohio female convicts described in *Prisoner's Friend.* This scene represents the birth of Margaret's interest in penal reform.

Incarceration plays a defining role at every stage of Margaret's life. Her passage from youth to maturity occurs with the execution of another brother, Chilion. In a purposefully ambiguous and bizarre series of events, the intoxicated Chilion hurls a file toward a man making sexual advances on Margaret during a husking bee. Though Chilion's intent was merely to scare off the offender, a fatal injury ensues, and Chilion is convicted of murder; Judd uses the story to promote an anti-gallows agenda. Placing no fewer than six of Margaret's closest friends and relations in prison at one point or another in the story (her biological mother and father, her adoptive father, her beloved tutor, and two of her adoptive brothers), Judd thoroughly establishes his heroine's motivation to improve conditions among the incarcerated. Moreover, much as Southworth would in *The Hidden Hand,* Judd hints at an implicit link between his heroine's marriage and the subject of imprisonment. When Margaret meets Mr. Evelyn, the man who will become her husband, and shocks him with her unconventional sentiments about religion, she observes, "I frighten you, Sir," and wonders if he "will have me put in Jail right off" (228). Her words prove prophetic: though Margaret does not go to jail "right off," she and Mr. Evelyn end up intimately involved with the town's penal institution.

Judd's imaginative transformation of the formula whereby a woman's worthiness for domestic happiness is predicated on her dedication to helping the incarcerated begins with the heroine's marriage. After the discovery of her parentage makes her an heiress, Margaret marries her spiritual tutor, Mr. Evelyn. The two of them subsequently use their vast fortune to refashion the town of Livingston into a utopia known as Mons Christi, allowing Judd to demonstrate the social utility of the era's reform movements. A complete renovation of the town's jail is one of the couple's earliest and most important reforms. Margaret describes the scene in a letter:

> At the time they were rebuilding the Jail, Mr. Evelyn proposed to the Commissioners if they would consent to an establishment on an enlarged scale, with rooms more commodious, windows more numerous, and better conveniences for warmth in winter, he would bear the additional cost. . . . Each room, Mr. Evelyn furnished with a good bed, books, lights, looking-glass, washstand and flower vase. The windows have green blinds, which by a simple contrivance the prisoners can open and shut at their pleasure. The horrors and discomforts of the old Jail I have myself too sensibly realized. A new keeper has been appointed in place of Mr. Shooks. At the last Town Meeting the Selectmen were instructed to look after the moral condition of the prisoners. (410)

Do the changes to the town jail, though, trace their origins primarily to Mr. Evelyn? Judd productively obfuscates authority for the reforms by having Mr. Evelyn write to a correspondent about the many changes the town has witnessed: "I do not intend to overtax her modesty . . . beyond what is meet; but in truth I must declare, the first person in [Margaret's] letters would be more fitting and exact, than any second; it is she herself, and not we, who is, under God, and in Christ, the soul of all that which we now behold" (439). Margaret coyly accepts his shifting of responsibility: "Mr. Evelyn would make you believe that I have been personally interested in this rejuvenescence of the town; so mote it be" (449). Perhaps this canny formulation allowed antebellum readers to impute to Margaret as much or as little agency as suited their individual notions of feminine propriety, but Judd implicitly credits Margaret with being, at the least, an equal partner with her husband in a broad program of social reform centered on a reconceptualization of the town's penal institution.

The notable unity of purpose shared by Mr. Evelyn and Margaret in carrying out their plans aligns Judd's novel with radical sentiments on the subject of marriage as expressed, for example, in Margaret Fuller's essay "The Great Lawsuit," published in *The Dial* in 1843. Fuller conceived of the ideal marriage as a union of two souls engaged in "pilgrimage towards a common shrine," a phrase that perfectly describes Mr. Evelyn and Margaret's joint efforts to remake Livingston as a utopia.[34] A shared commitment to penal reform therefore provides one of the vehicles through which Margaret and Mr. Evelyn model a Transcendentalist revision of marriage and gender roles along egalitarian lines. Margaret's participation in the reconceptualization of the jail significantly enhances her social utility over that of the conventional angel of the penitentiary, whose work typically involved merely facilitating individual moral conversions within an existing penal structure.

In the hands of Margaret and Mr. Evelyn (echoing the detail-oriented proponents of the Auburn and Pennsylvania programs), no aspect of the disciplinary regime, down to the color of the window blinds, escapes the attention of a dedicated reformer. Their interest in the moral condition of the prisoners puts them squarely in the mainstream of reform opinion in the antebellum era. Moreover, in accordance with Judd's faith in social progress, the reforms work spectacularly. In the service of confirming their efficacy, Judd shrewdly embeds in the novel resistance to the humanitarian impulses of prison reformers. After initial implementation of the town's reforms, state authorities become concerned by Livingston / Mons Christi's disproportion-ately small contribution to the population of the state penitentiary. An inves-tigative committee spends several weeks in the town before filing a report endorsing its new penal measures. In Margaret's words to a correspondent, "They say that during the last four years since the enlargement of the Jail, the addition to the comfort of the inmates, and the practice we have of visiting them frequently, and attending to their moral condition, the *recommitments* have almost entirely ceased . . . and they consent that our mode tends really to reform the prisoner, and restore him a useful citizen to the State" (435–36). Margaret's efforts as an angel in the penitentiary transcend the reform of a few individual inmates to become the cornerstone of a social reform agenda to whose efficacy state authorities enthusiastically attest.

Sensitive to literary trends ennobling women who devote themselves to the problem of criminality, Judd creates the ultimate embodiment of the female prison reformer, a character indebted to a number of real and fictional models, including Fry and Farnham. But Judd surpasses his models by giving Margaret an unprecedented degree of agency in overseeing the town's penal reforms. Margaret does not merely cross the threshold of a prison to minister to its inmates on an individual level; she participates in the redesign of the entire institution from the ground up, becoming not so much the angel of the penitentiary as its architect. Judd's placement of prison reform at the center of *Margaret*'s utopian vision conveys the importance of this movement to radical thinkers of the 1840s, while his innovative adaptation of the angel-in-the-penitentiary motif implicitly endorses the most far-reaching possibilities for female agency imagined by feminists such as Fuller. Looking at *Margaret* with an eye to how other writers of the period portrayed women in prisons confirms Gavin Jones's claim that the novel "redefines the limits in which a female protagonist usually moved."[35]

While Judd did not work exclusively or even primarily within the sentimental mode, his portrayal of Margaret's coming of age partakes of various sentimental elements, territory usually ceded to writers such as Susan Warner and Maria Cummins. Judd's achievement in transforming an angel of the penitentiary into the co-founder of a utopian community recalls Glenn Hendler's assessment of how certain writers working within the sentimental tradition manipulated generic conventions in the name of entailing upon their works a significant public or political role, "carrying the internal workings of a convention to places it might not otherwise have traveled, but not rejecting the form outright."[36]

Women and Incarceration in *The Hidden Hand*

By the late 1850s, the figure of the angel in the penitentiary had become so familiar to antebellum readers that an author could meaningfully conjure the archetype with a few deft strokes. Harriet Beecher Stowe applies the formula to a minor but significant character in *Dred: A Tale of the Great Dismal Swamp* (1856). When protagonist Edward Clayton visits a prison on an errand of mercy to a woman who has defiantly confessed to killing her children to spare them the agonies of slavery, he finds he has been anticipated by another visitor, who leads the woman in prayer. Clayton notices that the beautiful young woman visiting the prisoner wears "the expression that comes from communion with the highest and serenest nature." The visit has had the requisite impact on the incarcerated slave, who now appears in a "softened mood" with "traces of tears on her cheek, and an open Bible on the bed." The anonymous comforting figure disappears from the novel for hundreds of pages, until Clayton encounters Livy Ray, a schoolmate of his deceased fiancée Nina Gordon, whom Nina had always regarded with a kind of reverent awe as the embodiment of all feminine virtue. When Stowe reveals that Livy Ray is in fact "the lady [Clayton] had met in the prison in Alexandria," readers need no further assurance that she has been vetted as an appropriate romantic interest for Clayton.[37] A year later, the pattern surfaced in Dickens's *Little Dorrit* (1857), in which Amy Dorrit is raised in the Marshalsea debtors' prison and returns there to care for her beloved after he suffers a financial reversal; eventually the narrative rewards her with marriage and prosperity.

Taking such a familiar, archetypal character in a novel direction required remarkable self-consciousness on the part of an author, especially one working within the constraints of a popular mode. Such a level of generic self-awareness is apparent in one of the most popular novels of the 1850s, Southworth's *The*

Hidden Hand; or, Capitola the Madcap, first serialized in the *New York Ledger* in 1859. Southworth embeds within the novel both of the plots that circulated during the period about women in prison: the ungovernable female inmate who becomes feminized by her imprisonment and the affluent heroine who proves her virtue through ministry to the incarcerated. Both tropes prove susceptible to sly authorial manipulations, however, registering a broad critique of antebellum culture's assumptions about feminine identity alongside a more focused indictment of the vicissitudes of the criminal justice system, concerns Southworth addressed repeatedly in her long and successful career.

The first of the paradigmatic narratives of women in prison is embodied by Mrs. Capitola Le Noir, mother of Capitola Black, Southworth's heroine. In the novel's complicated plot, Mrs. Le Noir is confined in a house for a period of years by her evil brother-in-law, Gabriel Le Noir, who is intent on securing the family fortune. Eventually Gabriel transfers Mrs. Le Noir to an elegant lunatic asylum in Louisiana, where she meets the kind physician Traverse Rocke, one of the novel's heroes. Though not technically a prison, an insane asylum figured within antebellum thought as a parallel institution to the penitentiary. Fuller, for example, placed her account of the Utica and Pennsylvania Asylums for the Insane in her lengthy article "Prison Discipline," offering this rationale: "We do believe that advancement in thought and wisdom of treatment in both of these departments are and will be simultaneous. When there is a well-digested system of treatment for the one, that for the other will not be far behind."[38]

Southworth is explicit about the carceral function of the institution, which the narrator describes as "a prison for the insane," language that Mrs. Le Noir echoes when she implores her newfound benefactor to "succeed in freeing me from this prison."[39] Like the women who serve as her analogs in prison reform literature, Mrs. Le Noir enters confinement prone to bursts of unruly behavior. The institution's director tells Dr. Rocke that she "used to become so violent that we would have to restrain her" (443), and Mrs. Le Noir herself affirms that a "nervous irritability, to which every woman is subject," makes her "rave with impatience and excitement" (446). Eventually, though, Mrs. Le Noir becomes resigned to her confinement, a psychological adjustment reflected in her appearance. Rocke tells her that her face "speaks equally of profound sorrows and of saintly resignation," and sees in "the calm depth of those sad eyes" that she is not insane as reported (446).

In the personal history she furnishes to Rocke to convince him of her mental stability, Mrs. Le Noir reports a conversion experience that echoes the rhetoric of prison reformers:

> I was sinking into an apathy when one day I opened the little Bible that lay upon the table of my cell. I fixed upon the last chapters in the gospel of

John. That narrative of meek patience and divine love! It did for me what no power under that of God could have done. It saved me! it saved me from madness! it saved me from despair! . . . I have learned patience with sinners, forgiveness of enemies, and confidence in God. In a word, I trust I have learned the way of salvation, and in that have learned everything. (456)

Reformers averred that the combination of silence for reflection and the presence of a Bible were the necessary conditions to inspire penitence and submission in penal subjects. Institutionalization apparently functions this way for Mrs. Le Noir, whom the narrative refines and Christianizes in preparation for restoring that ultimate blessing of femininity, maternity, in the form of reunion with her long-lost daughter. In these ways, Southworth seems deeply indebted to the trope of the converted female inmate, as Mrs. Le Noir's saintly resignation and deep, calm eyes call to mind the submissive female prisoners observed by Dickens and Marryat.

Unlike the women featured in the period's nonfictional prison reform literature, however, Mrs. Le Noir is guilty of no crime. This is a very salient distinction. What is the meaning of a conversion experience for a woman who has been unjustly imprisoned, a woman with no crime for which to repent? For Southworth, Christian patience and meek resignation represent not the restoration of the femininity forfeited by turning to a life of crime but rather the disposition most suitable to preserving Mrs. Le Noir's sanity in response to a confinement that has been violently and unjustly imposed upon her. What prison reformers and the culture at large regarded as personality traits inherent to the female character, and reawakened by the carceral experience, Southworth depicts in *The Hidden Hand* as necessities to which a woman is driven in order to cope with a psychologically intolerable denial of liberty. Mrs. Le Noir's imprisonment within an elegant asylum masquerading as a pleasant home (it resembles "the luxurious country seat of some wealthy merchant or planter" [439]) neatly serves, madwoman-in-the-attic style, as a metaphor for the wider regime of confinement and domestication Victorian-era women endured, a regime "to which every woman is subject," in Mrs. Le Noir's resonant phrase. The trope that prison reformers used to imply that prison restored to women the traits of passivity and resignation that was their natural birthright is used to the opposite end by Southworth, who implies through Mrs. Le Noir that women may instead cultivate these traits as a self-protective response to a quite unnatural state of confinement.

In Southworth's appropriation of the second key antebellum narrative of women and incarceration, *The Hidden Hand* invests its angel of the penitentiary with something more than just the power of sympathy. The novel gestures toward a conventional denouement, in which the heroine's eligibility for marital happiness depends on the attention she devotes to an incarcerated criminal, when it links the fates of Capitola and the bandit Black Donald.[40] The narrative forges this link in various ways, most notably when the governor postpones Black Donald's execution until the date of Cap's wedding (476). The eve of execution finds Black Donald, who has previously confronted his impending execution with bravado, trying unsuccessfully to pray, "very pale and haggard from long imprisonment and great anxiety" (479). Conventions governing prison narratives would suggest that Black Donald requires an angel to seal his emergent impulse toward redemption, a role Cap appears to fulfill. On Cap's unexpected appearance in the jail, Black Donald notes that she is distinguished among women by her superior virtue, being "the first female that has been in my cell since my imprisonment" (479). With the words "God redeem you, Donald Bayne," Capitola achieves the incarcerated criminal's conversion. Black Donald replies, "And God forsake me if I do not heed your advice!" (481). Though Capitola decides to help him escape and freely offers Black Donald her beloved pony Gyp to aid his getaway, she finds the next morning that he is now too scrupulous even to accept this gift, deciding instead to "purchase" another horse from the stables at the Hurricane Hall plantation, leaving a bag of money to compensate the owner. Significantly, the note accompanying the money is signed "Black Donald, Reformed Robber" (484).

The Hidden Hand's departures from the standard angel-in-the-penitentiary narrative involve two related plot elements: Black Donald, though a criminal, claims not to be guilty of the capital crime for which he has been condemned to death, and Capitola not only reforms but also liberates him. Although Black Donald's leadership of a criminal gang is not in question, he tells Capitola that he "never was guilty of murder" (479). Capitola accepts this claim (the text leaves its truth murky, but readers are presumably supposed to trust Capitola's intuition) and provides him with tools to aid his escape, recognizing that community sentiment made an unbiased trial impossible. Southworth's narrator reminds readers that Black Donald's conviction rested on unreliable evidence: "He was indicted upon several distinct counts, the most serious of which . . . were sustained only by circumstantial evidence. But the aggregate weight of all these, together with his very bad reputation, was sufficient to convict him, and Black Donald was sentenced to death" (465). Other novels from this period in Southworth's career include warnings about the danger and insufficiency of circumstantial evidence, for which executive pardon serves as an indispensable legal remedy. In *The Lost Heiress* (1854), a governor rejects the petition for pardon of a defendant convicted of murder on circumstantial evidence, only to find after the execution that the man was innocent. Southworth includes an explicit critique of "the nature, history, and tendencies of circumstantial evidence" in *The Gipsy's Prophecy* (1861), another novel in which an innocent man is convicted of murder and a government authority figure refuses to stay his execution.[41]

These novels suggest the pardoning power as a pertinent context underlying Capitola's liberation of Black Donald. After attempting unsuccessfully to petition the governor for a commutation of Black Donald's sentence (no one in the community is willing to sign her petition), Capitola usurps the prerogative of the governor and, in effect, grants Black Donald the pardon he deserves: as she puts it, "*I* of all others have the best right to pardon you and set you free" (480). Not unlike Judd's Margaret, Capitola leverages her position as an angel in the penitentiary into an exercise of broader judicial authority; in Paul Christian Jones's words, she represents "an embodiment of the justice system."[42] Sentimentalism is incontestably at work in the scene, insofar as a young, virtuous, and soon-to-be-married heroine earns domestic happiness by miraculously converting a criminal through the power of her sympathy. But Capitola combines sympathy with the intelligence to discern a grievous miscarriage of justice and the capacity to right the wrong. Southworth allies sympathy with intellect and agency in a female character who embodies, but also exceeds, the angel-in-the-penitentiary trope.

Critical opinion differs on the question of Capitola's divergence from gender norms, with Michele Ann Abate offering the assessment that, contrary to the views of many critics who credit Southworth with feminist leanings in *The Hidden Hand,* Capitola "is actually more gender normative than past or present criticism has been willing to concede."[43] Southworth's careful manipulation of conventions dictating what should happen when a female character enters a prison cell suggests to me a middle ground of interpretation, in which she capitulates to the pressures of genre to satisfy readers' expectations but demonstrates an astute awareness of precisely how far such conventions can be modified in the direction of challenging limits on female agency. Discussing Southworth's adherence to the convention that novels about women should end in marriage, Cindy Weinstein captures the dynamic perfectly in describing the author's "vexed relation to a literary tradition that demanded an ending of which she was deeply suspicious."[44] In the difference between Emily Reed of "A Thunderbolt to the Hearth" (whose primary function within the story is to soothe her condemned husband's anguish) and Capitola in *The Hidden Hand* (who overturns a trial verdict and pardons a condemned criminal), it might be possible to trace Southworth's emerging willingness to experiment with convention, as she explored the possibility for women's agency implicit within the sentimentalized figure of the angel in the penitentiary.

As a way of confirming the power and endurance of the tropes discussed in this chapter, I invoke the final paragraphs of Rebecca Harding Davis's "Life in

the Iron-Mills" (discussed in chapter 3), which betray a debt to many previous
stories of women and imprisonment. After millworker Hugh Wolfe's prison
suicide, a peaceful female figure drifts into his cousin Deb's jail cell. Until
this point, Deb has behaved with the unwomanly deportment sometimes
associated with incorrigible female criminals. Noting that she guards Hugh's
corpse with "the ferocity of a watch-dog," the narrator describes Deb's features: "There was no meekness, no sorrow, in her face; the stuff out of which
murderers are made, instead."[45] But the presence of the visitor, who brings
"a vase of wood-leaves and berries" into Hugh's cell (449), inspires a nearly
instantaneous transformation in Deb's demeanor: "As she looked, a shadow of
[the clouds'] solemn repose fell on her face; its fierce discontent faded into a
pitiful, humble quiet" (450).

The dignified visitor, Davis's readers would not have been surprised to
learn, is "a Quaker, or Friend, as they call themselves," an identity that Davis
emphasizes by giving the character no other name (449). A latter-day incarnation of Quaker prison reformer Fry, this woman initiates the process that will
ultimately convert the wild and morally confused Deb into a paragon of feminine virtue. We see her three years later: "There is a woman, old, deformed,
who takes a humble place among [the Quakers]: waiting like them: in her
gray dress, her worn face, pure and meek, turned now and then to the sky.
A woman much loved by these silent, restful, people; more silent than they,
more humble, more loving" (450). Humble, silent, restful, and loving, the
reformed Deb resembles the perfectly serene female inmates who captivated
Marryat and Dickens. With remarkable economy, Davis tells both of the
stories about women in prison that fascinated antebellum readers: the fierce
incarcerated criminal who reclaims her feminine identity, becoming newly
receptive to the influence of nature, and the angel in the penitentiary, the
pious and benevolent middle-class woman who abets the transformation. The
economy is possible precisely because the stories were so well known.

Although, in the name of literary realism, Davis pointedly avoided applying the shopworn formula of carceral conversion to Hugh, the subplot with
Deb and the Quaker woman relies on familiar sentimental tropes governing the depiction of women in prison. The reversion to generic conventions
(whether defined as romantic, pastoral, or sentimental) inconsistent with an
otherwise realist project has been noted and analyzed in recent criticism. For
Adam Silver, "the Quaker woman's presence suddenly transforms the text
from an accusatory narrative of class conflict to a conciliatory narrative of
class assuagement," undercutting the text's radicalism.[46] Jill Gatlin sees Davis
using this subplot somewhat more self-consciously, providing readers with a
vision of pastoral redemption in which her own faith is "incomplete" before
returning to the more troubling realities of Hugh's korl sculpture and the mill

town at the end of the story.[47] The presence of a magically reformed female prisoner and an angel in the penitentiary in "Life in the Iron-Mills" appears to register the influence of decades of prison reform discourse on American literature. The way these familiar and (for antebellum authors and readers) beguiling tropes unsettle Davis's realism also shows how confining conventions governing the representation of women in prison could be.[48] Judd and Southworth therefore displayed noteworthy resourcefulness in discovering ways to refashion such pervasive stereotypes in directions consistent with an expanded vision of female agency.

Matron of the Female Department at Sing Sing from 1844 to 1848, Eliza Farnham was a celebrity among advocates of prison reform, who credited her with working wonders among the female inmates under her charge. Walt Whitman trumpeted her efforts in the *Brooklyn Daily Eagle* on September 2, 1846: "That lady [Mrs. Farnham] is identified with the principle of prison reform— and, *if she has a fair chance,* we for one are content to let it stand or fall with her efforts, and their success or failure."[49] A few months earlier, Whitman had featured a story in which Farnham entrusted an African American girl with working among flowers on the prison grounds: "On returning to her at the end of half an hour, Mrs. F. found her face bathed in tears." When asked why she wept, the girl replied that she "had never, since her imprisonment (three years,) felt so keenly the loss of her innocence and her rectitude; and that the flowers reminded her of her early home and the plants that her mother used to nurse so carefully upon the window-sill, in broken pitchers and pots."[50] At about the same time that Whitman was retailing this sentimentalized account of Farnham's reformation of a female convict, Margaret Fuller enthusiastically praised Farnham's prison reform efforts in the pages of the *New York Tribune*: "May she never turn aside from this cause till she has made a mark that cannot be effaced upon its history!"[51]

Farnham's claim on the attention of Whitman and Fuller was based on her sincere and humane efforts to improve the lives of female prisoners during a moment when penal reform was of widespread interest among readers. Her prominence within the movement may also be traceable, however, to the degree to which she modeled the culture's underlying assumptions about criminality and womanhood. Antebellum Americans loved to read about women from respectable backgrounds who carried their incorruptible aura of virtue into the prison. If the details of Farnham's biography did not perfectly square with an image of middle-class piety (raised as an orphan by an atheist aunt and alcoholic uncle, the freethinking Farnham was a forceful and ambitious personality), supporters overlooked these traits in their celebrations.[52] As Janet Floyd has written, "It must surely have been an interesting prospect to see a woman in her mid-twenties come from 'nowhere' in terms of birth and education, intellectual and cultural capital, experience or social status—as Farnham did—and take the helm of a new kind of institution."[53] Farnham served antebellum writers as a contemporary exemplar of sentimentalism's core values, a real-life angel in the penitentiary on the model of Fry.[54] The culture's readiness to embrace such a figure may help to explain Farnham's swift rise to celebrity. That Farnham herself skillfully traded on the language of sentiment to gather support for her efforts seems apparent from the letter to the *New York Tribune* quoted earlier, where she describes the tearful responses of the inmates under her care to a rendition of the song "My Mother's Bible."

Farnham's career suggestively resonates with—yet also differs from—that of Judd's character Margaret. (Judd published *Margaret* about a year after Farnham assumed her duties at Sing Sing.) Farnham leveraged the cultural capital she acquired as an angel in the penitentiary to assume an ambitious role as a prison reformer. In 1846 Farnham "edited" for an American audience English journalist Marmaduke Sampson's *Rationale of Crime and Its Appropriate Treatment,* which promoted phrenology as an approach to dealing with crime. I put quotes around the word "edited" because the word hardly does justice to Farnham's remarkable transformation of her source material. Farnham excuses any impropriety in "undertaking a task which . . . might seem presuming in one of her sex" by claiming that her office "is very humbly discharged."[55] Farnham's disclaimer functions similarly to the epistolary exchanges in *Margaret* that coyly obfuscate Margaret's degree of agency in enacting the social reforms of Mons Christi. *Rationale of Crime* under Farnham's editorship was, despite her demurral, a boldly experimental project. The explanatory notes Farnham added to Sampson's original text at times virtually crowd out Sampson's prose altogether; in some of the book's appendices, Farnham's paratext takes up double the space of Sampson's original commentary. Moreover, to the chagrin of prison chaplain John Luckey, Farnham arranged to have Mathew Brady take daguerreotypes of criminals at Sing Sing; she includes the daguerreotypes, along with extensive analyses of how they illustrate the tenets of phrenology, in a final appendix whose authorship is entirely her own.[56]

Farnham shrewdly took advantage of public interest in antebellum prisons to transform herself from sentimentalized angel abetting individual women's conversions to theorist of prison reform. In contrast to her fictional counterpart Margaret, however, Farnham did not enjoy universal admiration for her efforts. *Rationale of Crime* was praised in some quarters but denounced in others, where phrenology's attribution of criminal behavior to physiological sources reputedly absolved criminals of accountability; Farnham's detractors used the controversy to help justify removing her from her post. The argument here is not that the shape of Farnham's career at Sing Sing is reducible to a narrative in which she steps outside of the culturally assigned role of angel in the penitentiary and is slapped down for her presumption, because the causes of her dismissal, which have been well documented, were complex.[57] I merely contend that the angel-in-the-penitentiary story that saturated American print culture in the 1840s (and beyond) may have provided a frame through which journalists and the public understood Farnham's role within the prison, a frame that eventually proved inadequate to contain her social reform ambitions. If the penitentiary's visibility in antebellum print culture provided Farnham with a unique platform for engaging in social activism, the horizons of possibility associated with such a platform were not unlimited.

Conceived of as collaborators in the shaping of American literary sentimentalism, unsung writers such as Farnham and Ohio prison chaplain Finley deserve credit for, if not inventing, at least popularizing and spreading narrative patterns that later literary authors found almost irresistibly appealing. The related stories of self-sacrificing heroines who carry a sanctifying presence across the threshold of a prison to convert criminals, and female criminals whose femininity is restored by the workings of a carceral regime, exerted an enduring impact on nineteenth-century American literature and culture. Whereas these sentimental narratives tended to follow formulaic lines in the reform periodicals, newspapers, and popular magazines in which they initially appeared, novelists such as Judd and Southworth discovered untapped potential for redefining the limits of feminine agency in these culturally resonant stories. In Judd's hands, the angel in the penitentiary became a vehicle for promoting a radical Transcendentalist revision of gender and social norms, while Southworth tweaked narrative conventions associated with women in prison just enough to voice her own challenges regarding the failings of the criminal justice system and the limits imposed on women by Victorian notions of feminine propriety. Prison reform discourse gave birth to a separate set of narrative conventions governing stories about inmates leaving the penitentiary and rejoining society. Literary experimentation with these conventions forms the subject of my next chapter.

5

"Branded with Infamy"

Discharged Convicts in Antebellum Crime Novels and *The House of the Seven Gables*

While critics often invoke the significance of Nathaniel Hawthorne's careful avoidance of the word "adultery" in *The Scarlet Letter*, less frequently (if ever) remarked upon is the absence of the word "penitentiary" from *The House of the Seven Gables* (1851).[1] Hawthorne's initial mystification of the nature of Clifford Pyncheon's thirty-year removal from society—eventually, of course, the narrator makes it clear that Clifford has been unjustly imprisoned—may have something to do with a critical failure to situate the novel within the context of the period's penal reform movement. Because it was widely recognized that the post-institutional life of the discharged convict was one of the primary benchmarks by which to judge the success of a given method of incarceration, released inmates such as Clifford occupied a significant position in antebellum prison reform discourse. As with *The Scarlet Letter*, Hawthorne surely did not intend to position *The House of the Seven Gables* with respect to the narrowly focused Auburn versus Pennsylvania carceral debate. The novel's portrait of Clifford, however, draws elements from numerous contemporary accounts of inmates attempting to find a place in the community after prolonged periods of incarceration.

Hawthorne's attention to the subject of life after prison can be profitably contrasted with the work of crime novelists Ned Buntline, George Thompson, and George Lippard, who depicted the hardships of the discharged convict in novels of the 1840s and 1850s. These novelists looked skeptically at the idea frequently promoted by optimistic prison reformers that the discharged convict could shake off the stigma of incarceration to rejoin society, as Clifford achieves—more or less—in the famously problematic ending of *The House of the Seven Gables;* they insisted, instead, that the discharged convict's experience branded him for life, physically and psychologically. Degree of complicity with antebellum print culture's most complacent narratives of prisoners' post-carceral lives offers a novel standard by which to examine Hawthorne's reputed failure of nerve at the end of the book, while the idea of a permanent post-carceral brand imagined by the crime novelists provides a new perspective on the racial motifs that have generated some of the work's most astute commentary in recent years.

Like Hawthorne, Lippard embedded the story of a discharged convict within a novel that spoke more broadly to the problem of criminal justice institutions beholden to entrenched networks of wealth and power. And also like Hawthorne, Lippard relied on and adapted widely circulating narratives about post-carceral life when he decided to make a charismatic former convict called Number Ninety-One a prominent character in *The Empire City* (1850) and *New York: Its Upper Ten and Lower Million* (1853). But in compelling his readers to confront the most unsavory aspects of America's experimental carceral regime, it was Lippard who offered the more searching assessment of the meaning of incarceration for those who had lived through the experience.

Incarceration and Discharge in Penal Reform Discourse

The conversion experience at the center of penal reform discourse, which promised to "transform the inmate's character so that he would leave the institution a different person," led to two important consequences.[2] First, emphasis on the inmate's personality meant that the psychological effects of extended periods of incarceration became a crucial ground of contestation between competing camps of prison reformers: Did incarceration always inspire penitence, or could it have far less salutary effects on inmates' mental health? Second, the success or failure of discharged criminals to become productive members of society was regarded as a key marker of a penal system's efficacy. Observers, prison inspectors, and journalists therefore devoted close attention to how inmates fared under imprisonment and speculated about (or, if possible, tracked) their post-carceral lives.

While the Auburn (or congregate) method, being cheaper to implement, was by far the more widespread system of incarceration in the United States, the Pennsylvania (or separate) method, which was adopted in many European countries after its endorsement by an international conference of penal reformers in 1846, was sufficiently prominent to ensure continuation of a penal reform debate up to the Civil War. Almost from its inception, the separate system of confinement was suspected of inflicting grave psychological damage on its subjects.[3] A new arrival to the Eastern Penitentiary in Philadelphia, where the Pennsylvania system originated, was hooded while

being escorted to his cell, inducing disorientation and terror. After this, the
inmate's only human contact was with inspectors or prison administrators.
Supporters of the separate system, including prison physicians, downplayed
the psychological damage of this regime in official reports and the popular
press, sometimes citing authoritative-looking statistics about the incidence
of insanity in a given prison. In contrast, skeptics circulated compelling stories of the individual criminal's mental health slowly deteriorating under the
psychological duress of (nearly) absolute solitude, as in this passage from an
article on prison reform in the *North American Review:*

> Certainly, it is possible to effect an apparently moral reformation of the con-
> vict by reducing him to a state of mental imbecility. . . . So a raving maniac
> may be stunned by heavy blows on the head, or stupefied by large doses of
> opium, and thus be reduced to quiet; yet this is not the way to cure, but to
> kill him. The moral torture of long-continued solitude, the ceaseless blows
> it inflicts till reason totters on her throne, may be less savage in appearance,
> but are far more terrible in reality, than any attempt to subdue a madman
> by brute force.[4]

The prison inmate whose mental faculties are compromised by incarceration
became a familiar character in the period's literature, no doubt in part owing
to the circulation of images like these. That Dr. Manette in *A Tale of Two Cities* (1859) anxiously reverts to cobbling in moments of post-carceral stress, for
example, owes something to Charles Dickens's 1842 visit to the Eastern Penitentiary, where shoemaking was one of the principal trades isolated inmates
were allowed to practice in their cells.

In their widely publicized visits to famous prisons, British travel writers
picked up and amplified ideas about incarceration and discharge held by their
American hosts. (Indeed, the international scope of penal reform ensured
that British writers would be familiar with its basic assumptions.) Quickly
reprinted in the United States, these volumes were carefully scrutinized by
American reviewers concerned about the nation's reputation abroad. In *Society in America* (1837), Harriet Martineau took a firm stand in favor of the
Pennsylvania system, partly on the grounds that it offered inmates the best
chance to rejoin society after their sentences were served. The inmates she
interviewed at Eastern Penitentiary (also known as Cherry Hill) felt that they
were being treated with respect under this regime, with its relative lack of
degrading corporal punishment, a central feature of the Auburn experience.
According to Martineau, the inmates in Cherry Hill believed that isolation
from other prisoners would help them avoid the problem of being identified
as former convicts upon release; they would be able to live "without the fear

of being waylaid by vicious old companions, or hunted from employment to employment by those whose interest it is to deprive them of a chance of establishing a character."[5] Supporters of the Pennsylvania system often touted the convicts' anonymity as one of its key advantages over the Auburn system, in which inmates who had worked together would be able to identify one another after release.

Frederick Marryat, in *Diary in America* (1839), also endorsed the anonymity argument. Marryat provided abstracts of interviews he conducted with ten separate inmates in the Eastern Penitentiary, in which he inquired about their backgrounds, their crimes, and their assessments of the disciplinary regimes to which they were subjected. The difficulty of life after incarceration was foreseen by one inmate, an Irishman, who "was fearful of only one thing: his time was just out, and where was he to go? If known to have been in the prison, he would never find work." Marryat shared this concern about the fate of convicts after discharge: "There is one decided advantage in this [Pennsylvania] system, which is, that they all learn a trade, if they had not one before; and, when they leave the prison, have the means of obtaining an honest livelihood, if they wish to do so themselves, and are permitted to do so by others." Marryat placed high value on the discharged convict's supposed ability to overcome or avoid the stigma of incarceration; learning a trade was a necessary but insufficient feature of imprisonment if this stigma followed the inmate out of the institution. Marryat's approval of the Pennsylvania system was qualified, however, by concern over the mental health of inmates. One prisoner Marryat interviewed, who had not yet been assigned any employment within the prison, showed signs of mental disquietude after only six weeks under the separate regime. Of him Marryat observes, "The want of employment appeared to have completely prostrated this man."[6]

Struck even more forcibly than Marryat with the mental prostration of inmates in the Eastern Penitentiary, Dickens excoriated the separate system in *American Notes* (1842). Chapter 7 of the book is titled "Philadelphia, and Its Solitary Prison," and description of the prison takes up almost the entirety of Dickens's observations on Philadelphia. Though he did not question the motives of the solitary system's supporters, Dickens charged that "those benevolent men who carry it into execution, do not know what they are doing. . . . I hold this slow and daily tampering with the mysteries of the brain, to be immeasurably worse than any torture of the body." Like Marryat, Dickens offered detailed descriptions of individual inmates. Of a German who had served two years of a five-year sentence, Dickens observes, "A more dejected, heart-broken wretched creature, it would be difficult to imagine." One prisoner tended rabbits as a hedge against his solitude, and his pathetic solicitude for them led Dickens to wonder "in what respect the man was the nobler animal of the two." The most distressing case of mental incapacitation was a sailor whose release was imminent after eleven years of incarceration:

> Why does he stare at his hands, and pick the flesh upon his fingers, and raise his eyes for an instant, every now and then, to those bare walls which have seen his head turn grey? It is a way he has sometimes. . . . It is his humour too, to say that he does not look forward to going out; . . . that he has lost all care for everything. It is his humour to be a helpless, crushed, and broken man.

Such observations led Dickens to the "fixed opinion that those who have undergone this punishment, MUST pass into society again morally unhealthy and diseased."[7] Given the short period of their visits, of course, British travelers were unable to assess the post-carceral lives of the subjects they interviewed and could only speculate about the long-term effects of a given regime.

American prison reformers, however, could and did track the outcomes of individual prisoners. Dickens's charges about the perils of the Pennsylvania system were so compelling and potentially damaging to the cause that they demanded a response. The *Pennsylvania Journal of Prison Discipline and Philanthropy* therefore published a letter from William Peter, Great Britain's consul general for the state of Pennsylvania, outlining his approval of the separate system as run by the Eastern Penitentiary and specifically addressing the condition after release of the inmates Dickens had interviewed. Peters thought that the German, for example, was in "as excellent health and spirits as mortal need be," and had simply exploited Dickens's too tender heart. The man who kept rabbits "now resides in Canada, and (according to letters received from him by his countrymen) is doing well." Peters noted that the sailor had been incarcerated for rape, as if this were a pertinent fact that Dickens's account purposefully left out for the sake of garnering sympathy. Duly released, the sailor was now "in the employment of a farmer in the interior of the State, and said to be conducting himself well." Throughout the article Peters emphasized the post-incarceration success stories that Dickens could not have foreseen, including one of Dickens's interview subjects who "now earns a comfortable livelihood by his labours as a journeyman printer," another who "is now in respectable business, reconciled to his father, and respectably married," and a third who "is now employed in a large apothecary's establishment in South America, and conducting himself with propriety."[8] Though it reads now as a partisan whitewash of the Pennsylvania system, the article reveals how the fate of the discharged convict inevitably became a key piece of evidence in ongoing carceral disputes.

In the mid-1840s, lending aid to discharged criminals became a new front among supporters of penal reform. For example, John Luckey, the newly appointed chaplain at Sing Sing, began trying to find jobs for discharged inmates in New York City and visiting them periodically to assess their progress.[9] As one author advocating the establishment of an asylum for discharged convicts put it in *Prisoner's Friend,* "Branded with infamy wherever he is known; shut out from the common avenues of industry, [the discharged convict] finds it almost impossible to regain a respectable standing, even in the lowest ranks of society."[10] According to reports of the time, older convicts were in particular danger of feeling disoriented by life after prison. One article in *Prisoner's Friend* told of several aged men who found themselves so "lonely and abandoned in a world of strangers" upon release from prison that they deliberately committed crimes in order to be re-incarcerated.[11] A prison chaplain wrote of a long-imprisoned inmate who was afraid to reenter society on his day of discharge, since "his long confinement" had taken from him "all his knowledge of the affairs of life" and left him "as ignorant and as helpless as a child." The chaplain went on to advocate societies to assist discharged convicts in transitioning to a new life on the outside.[12]

One of the primary goals of the New York Prison Association (NYPA), founded in 1844, was to render assistance to discharged convicts to help them avoid a return to criminal habits. Hawthorne's friend and patron John L. O'Sullivan took the position of secretary of the newly formed association.[13] As part of a longer article titled "Prison Discipline," O'Sullivan published a detailed account of the first meeting of the NYPA in the August 1846 issue of the *United States Magazine, and Democratic Review* (where it appeared along with a selection titled "Papers of an Old Dartmoor Prisoner," edited by Hawthorne). The organization's committee on discharged convicts had a seven-point mission, which included keeping an office in New York "where discharged persons may apply for aid and advice," maintaining correspondence with prison officials to ascertain the job skills and character of inmates about to be released, keeping a record of local employers willing to hire discharged inmates, and locating boardinghouses where the discharged prisoners would not be subject to "corrupting influences."[14] The New York City office of the NYPA was managed by Quaker reformer Isaac Hopper and came to be known as the "Hopper House." Hundreds of former inmates found jobs through Hopper's efforts.[15] *Prisoner's Friend* reported in 1849 the comments of the newly appointed warden of Auburn Prison, E. L. Potter, on the importance of providing for inmates' welfare after release: "Intimately connected in importance with the abridgement of the term of first sentences, is some provision for the employment and encouragement of discharged convicts. The taint of suspicion is apt to rest upon one who has been subjected to the restraint of prison walls."[16] This concern for the formerly incarcerated was not confined to New York; the Massachusetts Society in Aid of Discharged Convicts was founded in Boston in 1845.[17]

Lydia Maria Child reported on the foundation of the NYPA for the *Boston Courier,* including an anecdote Hopper related at the meeting. Hopper had interviewed an inmate named Mary Norris, who yearned to leave prison yet seemed resigned, even should that happen, to re-incarceration. When asked why, she told Hopper: "When I go out of prison, nobody will employ me. No respectable people will let me come into their houses. I must go with such friends as I have. If they steal or commit other offences, I shall be taken up with them. Whether I am guilty or not, is of no consequence; nobody will believe me innocent." Moved by her story, Hopper procured Norris's release and found her work as the head nurse in a hospital for the poor, where she remained for seventeen years and "discharged the duties of her situation so faithfully, that she gained the respect and confidence of all who knew her." Child reports that this anecdote received a "cordial response."[18] Undoubtedly it did. This story of a penitent criminal successfully discharged from prison into a productive life on the outside struck a chord with hopeful readers. It was reprinted from the *Boston Courier* in *Prisoner's Friend* in January 1845, told again by a different author in *Prisoner's Friend* in February 1846, and retailed once more, in the same periodical, in October 1848. The anecdote was also reprinted in the article "Prison Discipline" in the August 1846 issue of the *United States Magazine, and Democratic Review* mentioned earlier.[19] The story's reiteration, while partially attributable to the reprint practices common to the era, demonstrates not only how attractive this narrative of a successful post-carceral life was to editors but also, quite possibly, just how rare such experiences actually were: if other individual examples were available, why keep recycling the same anecdote?

Prison reform advocates recognized the stigma of incarceration as one of the heaviest burdens placed on discharged inmates. A former convict became an easy scapegoat for any crime subsequently committed in his or her neighborhood. In the meeting establishing the NYPA, Hopper also told the story of an Irishman named Patrick McKever, who spent ten years in jail as the penalty for burglary. After discharge, McKever "returned to his trade, and conducted [himself] in a very sober, exemplary manner." Some time after his return, though, he was arrested for a burglary he did not commit. Though no evidence linked him to the crime, Philadelphia officials maintained, "He is an old convict, and that is enough to condemn him." Hopper succeeded in securing bail and eventually McKever was proven innocent, but the tenuousness of his escape from re-incarceration troubled the author of the article, who asked what would have happened had Hopper never intervened on McKever's behalf.[20]

Interest in the fate of the discharged convict had literary as well as social implications. The line between fictional entertainment and nonfictional advocacy was sometimes blurred in the discourse of penal reform, as it was across the antebellum reform landscape. Child crossed this line effortlessly, following up the presumably nonfictional anecdote about Mary Norris with a fictional work, "The Irish Heart," which appeared in the *Columbian Lady's and Gentleman's Magazine* in July 1845. The story tells of an Irish immigrant named James, who is cheated into accepting counterfeit money, knowingly passes the fake bills, and ends up in prison. After five years served, James stops for help at the NYPA, which Child pointedly inserts into the narrative. Receiving kind advice and tools to help him ply a trade, James lives out his life as a virtuous mechanic raising a family with the true love who waited for his release.[21] Writing on behalf of the prison reform movement, Child circulates the most hopeful version of the post-carceral narrative. However well-meaning Child's portrait of James may have been, this kind of story had the unintended effect of minimizing the former inmate's experience of incarceration. Conferring upon the discharged inmate post-carceral anonymity also suggested that whatever suffering he endured in prison was temporary and effaceable, carrying no meaning or importance after incarceration ended.

Branded with Infamy: Discharged Convicts in Crime Fiction

Not all literary versions of the discharged convict's reentrance into society were as optimistic as Child's in "The Irish Heart." Appearing in *Godey's Magazine and Lady's Book,* Emma C. Embury's story "The Convict's Daughter" tells of a man released from twelve years of incarceration into the care of a loving daughter. Although the young woman attempts through gentle moral suasion to save the man from further disgrace, the penitentiary system has obliterated any shred of decency to which she might appeal: "Hard labour, coarse food, the want of healthful exercise, and, above all, a daily contact with vice and crime through so many long years, had effaced every trace of a better nature even in the physical man."[22] The father returns to the scene of his crimes, digs up the long-buried spoils of his larceny, and lives dissolutely until he contracts a fatal illness while extracting a buried fortune from a plague-tainted graveyard. Embury's story is notable for rejecting the premise that a woman's beneficent moral agency can redeem a discharged convict, even more so given its appearance in a periodical generally associated with uncritical celebration of the power of female sentiment.

The antebellum authors who betrayed the most skepticism regarding the outcomes of the formerly incarcerated were crime novelists such as Buntline,

Thompson, and Lippard. As former prison inmates, Buntline and Thompson brought a perspective to the issue to which few other published novelists could lay claim. Buntline spent a year in prison after being convicted of participation in the 1849 Astor Place Riot, which, as a nativist supporter of American actor Edwin Forrest, he had plotted to incite. Sentenced to a year's hard labor at Blackwell's Island, Buntline seized the occasion to write a self-aggrandizing novel called *The Convict; or, The Conspirators' Victim* (1851), with a subtitle prominently proclaiming that it was "Written in Prison," perhaps in the hope of deriving credibility among like-minded readers for his personal sacrifice to the nativist cause, or more broadly intending to capitalize on the period's widespread interest in all things related to incarceration.[23]

According to his autobiography, *My Life,* George Thompson was arrested for assault and battery after an altercation at a theater and imprisoned for six weeks awaiting trial in Boston's Leverett Street Jail (though he was eventually found not guilty). In a limited way, Thompson himself might be regarded as a prison reformer, insofar as he wrote from jail a series of newspaper editorials titled "Mysteries of Leverett Street Jail." He took credit in his autobiography for exposing the cruel treatment of the jail's "petty tyrants" and for "producing a far better state of affairs in the interior of the 'stone jug.'"[24] Whatever his efforts to improve conditions in a particular jail, though, Thompson cannot be classed with the ministers, philanthropists, and other figures who devoted themselves to advancing the broader philosophy of moral reform via incarceration; in fact, he frequently satirized them in his crime novels.[25] The crime novelists shared with prison reformers a keen interest in the social position of the discharged inmate, but they did not soft-pedal the former inmate's hardships.

Thompson's novels consistently resist the notion of the inmate being welcomed back into society after incarceration. Invoking the metaphor of branding, Thompson's Jack Harold, when asked whether he repents of his life of crime, answers that the stigma of incarceration makes repentance impossible: "The woman who falls from virtue can never rise again; the man who swerves from honesty must remain forever a branded Outlaw!"[26] In *Life and Exploits of Bristol Bill* (1851), Thompson exposes the obstacles placed in the way of discharged convicts who try to go straight. Finding himself in poverty in New York, Bristol Bill (an alias of real-life criminal William Darlington) resolves to become an honest man and takes a job at a factory, where his skills as a machinist recommend him to the owner. But "conceiving that this was merely a scheme to further some villanous [sic] design, the police informed the manufacturer as to the character of his newly-hired workman, and Bill was of course forthwith discharged."[27] The same thing happens when Bill takes a job at a sawmill in Connecticut; bereft of other options, he eventually returns to a life of crime. Recalling real-life discharged convict McKever, Bristol Bill remains at the mercy of predatory police officers, without a kind-hearted reformer like Hopper to intervene on his behalf.

Lippard, too, consistently portrayed the discharged convict as being marked by the experience of incarceration in such as way as to prevent reintegration with society. In *The Nazarene* (1846), Lippard foregrounds the convict's telltale clothing with emphatic capitalization, describing a character as "clad in a coarse grey roundabout and pantaloons; the uniform of the Eastern Penitentiary. In one word he was a DISCHARGED CONVICT."[28] Sometimes the signs by which a formerly incarcerated person is identifiable are left unstated. In Lippard's 1850 novel *The Killers*, Elijah Watson serves a four-year sentence in Philadelphia's Eastern Penitentiary for passing counterfeit notes. After release, Elijah takes employment as a compositor at a large Philadelphia printing house. But when a fellow workman identifies the pale, downcast, and quiet new workman as a former inmate (in a moving chapter called "The Silent Compositor"), employer and co-workers gather to bully Elijah off the premises. Struggling with emotion, Elijah makes a sad but dignified exit. Later he complains to his mother that he faces this prejudice at each new place of employment (he also tries to work as a shoemaker and a porter): "And now when I comes out of jail, the word 'Convict' follers me everywhere, and shuts me out from every hope of gettin' an honest livelihood."[29] Lippard neglects to inform readers how Elijah's co-workers consistently intuit his former status.

Intriguingly, the crime novelists return again and again to the idea that the discharged convict is "branded" by his crime. Reformers used this term metaphorically, as when a writer in *Prisoner's Friend* lobbied for an asylum for discharged convicts by noting that the formerly incarcerated individual was "branded with infamy wherever he is known."[30] But the crime novelists frequently literalized this metaphor, insisting that the formerly incarcerated individual bore visible and permanent marks of imprisonment. In these figurations, inmates carried their stigma everywhere, not just "wherever [they were] known." As I discuss shortly, Lippard's Number Ninety-One, a prominent character in *The Empire City*, bears scars on his face and head from torture suffered at the period's two most famous prisons. A villain in Thompson's *Venus in Boston* (1849), the Chevalier, has the words "Convicted Felon" branded on his chest, a mark that prevents him from violating a young woman he has married under false pretenses.[31] Thompson uses similar imagery to tell the story of Bristol Bill, who sports ineradicable scars on his back from enduing whipping and torture in prison in *Life and Exploits*.[32] Thompson's geographical projection of these acts of torture onto Australia's Botany Bay prison colony (where both prisoners ostensibly received their scars) allows him to retain a certain verisimilitude (American penitentiaries did whip but did not brand convicts) even while presenting the idea that incarceration is far more deeply ingrained in the former convict's identity than simplistic narratives of successful discharged convicts allowed for.

Perhaps the most horrifying scene of a former inmate's vulnerability to a visible stigma of incarceration is found in Buntline's *Mysteries and Miseries of New York* (1849). At one point in the novel, the (white) villain Butcher Bill strolls into Pete Williams's Five Points saloon (which Dickens had famously chronicled as the site of interracial debauchery in *American Notes*) looking to indulge his penchant for violence by fighting a black man. After compelling a number of black women to dance with him, Butcher Bill walks directly up to one of the saloon's terrorized patrons and says, "Your name is Zack Reed, and you're a states-prison bird!"[33] Bill taunts the reluctant Reed into fighting and beats him until, badly bloodied, Reed pleas for mercy. As with Elijah Watson's co-workers in Lippard's novel *The Killers*, Buntline does not explain how Bill possesses this information about Reed's identity.

Buntline's charged treatment of the subject suggests that a racial component may be involved in the crime novelists' insistence that discharged convicts were permanently marked by a prior condition of unfreedom. That incarceration and slavery were in some ways parallel institutions was readily apparent to contemporary observers. In fact, the similarity would be acknowledged within the language of the Thirteenth Amendment to the U.S. Constitution in 1865: "Neither slavery nor involuntary servitude, except as a punishment for crime whereof the party shall have been duly convicted, shall exist within the United States, or any place subject to their jurisdiction."[34] In the most influential recent reading of the poetics of incarceration, Caleb Smith describes antebellum American prison inmates experiencing a legally defined condition of "civil death" that "brought them very close to the 'social death' of the slave."[35] Colin Dayan, too, has noted how "the power of competing analogies to redefine liberty permitted the conversion of slave into prisoner and prisoner into slave" during the nineteenth century.[36] In addition to the obvious fact that inmates and slaves were denied liberty, both groups suffered the infliction of degrading corporal punishments. Inmates and slaves were also subjected to similar (though, of course, not identical) regimes of coerced labor. This was especially true in the many states adopting the Auburn system of incarceration. Just as slave owners sometimes hired out slaves to third parties, these states sold inmates' labor to private contractors. Labeling this system "contractual penal servitude," prison historian Rebecca M. McLennan notes that many states embraced the Auburn model for its presumed economic efficiency during the period 1825–1850.[37]

Convicts subjected to denial of liberty and forced labor potentially destabilized a border between white freedom and black servitude upon their return to society. Former inmates wishing to break free of the signs of imprisonment and reenter society on equal terms with their fellow citizens call to mind the situation of mixed-race former slaves who left behind the traces of their African ancestry and condition of past enslavement to pass as white. (Characters who passed across the color line, though not unknown in the antebellum period, would increasingly populate American fiction in the post–Civil War years.) Such fluidity of identity on the part of a discharged convict did not trouble Child; she celebrated the possibility of the convict transitioning unobtrusively back into society in "An Irish Heart." But Child was, perhaps not coincidentally, an ardent abolitionist who had sympathetically depicted an interracial (white-Indian) union in her first novel, *Hobomok* (1824), and decried anti-miscegenation laws in her 1833 abolitionist tract *An Appeal in Favor of That Class of Americans Called Africans.* If Child did not see incarceration as imparting a permanently stigmatizing racial coding, this endorsement of the convict's "passing" is consistent with the egalitarian spirit found across her body of work.

In contrast with Child, authors of sensational crime fiction may have sensed something troubling about the possibility of the discharged convict blurring a line between coerced (black) labor and free (white) labor, especially given a white working-class readership whose own sense of identity was sometimes asserted through contrast with the condition of enslavement.[38] In Buntline's *Mysteries of New York,* Butcher Bill identifies black saloon patron Zack Reed not only as a former inmate but also, more specifically, as a "*states*-prison bird," as if incarceration in a state penitentiary (where he would have been subjected to forced labor) implied a uniquely degrading condition. As a former inmate who is also black, Zack Reed carries the burden of a doubled stigma, perhaps in some way accounting in the eyes of antebellum readers for Butcher Bill's otherwise mysterious, instantaneous identification of his prior condition. Of course, the crime novelists assign this identifying stigma to white former inmates as well, including sympathetic ones such as Lippard's silent compositor Elijah Watson and Thompson's quite unsympathetic would-be rapist in *Venus in Boston.* In asserting that inmates were permanently marked by the experience of incarceration, crime novelists picked up on similarities between slavery and forced prison labor, recognizing that a regime that (in some ways) treated inmates like slaves implied such a compromise of a white inmate's racial status that it could not but leave behind a sign. The threat to white privilege embodied by people passing across a line between civil/social death and legal personhood is contained in these novels by the implication that the discharged convict never fully sheds the stigma of incarceration.

The idea that prison left its mark on convicts, preventing their seamless reintegration into society, posed a broad challenge to reformers' hopes, even as it more pointedly belied claims made on behalf of the solitary system of incarceration, whose advocates often cited preservation of post-carceral anonymity as one of its most important features. Although their depictions of the discharged convict varied widely in tone, these sensational crime novels collectively suggested that returning to society from the penitentiary would never be an uncomplicated transition; one way or another, the convict's past would come to light. Suggestively imbuing incarceration with racial overtones through the imagery of branding and marking of bodies, the crime novelists captured the culture's anxiety regarding a carceral policy that, as contractual penal servitude gained ground, increasingly exposed white men to a labor system analogous to plantation slavery.

The Travails of Number Ninety-One

Although all three novelists charted the travails of discharged convicts, Lippard brought greater depth and sensitivity to the subject than Buntline or Thompson. Lippard's extended depiction of the experience of a discharged convict across two 1850s novels reflects his awareness that to believe in an inmate's quiet reintegration into society was to ignore the suffering that incarceration had imposed on him and, ultimately, to absolve readers of complicity with the cruelties of the penal system. The inmate who aspired to post-carceral anonymity accepted silence as the price of reintegration, which effectively prevented the most meaningful testimony about the experience of incarceration from reaching the public. Refusing to buy in to this effacement, Lippard insisted that the former inmate's suffering be recognized by a culture that otherwise seemed all too complacent about the success of its prison experiments.

As discussed in chapter 1, Lippard began his literary career reporting on arrests and trials for a socially radical Philadelphia penny paper. The experience heightened his awareness of disparities in the criminal justice system and eventually developed into sympathy for the socially oppressed, including those who found themselves on the wrong side of the law. Given his wide-ranging interest in social reform, Lippard was bound to take an interest in the subject of prison reform, which he briefly addressed in his first and still most famous novel, *The Quaker City* (1845). Late in the novel, a virtuous young woman named Izolé (formerly Mabel) enters a trance state and articulates a utopian vision of Philadelphia in the distant future. Among other reforms, the prison no longer anchors the criminal justice system: "There are no rich; there are no poor; I see neither church nor gaol, priest nor gaoler, yet—yet—all are happy!" Izolé relates the fate of a murderer in a society where crime is rare: the city has seen only two murders in the course of two centuries. The criminal begs for execution to relieve him of the pangs of conscience, but no official penalty is imposed. Instead, "he goes to his home—his friends and neighbors gather round him, they seek to comfort him. Hark that voice! 'Crime is a disease to be cured, not an ulcer to be cut off.'"[39]

Whereas sympathy for criminals and belief in their potential for redemption were widespread within and beyond the prison reform movement, these ideas were predicated on the assumption that incarceration simultaneously punished the criminal for wrongdoing and provided the opportunity for him or her to achieve penitence. The sentiment that the penitentiary itself would eventually be regarded as an outmoded response to criminality put Lippard outside even the liberal vanguard of reformers.

Lippard published two novels in the 1850s that included a discharged convict as a prominent character: *The Empire City* and *New York: Its Upper Ten and Lower Million.* These formally experimental novels cover the same time period of December 23–25, 1844, and both build toward a denouement on Christmas Day, when the immense fortune of benevolent New York aristocrat Gulian Van Huyden will pass, according to the terms of his will, into the hands of his heirs, some twenty-one years after his (apparent) suicide. The novels trace the fortunes of the surviving heirs in the days leading up to the settlement of the will. As discussed in chapter 2, these novels jointly critique the failings of American criminal justice, particularly through their portrayal of vigilante courts that punish various evildoers whose wealth and power would otherwise insulate them from prosecution. Lippard therefore embeds the story of a discharged convict within a larger portrait of criminal justice institutions corrupted to serve elite interests.

Unlike Hawthorne, Lippard chooses not to mystify the past of the discharged convict who first appears in *The Empire City* on a train, generously sharing his meal with a starving fellow passenger. When asked his name, the character replies: "*Where I was last,* they called me Number Ninety-One. Yo' see they are werry pertickler about their scholars in the school were I've been gettin' my larnin.' They're so 'fraid they might lose 'em that they *numbers* 'em."[40] H. Bruce Franklin notes that convicts writing books using their numbers as pseudonyms became a cliché by the late nineteenth century, but Lippard anticipates those writers by fifty years in choosing this nomenclature to emphasize the dehumanizing effects of incarceration.[41] By refusing to reclaim his pre-carceral name, Number Ninety-One emblematizes the crime novelists' insistence that incarceration permanently affected an individual's identity. Even had he not verbally identified himself as a discharged convict, Number Ninety-One's status would have been perceptible to his fellow passengers; the narrator notes that he is "clad in a loose jacket and wide trowsers [*sic*] of coarse grey stuff, very much like the uniform of starvation or felony; the court dress of the poor-house or penitentiary" (47). Inmates discharged from Auburn Prison were provided with ill-fitting clothes purchased by the warden from secondhand garment dealers, leading the NYPA to complain of the unfairness of returning a former convict to the community "with the mark of a *jail bird* on his very clothing."[42] The shabby clothing with which inmates were discharged into the community was the first barrier to their reintroduction on equal grounds with their fellow citizens.

The evidence of Number Ninety-One's incarceration is not merely visible in his clothes; it is also etched upon his body. Like Thompson and Buntline, Lippard portrays the scars of incarceration as ineffaceable. It was not unheard of for repeat offenders to have experienced both the Auburn and Pennsylvania systems of confinement. Martineau had interviewed such inmates in coming to her conclusion in favor of the Pennsylvania regime. Number Ninety-One is one such prisoner, who confesses to (or boasts of) having endured both methods of incarceration. Pointing to a scar, he says, "That's the mark of the gag that was put in my jaws at Cherry Hill!" (51). Then indicating a bald spot on his head, Number Ninety-One announces, alluding to a form of water-drop torture: "There's where they *baptized* me. . . . Yes: it was in Auburn prison" (51). Later in *The Empire City,* Ninety-One claims to have suffered "lashes, chains, dark dungeons, and drops of water" during his eleven years of confinement (147). In the minds of antebellum readers, the distinction between the Pennsylvania and Auburn systems was the crucial remaining point to be decided on the question of penal reform.[43] Number Ninety-One acknowledges no significant difference between the disciplinary regimes. Pointedly endowing his character with personal experience of both types of prison, Lippard implies that the Auburn versus Pennsylvania debate implies a false distinction. Where the torture of inmates is routine, the question of congregate or solitary labor becomes comparatively trivial.

Charges of deliberate torture were not often made in penal reform literature. A rare exception was an investigation of administrative malfeasance and disciplinary cruelty at the Eastern Penitentiary in 1834. The inquiry was spurred, in part, by the death of a convict who had been subjected to punishment with an iron gag—the same punishment (at the same institution) that Number Ninety-One claims to have endured. After inspectors gave the prison a "clean bill of health with a few mild reprimands and suggestions for reform," inspector Thomas B. McElwee filed a minority report in which he charged "cruel and unusual punishment inflicted by order of the Warden upon refractory convicts" and went on to detail freezing water thrown on convicts in the dead of winter, iron gags forced into prisoners' mouths, and a "Mad Chair" forcing inmates into prolonged stress positions.[44] McElwee's exposé, which he published over the objections of the Pennsylvania legislature, was unusual. Readers could indeed find statistics on the discipline meted out to convicts; the only punishments acknowledged, however, were stripes and days of solitary confinement.[45] An inmate's death by flogging at the Auburn Prison inspired an investigation in 1846, leading Walt Whitman to ask in the pages of the *Brooklyn Daily Eagle*, "If we can govern crazed people, idiots, and brutes, so much better by mild means, than by force, is it not monstrous to think we cannot also govern those who, though criminal, yet possess the godlike faculty of mind?"[46] Dorothea Dix wrote of such punishments as the gag, leg irons, and the "shower bath" in use in American prisons, but she downplayed their frequency of use and defended their necessity in individual cases.[47]

In the response of Number Ninety-One's horrified interlocutor, Lippard anticipates the likely reaction of most readers on hearing of deliberate and systematic torture in American prisons: "'It is too horrible—I cannot believe it!' muttered the young man" (51). With his forthright and graphic exposure of torture masquerading as discipline, Lippard provocatively directs readers to consider that prison reports authored by interested parties may not have told the whole truth about the nature of incarceration.[48] In this Lippard antici-pated Michael Meranze's analysis, which found that corporal punishment was not, as most of its supporters would have claimed, extraneous to the solitary system; it was an inevitable corollary to its assumptions. When solitude failed in disciplining or reforming a refractory inmate, "prison officials had nowhere else to turn than to the body itself."[49]

Lippard is sensitive to the community's alarmed and biased response to the appearance of a discharged convict in its midst. In *The Empire City*, a valise containing $71,000 goes missing on the train in which Number Ninety-One is a passenger. Suspicion immediately turns to two people, Number Ninety-One and a second character called Nameless, the sharer of Number Ninety-One's meal and himself a recent escapee from an asylum for the insane. When the victim of the apparent robbery asks for a personal search of the suspicious men, Nameless's appeal to his fellow citizens is met with ridicule: "'Have I not a friend in the car, who will protect me from this outrage?' There was such a contrast between the tone of the man, and his poverty-stricken garb, that the passengers burst into a simultaneous roar of laughter" (96). The search is forcibly carried out on Nameless, who manifests "a blush of burning shame" at the humiliation he endures (97). Number Ninety-One evades search by whispering a single word to the well-dressed fellow passenger named Colonel Tarleton who presides over the scene: "Every one heard the word, uttered dis-tinctly by the convict, Ninety-One: it was apparently idle and meaningless, and yet its effect upon the Colonel was incredible. 'Thirty-Nine!'" (97). The stigma of incarceration is so powerful that the novel's chief villain, Colonel Tarleton, immediately relents in his persecution of Number Ninety-One lest he, too, be outed as a former inmate.

The irony of the scene is that Number Ninety-One and Nameless had indeed been hatching a plan to steal the valise, though they do not carry it out. Number Ninety-One went into prison an innocent man: the novel later reveals him to be honest mechanic John Hoffman, framed by Colonel Tarleton for reasons I discuss shortly. But his treatment while incarcerated has made him vengeful: "'And yit, with all this,' cried Ninety-One, his mouth wearing that indescribable sneer—'with all this, the gag and the dark dungeon at Cherry Hill, the drop o' water at Auburn, I'm not a bit better, but on the con-*trairy* much *wuss* than ever'" (51). Number Ninety-One's turn to crime is the result rather than the cause of his imprisonment. As he puts it, he was discharged from prison "a miserable wreck of a man with no chance of honest employment" (147). If the narrative the culture preferred to tell itself about incarceration was of the guilty criminal redeemed by his or her experience in prison, Lippard offers here its reverse: an honest man morally perverted by the unspeakable cruelties of the penitentiary.

The politics of the workingmen's movement of the antebellum period magnified the challenge that Lippard took up in fashioning a sympathetic character out of a discharged convict. With the introduction of the Auburn system of congregate labor in New York's penitentiaries, mechanics complained bitterly of the unfairness of having to compete in the labor market with prison workers. According to McLennan, "Whereas many mechanics had shown some empathy for convicts in the early 1830s, many hardened their attitudes toward convicts in the years after 1834."[50] New York mechanics repeatedly petitioned the state legislature for relief; the "gravest concern" of New York City's General Trades' Union in 1834 "was over state prison labor, an offense to all journeymen and something of an economic threat to men in the building trades."[51] Inmates not only produced below-cost goods while in prison; they also learned trades that allowed them to compete with mechanics after they were discharged. Economic self-interest pushed urban mechanics, almost certainly a large segment of Lippard's readership, toward an unapologetically bigoted view of prison inmates. Prison historian Orlando Lewis summarizes the attitude toward discharged convicts expressed by mechanics in a petition to the New York State Assembly: "Masters would, unaware, be taking discharged convicts into their own homes, among their wives and daughters. . . . Robbers, ravishers, false swearers and thieves ought not to be benefited to the injury of those honest persons who had a claim on the laws for protection. Rogues are no legitimate part of the community."[52] This same resentment surfaced in Lippard's hometown of Philadelphia in 1835, when a shoemakers' union objected to competition from convict laborers at the Eastern Penitentiary.[53] Asking an audience of mechanics to be sensitive to the hardships of the discharged convict was a hard sell for a novelist in Lippard's position. By making Number Ninety-One a likable rogue who had never committed a crime before his unjust imprisonment, Lippard carefully guided his readers into considering the claims of a group that they legitimately distrusted and feared as an economic threat. That Number Ninety-One does not survive long enough to reenter the labor market at the end of *The Empire City* may have served as a further appeasement of wary mechanics among his readership.

The Empire City employs the plot contrivance of a disputed inheritance whose secrets are revealed in the final chapters. While Lippard generally capitulates to the demands of literary convention, dispensing rewards to the virtuous and punishments to the vicious in accordance with the melodramatic principles of sensation fiction, the fate of Number Ninety-One tellingly violates the formula. At first glance, as the legal guardian to one of the decedent's two legitimate heirs (he is the adoptive father of Gulian Van Huyden's son), Number Ninety-One would seem to have a reasonable prospect of securing a portion of the immense Van Huyden estate. Number Ninety-One learns in the course of *The Empire City* how Colonel Tarleton (who turns out to be the evil brother of Charles Van Huyden) framed him for the crime that initially landed him in prison. Tarleton needed to get John Hoffman and his adopted son, the true heir, out of the way to allow his own child access to the family fortune. Apprised of this history, and of Tarleton's subsequent attempt to frame him for another murder, Number Ninety-One takes his fate into his own hands. Pursued by police while hunting down his enemy, Number Ninety-One chases Tarleton to the roof of a building, seizes him, and leaps, killing both men in the process: "By gosh, boys, he's smashed at last! The old jail-bird has jumped clean off this four-story roof" (203). In a grimly fatalistic ending, Lippard's discharged convict meets his death locked in violent combat with another ex-con.

In Lippard's jaundiced retelling of the culture's preferred narratives of penology, the legacy of incarceration for Number Ninety-One includes the physical and emotional scars left by torture at the hands of prison guards, a propensity for violence, and exclusion from the economic prosperity he (as adoptive guardian of Gulian Van Huyden's son) figuratively step-fathered. Permanently defined in the eyes of society by his former carceral status ("the old jail-bird"), Number Ninety-One cannot, even in death, escape the stigma of incarceration.

The Discharged Convict in *The House of the Seven Gables*

Treatment of the discharged convict across a range of antebellum sources provides the necessary context for evaluating Hawthorne's characterization of former prison inmate Clifford Pyncheon in *The House of the Seven Gables*. With his usual diffidence, Hawthorne withholds any specific identifying information regarding the prison where Clifford spent thirty years. But the institution that would have received a convicted murderer in Massachusetts was the state prison at Charlestown, a prison that was much in the news in the late 1840s. In its early days, the institution had relied on vicious corporal punishments and terms of solitary confinement that one historian has described as "reformation by terrorism."[54] But in 1829 a new building was erected and the prison adopted the Auburn scheme of administration. A religious revival swept through the prison in 1842, in which "from thirty to forty" inmates had "become subjects of renewing grace" according to one report, which declared the movement "a glorious display of divine power."[55] In 1843 the new warden, Frederick Robinson, drastically curtailed the prison's reliance on flogging as a form of discipline and permitted conversation among inmates, in contravention of the normal Auburn system insistence on absolute silence. The institution was thereafter lauded in the press as a model prison. The *New York Evangelist* reported on the formation among the prisoners of a "Massachusetts State Prison Society for Moral Improvement and Mutual Aid" to encourage one another in their intellectual and moral progress. The article's author hails this development in the strongest terms: "Convicts have come to be regarded as *human* beings. . . . Carry out this principle in all our State Prisons and Houses of Correction, and convicts may yet very generally become *converts* to morality and to vital Christianity."[56]

Dix, by contrast, believed that reform had been carried too far at the prison: "I fear that the Inspectors, and also the Warden and Chaplain of the Massachusetts prison, have been somewhat too hasty in their conclusions in dispensing with some observances and rules generally connected with discipline."[57] Nevertheless, a correspondent in *Prisoner's Friend* defended Robinson and declared that under his management "the Prison is fast becoming, what every similar institution should be, a school of moral and intellectual reform."[58] *Prisoner's Friend* continued to chart developments at Charlestown, consistently defending the warden's efforts to end corporal punishment, even against the advice of some of his subordinate officers.[59] *Niles' National Register* surveyed recent reports on the prison and came to the conclusion that "the fruits of a mild and humane treatment manifest themselves" in the health and welfare of the prisoners. The journal focused specific attention on convicts discharged from the prison, who "go again into the world, many of them with

the purpose and the hope, by a correct course of conduct, of restoring themselves to their friends, instead of breathing out threatenings and vengeance
against their fellow men."[60]

Given Hawthorne's unsparing indictment of fictional prison reformer
(and devious monomaniac) Hollingsworth in *The Blithedale Romance* (1852),
it comes as no surprise to find him skeptical of the most utopian claims
of prison reformers. When Clifford first appears in *The House of the Seven
Gables,* he looks much more like the mentally incapacitated figures chronicled
by Dickens in Philadelphia's Eastern Penitentiary than the penitent subject
of a successful experiment in penal reform. Clifford totters through the
early chapters of the novel with a childlike frailty; the narrator likens him to
a "child" and a "wayward infant."[61] The recently discharged Clifford is also
prone to moments of mental abstraction: "Continually, as we may express it,
he faded away out of his place; or, in other words, his mind and consciousness took their departure, leaving his wasted, gray, and melancholy figure—a
substantial emptiness, a material ghost—to occupy his seat at table" (442).[62]
Without yet stating explicitly that Clifford has endured incarceration, the
narrator hints that "the soul of the man must have suffered some miserable
wrong from its earthly experience" (442). Clifford's moments of intellectual
lucidity, awakened by his cousin Phoebe's recital of poetry, are followed by
periods of fugue: "When the glow left him, he seemed conscious of a missing
sense and power, and groped about for them, as if a blind man should go
seeking his lost eyesight" (478). Incarceration for Clifford represents "a mysterious and terrible Past, which had annihilated his memory" (480).

Hawthorne may not have known (or cared) whether the Massachusetts
State Prison itself relied on an Auburn or a Pennsylvania disciplinary regime,
but he evidently drew on some of the most Dickensian descriptions of the
solitary system's mentally debilitating effects to flesh out his portrait of Clifford as a man whose intellect has been shattered by prolonged confinement.
No institution turning out a man in Clifford's state could pretend to a desig-
nation as a model prison.

Clifford faces the stigma associated with incarceration that reformers worried would prevent discharged convicts from successfully reentering society.
His and his sister Hepzibah's impulse to attend church is arrested by their
feeling of alienation from the rest of the community, "as if they were standing in the presence of the whole world, and with mankind's great and terrible eye on them alone" (497). Clifford foresees the likely reaction of other
churchgoers to his presence: "It is an ugly thought, that I should be frightful
to my fellow-beings, and that children would cling to their mothers' gowns,
at sight of me!" (498). Nor does Clifford underestimate the degree of latent
community hostility. As Lippard did in *The Empire City,* Hawthorne places

his discharged convict in proximity to a crime and allows readers to watch the community's reaction unfold. When a kinsman, Judge Jaffrey Pyncheon, turns up missing, suspicion immediately falls on the neighborhood's resident ex-convict and presumed murderer. Hawthorne's repository of community sentiment in the novel is Dixey, who (upon discovery of Judge Pyncheon's card on the doorstep of the Pyncheon house) whispers: "It would be no wonder if the Judge has gone into that door, and never come out again! A certain cousin of his may have been at his old tricks" (606). In *The Scarlet Letter,* Hawthorne examined the way a community projects its notions of sin onto a single transgressor; Puritan Boston reassured itself through the spectacle of Hester's "A" that its criminals were exposed and punished. In *The House of the Seven Gables,* Hawthorne continues this exploration by portraying the community suspicion that would make the formerly incarcerated a perpetually available scapegoat for any unsolved crime.

Even more shrewdly, perhaps, Hawthorne implicates the reader in such prejudices. Hawthorne's carefully ambiguous staging of Hepzibah's discovery of Jaffrey Pyncheon's corpse initially points the reader's suspicion toward Clifford. Hepzibah is "seized with a sudden intuition of some horrible thing" (566), while Clifford, with unaccustomed energy, exults over the dead body, even mocking it: "Let us leave the old house to our Cousin Jaffrey! He will take good care of it!" (567). At this point, Clifford and Hepzibah flee the scene by rail.

Though the astute reader probably intuits that Phoebe's charitable judgment of Clifford's character is accurate, Hawthorne allows the possibility of Clifford's guilt to linger in readers' minds for several chapters. Readers are invited to draw conclusions, like Dixey, on the basis of Clifford's previous incarceration. While Clifford is on the train, he fuels such suspicions by objecting to the telegraph's agency in the detection of criminals: "A bank-robber—and what you call a murderer, likewise—has his right, which men of enlightened humanity and conscience should regard in so much the more liberal spirit, because the bulk of society is prone to controvert their existence" (579). More outrageously, Clifford defends the claims of murderers, "who are often excusable in the motives of their deed, and deserve to be ranked among the public benefactors, if we consider only its result" (579). What makes this dialogue so crafty, of course, is the naïve reader's uncertainty as to whether it is spoken by a helpless victim of circumstance or the fleeing murderer of Jaffrey Pyncheon.[63] Holgrave, the Pyncheons' boarder, eventually dispels the mystery by telling Phoebe that "Judge Pyncheon could not have come unfairly to his end" (613), musing correctly that the flight of Clifford and Hepzibah throws "the worst coloring over this event, of which it is susceptible" (613). Only the daguerreotype Holgrave has taken, it is implied, finally stands between

Clifford and a second miscarriage of justice returning him to prison. Were it not for the near-miraculous intervention of this new technology, Clifford would face the same revolving door that likely awaited former inmates Mary Norris and Patrick McKever, had they not been rescued by the benevolence of their own Holgrave, Quaker reformer Isaac Hopper. Hawthorne's portrait of the devastating aftereffects of incarceration—mental instability, alienation from the community, and subjection to the constant presumption of guilt and threat of re-incarceration—relies upon (and finds untapped literary potential within) similar contemporary accounts.

Like Lippard, Hawthorne nestled his portrait of a discharged convict's hardships within a broader indictment of the criminal justice system, here subject over the course of generations to string-pulling by Salem's aristocratic Pyncheons.[64] Obviously, Colonel Pyncheon's role in the seventeenth-century execution of Matthew Maule for witchcraft represents the first offense against justice in the novel. Skipping ahead to the nineteenth century, the mechanism by which Clifford avoids execution (after his wrongful conviction for the death of his uncle) belies the notion of the law's impartiality: "The high respectability and political influence of the criminal's connections, had availed to mitigate his doom from death to perpetual imprisonment" (370). The theme of powerful interests manipulating the justice system reemerges in the novel's present with the information that Clifford's release from prison has been engineered by Jaffrey Pyncheon, corruptly invoking his authority as a judge and former member of Congress. As he asks Hepzibah, "Has it never occurred to you . . . that, without not merely my consent, but my efforts, my representations, the exertion of my whole influence, political, official, personal—Clifford would never have been what you call free?" (552). Destined (before his unexpected death) to be the beneficiary of a closed-door cabal designed to elevate him to the Massachusetts governorship, Judge Pyncheon cynically takes advantage of his connections to have Clifford pardoned, with the ulterior motive of learning the secrets of "the schedule, the documents, the evidences . . . of the vast amount of Uncle Jaffrey's missing property" (554).

Abuse of the pardoning power was a frequent target of radical writers of Lippard's ilk, who believed it allowed the socially prominent to evade incarceration (or shorten their sentences) through an avenue not available to members of the working class.[65] Personifying corruption in the criminal justice system, Jaffrey tells Hepzibah that as a judge he has the power to commit Clifford to an insane asylum if his designs are thwarted (555). Hawthorne's narrator sounds like Lippard or a like-minded member of socially radical circles in chapter 15 of the novel, "The Scowl and Smile," when Judge Pyncheon's outwardly unimpeachable character (for example, as "president of a

Bible society" and "treasurer of a Widow's and Orphan's fund" [550]) is contrasted with the hypocrisy, greed, ambition, and cruelty that readers know to constitute his true character.

Focusing on Hawthorne's adaptation of narratives about incarceration and discharge offers an index for assessing the success of the novel's social critique. The conclusion that emerges supports a long-standing critical consensus that the novel finally veers away from its own most pointed implications.[66] Notwithstanding its moving portrait of Clifford's post-carceral debilitation, for example, the novel finds a way to downplay the injustice of thirty years' wrongful imprisonment. Like Lippard's John Hoffman / Number Ninety-One, Clifford enters prison an innocent man, yet the effect of incarceration on the two men is radically different. On an existential scale, Hawthorne suggests, Clifford's moral preservation is achieved by his incarceration. One of the most curious passages in the novel is the narrator's contention that for Clifford, prison was a fortunate fall:

> It is even possible—for similar cases have often happened—that if Clifford, in his foregoing life, had enjoyed the means of cultivating his taste to its utmost perfectibility, that subtle attribute might, before this period, have completely eaten out or filed away his affections. Shall we venture to pronounce, therefore, that his long and black calamity may not have had a redeeming drop of mercy, at the bottom? (448)

In this regard, Hawthorne's novel betrays a surprising, and perhaps disturbing, affinity with the preferred cultural narrative in which incarceration inspires moral rehabilitation. The deprivations associated with imprisonment have, it would seem, allowed Clifford to preserve a certain indispensable moral faculty that he would have lost had he pursued the sybaritic lifestyle for which he was, by virtue of temperament, wealth, and social position, otherwise destined. No harm, no foul.

Hawthorne's tantalizing allusion to Clifford's "black calamity" raises the issue of race in *The House of the Seven Gables,* a subject that has generated some of the most provocative recent criticism of the novel. Inspired by Toni Morrison's observation of an "Africanist presence" that "informs in compelling and inescapable ways the texture of American literature,"[67] commentators have found that nearly every major character in the novel (not to mention assorted minor ones) is associated with racial blackness: through implication in the degradation of market exchange (Hepzibah); association with daguerreotypy, a new technology that promised to provide visual demarcations of racial difference (Holgrave); explicit comparison with the seventeenth-century Pyncheon slave Scipio (Matthew Maule); excessive consumption of racially insensitive baked goods (Ned Higgins); or imagery of a dark complexion and alliance with pro-slavery southern politicians (Jaffrey).[68] All of these readings attempt to understand *The House of the Seven Gables* as embodying (or challenging) nineteenth-century American attempts to define racial boundaries.

Evidence exists in the novel to assign a similar racial coding to Clifford, given the nature of his particular "black calamity." For example, Hepzibah thinks of her brother, "Oh, what a black shadow! Poor, poor Clifford!" (440), while Holgrave, invoking the legal notion of civil death that analogized the condition of convicts to slaves, describes Clifford as "another dead and long-buried person, on whom the Governor and Council have wrought a necromantic miracle" (538). If Clifford's status as a discharged convict is understood to "blacken" him along with so many of the novel's other presumptively white characters, then *The House of the Seven Gables* registers anxieties expressed elsewhere in the culture about the implication for one's white racial identity of imprisonment in a modern penitentiary.

But is Clifford, as in the crime novels of Hawthorne's contemporaries, permanently branded by a racially coded stigma of incarceration? When the idea is raised of the family pursuing some sort of official vindication of Clifford now that the truth about his uncle's murder has been revealed, the narrator endorses the decision not to put him through such a strain, stating unequivocally, "After such wrong as he had suffered, there is no reparation" (621). Yet although recovery of "the full measure of his faculties" is impossible, living among his newfound family, he is "evidently happy" (622). Positioned along a spectrum whose poles are defined by Child's narrative "The Irish Heart," where the discharged convict successfully "passes" into society free of the stigma of incarceration, and the novels of Buntline, Thompson, and Lippard, where incarceration imparts a permanent and racially inflected branding, *The House of the Seven Gables* stands, where one so often finds Hawthorne, occupying a middle ground. While Clifford has been grievously and to some extent permanently impaired by his long incarceration, the possibility of a somewhat normal post-carceral existence—and, by implication, a qualified reversal of his civil death—is not beyond imagining, enabled by his impending move to the Pyncheon country estate. *The House of the Seven Gables* reflects, finally, a guarded optimism regarding the post-carceral prospects of the discharged inmate. Whereas, in *The Scarlet Letter,* he forced readers to confront the physical marks left by moral turpitude on the bodies of Dimmesdale and Chillingworth, Hawthorne depicts the signs of Clifford's incarceration as, if not completely erasable, at least susceptible to gradual and partial effacement over time.

Like *The Empire City,* *The House of the Seven Gables* ends with the disbursement of a family fortune. The denouement unravels the mystery of the Pyncheon family's long-cherished but hitherto undocumented claims to a vast tract of Indian lands. Though the specific land the recovered "ancient deed" (624) represents is no longer reclaimable, its analog in the novel is the Pyncheon wealth that devolves from the grasping Judge Pyncheon to Clifford, Hepzibah, Holgrave, Phoebe, and Uncle Venner. Accumulated over centuries, this fortune suddenly lands in the hands of the deserving characters of the novel, including representatives of both the aristocratic Pyncheon and working-class Maule families. In contrast with the tragic fate Lippard assigns to Number Ninety-One, Hawthorne envisions a future that permits even the former prison inmate Clifford Pyncheon to partake of the nation's munificence. Clifford's not unhappy outcome is abetted by a move to the country, where his criminal past will no longer color community opinion. He seems poised, thanks to the Pyncheon family fortune, to outrun the stigma from which the working-class Number Ninety-One finds no means of escape. That the wealth by which Clifford obtains at least provisional release from a racially coded stigma of incarceration has its provenance in slave labor (from the slave Scipio through Jaffrey Pyncheon's advantageous alliance with pro-slavery political bedfellows) constitutes an irony of American history from which the novel cannot extricate itself.[69]

The stories of discharged convicts that surfaced as a particular focus of the prison reform movement in the 1840s and early 1850s provided Hawthorne and Lippard with a set of characters, images, and circumstances adaptable to various ends. Hawthorne recognized in the story of the formerly incarcerated an opening onto other narratives, such as an insular community's tendency to scapegoat its most vulnerable members and the criminal justice system's availability for manipulation by the wealthy and powerful. While both novelists employed the discharged convict as a symbol of oppression at the hands of a corrupt criminal justice system, they pursued this theme with different levels of emphasis and commitment. Hawthorne offers a portrait of an inmate who regains some degree of happiness, prosperity, and community standing after thirty years in prison. And although Hawthorne recognizes that no reparation the state can make would be commensurate with the degree of Clifford's suffering, any indictment of the criminal justice system *The House of the Seven Gables* aspires to make is ultimately mitigated by an ending in which wrongs are to some degree righted and even a thirty-year wrongful imprisonment can be interpreted as having a "drop of mercy" at the bottom. In *The Empire City*, Lippard foregrounds more insistently than Hawthorne the hardships that attended incarceration and discharge and looks more skeptically at the notion that the discharged convict over time would be welcomed as an heir to American prosperity on anything resembling equal footing with fellow citizens.

Well-meaning prison reformers did not fully recognize how optimistic stories of the discharged convict quietly rejoining society consigned former inmates to an anonymity that at once prevented their speaking out on the secret cruelties of incarceration and relieved the public of the responsibility to consider the methods, purposes, or effects of incarceration on a generation of its experimental subjects. In contrast, Lippard gives Number Ninety-One a platform from which to denounce torture in the country's most prominent penitentiaries, unsettling complacency about the presumed successes of a much-lauded carceral regime. Attempting to ennoble a member of a group whom his working-class readers had learned to view with distrust and hostility, Lippard finds room even within the confining generic requirements of sensational fiction to sketch a comparatively nuanced portrait of a discharged convict, one who remains noble at heart yet also possesses impulses toward crime and violence born of his carceral experience. *The Empire City* offers Number Ninety-One no escape from the legacy of incarceration.

As other commentators have noted, the experiences of prison inmates and slaves were bound together in nineteenth-century conceptions of racial identity. The crime novelists who consistently portrayed the discharged convict as "branded with infamy" understood that the civil death of the penitentiary inmate implicitly likened him to the figure of the slave. Resisting a prison reform narrative in which an inmate passes from a state of legal non-personhood back into citizenship, these novelists evidently policed a boundary between free (white) and coerced (black) labor that the institution of contractual penal servitude increasingly threatened to dissolve. Another opportunity for examining the intersection of incarceration and racial identity in the antebellum period is found within the memoirs of prison chaplains, texts that challenge recent claims that prison reform ideology categorically denied the capacity for rehabilitation to African American inmates. It is to these and other first-person nonfictional accounts of life in antebellum prisons that I turn in chapter 6.

6

Voices from Prison
Antebellum Memoirs of Incarceration

In the 1840s and 1850s, American readers turned their attention to a new generation of texts promising to bring readers inside the walls of the penitentiary. Continuing interest in prison reform united with the period's expanding publishing industry to give rise to new generic forms, including book-length memoirs by prison chaplains, exposés of prison conditions by abolitionists imprisoned in the South, and volumes of confessional poetry attesting to the salvific potential of incarceration. As different as these texts can be, they share significant unifying features. They promise readers nonfictional eyewitness testimony regarding the material conditions of prison life and the psychological experiences of inmates, and they tend to avoid the sensationalism that characterizes other varieties of prison exposé.

Literary historians have yet to devote significant attention to these books or to delineate with precision their generic properties. Karen Halttunen, for example, discusses exposés of asylum life that partake of a set of gothic literary conventions she helpfully identifies as "the cult of mystery."[1] These texts purport to bring readers behind the scenes of a normally invisible demimonde and to publicize the lurid secrets of the asylum. Many pamphlet-length novels exposing prison conditions discussed by Halttunen fit this model, but the nonfictional memoir of prison chaplain John Luckey, for example, has very little of the dark, sensationalistic tone that would make it comparable with the fiction in whose company she places it; nor does the poetry of incarceration, which falls outside of Halttunen's sphere of interest, dwell on underground architecture, secret passageways, or unspeakable tortures. H. Bruce Franklin discusses the revelations of prison life published by political prisoners including anti-renters and abolitionists in the nineteenth century, but the centuries-spanning scope of his book on the literature of the American prison prevents him from discussing these accounts in any detail; similarly, he devotes no more than a paragraph or two to antebellum poetry of incarceration.[2] Histories and analyses of crime literature in antebellum America also overlook these memoirs, which fall outside the better-known generic categories of crime fiction, trial pamphlets, or newspaper crime reports.

These antebellum voices from prison invite critical attention on multiple grounds. They provide new sources of evidence for assessing the racial attitudes underlying the prison reform movement, a subject that has preoccupied recent scholars working at the intersection of literature and criminal justice. Considered as nonfictional literature, these memoirs represent an unnoticed field of contextualization for various canonical works of the antebellum period. And, as Michele Lise Tarter and Richard Bell note in the introduction to their volume *Buried Lives: Incarcerated in Early America,* whereas scholarship on incarceration has tended to focus on disciplinary mechanisms from the perspective of their creators or theoreticians, downplaying the testimony of inmates themselves, some of these texts, in contrast, carry an intrinsic interest bound up with the promise of giving voice to penitentiary inmates, countering the anonymity to which even some prison reformers would have consigned them in the name of easing their reintroduction to society, as discussed in chapter 5.[3]

These memoirs cannot be regarded, however, as providing an unmediated truth about the antebellum penal experience. Understanding these memoirs requires careful case-by-case parsing of the complex rhetorical circumstances driving their publication. Interest in penal reform conferred new cultural authority on the individual who had witnessed or experienced incarceration: these memoirs, then, represent self-conscious attempts to appropriate that authority in support of varying agendas. In particular, the anthology *Voices from Prison* (1847 and 1849), a collection of poetry written by inmates at the behest of prison reformers, raises provocative questions about agency and authenticity in collaborations involving outsider authors and their patrons, while presenting the tantalizing case of an author whose poetry of incarceration apparently helped to effectuate his release from confinement—pending his second conviction and another prison sentence. Seizing the opportunity that prison reform discourse provided to demonstrate his penitence before state authorities, prisoner-poet (and counterfeiter) Christian Meadows appears to have managed one of the shrewdest rhetorical gambits in the antebellum literature and criminal justice archive.

Memoirs by Prison Chaplains: Appropriating Prisoners' Voices

At least three full-length memoirs by prison chaplains were published between 1850 and 1860, adding to the already voluminous literature of incarceration available to antebellum readers. All three chaplains served in Auburn-style penitentiaries during the height of the prison reform movement, to which their memoirs were self-conscious contributions. These memoirs can also be understood within the context of evangelical publishing, a significant sector of the nineteenth-century publishing industry whose contours have been defined by the historian of religion Candy Gunther Brown. Chaplains' memoirs resemble missionary memoirs, a "prominent biographical form" within evangelical publishing circles that combined models of piety with the appeal of describing exotic foreign locales.[4] A similar dynamic is at work in stories of pious chaplains carrying their religious mission into the confines of the prison. The chaplains' very entrance into the print marketplace says something about the culture's investment in dwelling upon the details of incarceration, as related by someone with intimate and otherwise unavailable knowledge of inmates' lives. The chaplains recognized and attempted to take advantage of the authority conferred by their proximity to incarceration to reclaim the literature of criminality from sensationalism and return it to the service of piety and clerical authority. Their memoirs also offer compelling evidence with respect to recent scholarly claims about the application of prison reform ideology to African American inmates.

The first full-length memoir by a prison chaplain published in the United States was apparently James B. Finley's *Memorials of Prison Life,* originally published in Cincinnati in 1850. Finley was the chaplain of the state prison in Columbus, Ohio, where he began working in 1846. Eleazer Smith's *Nine Years Among the Convicts; Or, Prison Reminiscences* was published in Boston in 1856. Smith had been the chaplain of the New Hampshire State Prison from 1846 to 1855. John Luckey published *Life in Sing Sing State Prison, As Seen in a Twelve Years' Chaplaincy* in 1860, recounting his employment at the famous prison from 1839 to 1851.[5] Title pages of the three books reveal publishers eager to capitalize on interest in the antebellum penitentiary. For example, the title page of Finley's book puts the words "Prison Life" in the largest type; Smith's title page devotes the largest typeface to the phrase "Among the Convicts," and Luckey's gives the phrase "Life in Sing Sing" the greatest prominence. Words like "chaplain," "chaplaincy," and "Rev." are placed in significantly smaller type on all three title pages. In other words, the title pages appear to promise an exposé-like attention to the hidden realities of prison life in the sensational mode Halttunen documents, rather than a sober account of the chaplains' efforts as missionaries to the incarcerated (which is what the books chiefly are), an angle of interest with appeal to a more limited audience of religiously like-minded readers. Whatever the assumptions on which readers grounded their purchase of these books, publishers accurately gauged public interest in the subject of an insider's view of incarceration, given the fact that both Finley's and Luckey's memoirs went through multiple editions.

The chaplains recognized widespread interest in penal reform as a useful vehicle for promoting secondary agendas. Whereas Finley claims in his preface that "every word can be relied on as fact," even the most cursory reading of his book makes it quite obvious that he freely refashioned prisoners' life stories to suit his ideological aims. Finley's bête noire throughout *Memorials of Prison Life,* for example, is the burgeoning denomination of Universalism. Finley regarded Universalism, which held that the Elect included all of humanity, as "the worst form of infidelity." Supporting Finley's theology, various prisoners (purportedly) confide to him that their belief in universal human salvation offered no disincentive to a life of crime. As one inmate puts it: " 'If all my sins cannot damn me, I will run the risk of the present life, surely,' said I, instantly, 'and as I may as well make a wholesale operation of my business I need not stick at trifles.' " The prisoner notes that the unsoundness of this reasoning from a theological perspective is clear to him now, though he overlooked it at the time. Writing during the rise of the Know Nothing movement (which was particularly strong in Cincinnati, where his memoir was published), Finley lodges similar theological grievances with Catholicism. After Finley asks a young Catholic what he thinks of the Protestant Bible he has been given, the man tells him, "Mother Church is wrong in many things, which I never could comprehend before," and, moreover, "if I had been taught to read and reference this book . . . I think I never should have been in such a place as this."[6] In chapter after chapter, Finley recounts interviews with penitent convicts, who become his proxies in attacking Catholicism, Universalism, drinking, Sabbath-breaking, and other threatening social ills.

Eleazer Smith's memoir often assumes an equally preachy tone. He warns readers against intemperance, neglect of early religious instruction, and other vices, ending chapters with pious exhortations: "Now let the youthful reader review the whole story, and judge whether even in this life, 'the way of the transgressor is *not* hard.' " Referencing the sensationalist tone of antebellum crime literature, Smith acknowledges that he courts criticism by publicizing the details of criminals' lives, insofar as familiarity with crime tends to lessen detestation of it. He argues, however, that the "cases of evident reform should be known, that good men may be encouraged to labor on in hope, and to pray with increased faith and fervor for the salvation of the guilty." In his preface Smith contrasts his own work with invented titles such as "The Thieves' Directory" or "The Best Methods of Committing Burglary," works he says he could have written, had his aim been to thrill readers with accounts of revolting crimes.[7] Smith's self-consciousness about the place of his memoir within antebellum print culture deserves emphasis. Because the ideology of prison reform gave prisoners a voice in the culture predicated on their status as exemplars of moral reform, the chaplain-authors recognized that their vocation provided them with an unusual opportunity to reclaim criminal biography from its lurid associations. Appropriating the voices of prisoners, the prison chaplains hoped to counter the racy sensationalism of daily arrest reports, city-mysteries novels, and pamphlet accounts of famous murder trials (among other forms), and return criminal biography to its roots in the execution sermons of early-eighteenth-century New England, a time when ministers, rather than journalists, novelists, or enterprising publishers, were the "chief mediators between criminals and readers" and the literature of crime presumably combated social deviance.[8] The relative popularity of these memoirs suggests that the prison chaplains may not have been entirely unsuccessful.[9]

Also at issue in the use of criminal life stories is the way the chaplain-authors altered prisoners' language to make it acceptable to a middle-class reading public. Given the humble social backgrounds and limited education presumably common among inmates, the dialogue attributed to them in these memoirs often rings quite false. In one bizarre chapter, Finley offers a fictionalized biography of a likable rogue, Alexander Jay Hamilton, a merchant-turned-criminal who waxes philosophic in language far too literary not to be fabricated: "Hope is the cordial of life; it comes to us in infancy, and attends us through the journey of life, frequently cheating us with anticipations we never realize." Hamilton continues on for pages in this strain, with fulsome praise of (none other than) his prison chaplain.[10]

Because Finley's ventriloquism is so clumsily performed, his memoir helpfully frames the issue of the mediation of prisoners' voices. All three chaplains readily convert what must generally have been the rough-hewn speech of working-class convicts into the high-flown language of sentiment, as in Luckey's rendering of the departing speech of an uneducated orphan whose formative years were, in Luckey's account, spent begging and stealing on the New York City docks: "In leaving your house my feelings are indescribable. It appears to me like parting from the only place on earth that I am permitted to regard as home, and bidding a final adieu to the only friends I have living."[11] Dialogue such as this reveals what Caleb Smith regards as the "peculiar new relationship between the prison interior and the mass public," in which a text's claim to authenticity predicated on exposing the truth of life behind bars is not at all compromised by the suppression of the rough details of actual prisoners' lives.[12] Unlike sensational authors for whom reproduction of "flash" speech was a particular selling point,[13] the chaplains routinely translated the language of convicts into an idiom more palatable for a middle-class (and, one suspects, evangelical) audience, as when Finley notes that, in transcribing an inmate's written life story, he made "only some corrections of a grammatical and rhetorical character."[14] Reproducing the known speech pattern of a given ethnic group provided Smith with one way out of this quandary of authenticity. Writing of an Irish Catholic whom he converted to Protestantism, Smith aimed for verisimilitude by reproducing the man's Irish accent. Tommy Carr complains to the chaplain that his prayers bring him "no pace," and asks "your riverence" what he should do. Smith prescribes attendance at Protestant prayer meetings, after which Carr exclaims: "O, glory be to Jesus! . . . I am blist! O, I *am* blist entirely!"[15]

What did prisoners really sound (or write) like? In *Life in Sing Sing Prison,* Luckey offers a rare glimpse of unedited prisoner discourse. He tells the story of an inmate who escaped by constructing a watertight coat that allowed him to walk under water, with the aid of breathing tubes ingeniously affixed to hollow "ducks" that floated above him in sight of the guards. (After making it across the river, he was eventually recaptured in New York City.) Luckey reproduces a "faithful copy, word for word, letter for letter, spelling for spelling" of the man's crudely written confession (the "tufs" are tubes; other misspellings are more or less phonetic):

> August 8, 1853. On the 8 I went to the age of the river and put my tufs in order and then waded out afout fifty yards and then med the fest of miy way for the villag when I got half way one of the tufs fusted I let go of the wates and come up to the curfes and then sunk all the aprates exet one tufe I cept by me in kase of the kramp for I had about holfe a mil to swem whe I got to the Dock I met with a man that give me a sute of close and 2 Dollars I went down to New York that nit the next day I went to se my frother he sent me in contery for a few wiks tell I cold live the contry when the time was expired I came to New York turd day I had feen in the city the Warden had information of me.

Luckey's facetious rationale for including the letter is that "variety of style" is a desirable quality and the reader "may be interested in a sample of our hero's writing and composing abilities," but he may also have intuited a conflict between the aim of telling the authentic story of prison life and bowdlerizing prisoners' language to make it acceptable for consumption by a polite readership.[16] In any case, this revealing fragment of a prisoner's actual written words establishes the baseline in a spectrum of mediation at work in these memoirs, from unedited reproduction of convicts' letters to the highly varnished, obviously invented dialogues routinely placed in inmates' mouths.

The chaplains published their memoirs as the Auburn system rose to dominate American penal practice. Rebecca M. McLennan has documented widespread adoption of the system she refers to as "contractual penal servitude," whereby prison administrators hired out convict labor to private contractors to defer the costs of incarceration.[17] Two of the chaplains criticized the excesses of forced prison labor. Finley lobbied for Bible classes and special prayer meetings to encourage reformation, claiming that a revival could sweep through the penitentiary, "were there as great an interest in the reformation of these men as in making money out of their hard labor."[18] With equal directness, Luckey complained that contract labor arrangements put financial considerations ahead of reformatory ones: "The whole contract system, as now managed, is full of evils. It allows no means of punishment but brute force, or that which occupies the shortest period possible, so as not to conflict with the contractor's pecuniary interest," a state of affairs that he forcefully denominated "miniature slavery."[19]

Without calling into question the humanitarian impulses driving these complaints, one might also observe that prison inmates offered all three chaplain-authors a set of life stories awaiting conscription for various rhetorical purposes, putting them in a position strangely analogous to that of the Auburn-system contractors whom Finley and Luckey deplored. While I am not claiming that the chaplain-authors' offense carries the same ethical import as the contractors' use of forced labor to make a return on investment regardless of inmates' health or well-being, their eagerness to seize on and manipulate the unwitting prisoners' words and life experiences nonetheless represents a subtle form of exploitation.[20] Attempting to accrue to themselves the credibility garnered from having experienced incarceration up close (if not quite firsthand), the chaplains, at times quite crudely, drafted prisoners' voices in the service of their own agendas. The chaplains' recognition that a voice from prison was intrinsically more compelling than a philosophical tract was an insight not lost on the abolitionist movement.

Chaplains' memoirs provide new evidence for evaluating the relationship between prison reform ideology and race. One assessment looks to Thomas Jefferson's comments on race in *Notes on the State of Virginia* (1787) and posits that African Americans were categorically excluded from the possibility of reform via incarceration: "According to Jefferson's categories, blacks were not endowed with the essential capacity necessary for penitentiary discipline, the power of *reflection*. . . . In the poetics of the penitentiary, 'individuals of the African variety' could be weakened and killed by solitude, but never redeemed."[21] This claim, however, is belied by the accounts of chaplains, who frequently recorded the conversions of African American inmates. One minister wrote in 1845 of a conversion that happened in the Philadelphia County Prison: "J. S., a coloured man, died *triumphant*. He had been afflicted about two months. I visited him daily, and had many happy scenes with him after his conversion, which was about six weeks before he died."[22] Prison chaplain Smith devoted an entire chapter of *Nine Years Among the Convicts* to a reformed black convict, Parker Paul. The turning point in Paul's conversion arrives after a period spent (not insignificantly) in solitary confinement, where he is compelled to reflect on the meaning of his crime: "There was a quietness and contentment so unlike his former self as to fix a strong conviction in the minds of all, that he was at heart *another* and a *better* man." Paul remains in a state of grace for the rest of his life, dying in prison, "in perfect consciousness and composure," and "commend[ing] his soul to the keeping of its great Redeemer."[23]

While it is indisputable that differential forms of criminal justice were meted out to blacks and whites in antebellum America, a generalization denying that prison reform ideology was applied to African American convicts because they were believed to lack the capacity for reflection invites skepticism. Jefferson's theories on race in *Notes on the State of Virginia* are notoriously fraught with logical inconsistencies, which were by no means invisible to antebellum readers (as David Walker's withering response in his 1829 *Appeal* makes clear). A generation or two after Jefferson published his sentiments, they may not have had the explanatory power attributed to them, especially among reform-minded northerners who found slavery abhorrent.

A more recent assessment refines and qualifies the earlier claim, arguing that prison reformers conceded salvific potential only to condemned black prisoners, basing other black inmates' "ineligibility for the transformative civic mortification and reanimation wrought by the penitentiary" on "their presumptive status as a deviant population of noncitizens."[24] While all of the reformed convicts just mentioned did indeed die in prison, accounts of converted African American inmates who were not condemned to death are also available. In 2001 Philip Gura published the memorandum books written by the Reverend Jared Curtis from 1829 to 1831, early in his decades-long ministry to the population of the Massachusetts State Prison. Curtis kept notes on interviews he conducted with prisoners, including brief accounts of each man's hometown, race, and criminal history, with additional assessments of the inmate's personality, intelligence, and prospects for reform. While Curtis was by no means free of racialist attitudes (he believed that "most negroes" were "unsteady and fond of frolics" and wrote of one black prisoner, "Think much better of him than of most of his fellows"), he often made positive evaluations of the potential for reform among black inmates under his care. He wrote of William Stevens, a twenty-year-old black inmate serving a five-year sentence for theft: "Possesses a good deal of sensibility. Is mild

& pleasant & very frank. Wept very freely. Appears much better than most prisoners." Curtis also held out spiritual hope for eighteen-year-old black inmate James Johnson, serving twenty months for larceny: "I have found but very few persons if any, who appear to profess as much sensibility & tenderness as Johnson. He weeps like a child, & thinks he shall never again be led astray."[25] Curtis clearly believed that redemption (followed by reintegration into society) was attainable for some of the African American inmates at the Massachusetts State Prison.

Luckey titled one chapter of *Life in Sing Sing State Prison* "Poor Jack— The Converted Negro" and told how he and the keeper selected "Negro Jack" from among *all* the inmates in Sing Sing to present to Governor Seward as an exemplary case of reform through penitentiary discipline and an eligible candidate for pardon. Jack testifies to his salvific experience within prison: "When I came here I could not read; I knew nothing about the great goodness and love of the adorable Saviour; but now I can read his blessed book, and rest my sin-polluted soul upon its many precious promises, which, I find to be 'yea and amen in Christ Jesus.' " After his pardon, readers are informed, Jack remained law-abiding and pious, becoming a preacher in an African American church. Later in the book, Luckey cites the experience of "J.P.," a "colored lad," who writes to the chaplain three years after discharge from Sing Sing, thanking him for his kindness and informing him that he is a church member in good standing.[26]

In their zeal to prove the reformatory potential of incarceration, to bear witness to the saving power of Christianity for an evangelical audience, or possibly to burnish their own credentials as spiritual authorities, chaplains reached for conversion stories among black inmates as eagerly as among other portions of the prison population. Granting the possibility that these stories are meant to insinuate that spiritual mentoring within the penitentiary could overcome even African Americans' presumed innate tendencies toward criminality, prison chaplains' openness to the possibility of reform among black inmates still belies recent claims about the movement's differential racial application. A wide variety of actors (wardens, inspectors, chaplains, propagandists), no doubt positioned along the full spectrum of racialist thinking that characterized antebellum America, fit under the umbrella of prison reform. Theories about the racial poetics of incarceration may take insufficient account of the potential for variation of thought among individual actors, or perhaps they underestimate the rhetorical value reformers found in appropriating African American voices, along with other inmates' testimony, to vouch for the value of their carceral mission.

Abolitionists in the Penitentiary:
Hybridizing the Prison Exposé

The chaplain-authors and their publishers capitalized on readers' interest in the hidden experience of prison life; the voices of prisoners simultaneously offered cultural cachet and a medium available for appropriation. Abolitionists, too, opportunistically (if less exploitatively) availed themselves of widespread interest in prison reform to serve their cause. Several books of the period simultaneously promote abolitionist and prison reform agendas. By the late 1840s, prison reform discourse had become so influential that abolitionists and their publishers came to recognize the potential value of textually linking the two movements; the resulting books were generic hybrids blending features of the prison exposé and the slave narrative or abolitionist tract.

J. C. Lovejoy's *Memoir of Rev. Charles T. Torrey, Who Died in the Penitentiary of Maryland* (1847) is one of the earliest books to combine an abolitionist message with a prison exposé. Originally from Massachusetts, Torrey (born in 1813) was a controversial abolitionist who moved to the Chesapeake Bay region to put his principles into action. Arrested and convicted of conveying several slaves across the Maryland border into Pennsylvania in 1844, Torrey was sentenced to six years in the state penitentiary in Baltimore.[27] He became a cause célèbre within abolitionist circles (although this status was somewhat compromised by his widely criticized and unsuccessful escape attempt), and after his death Lovejoy compiled Torrey's prison writings into a single volume along with newspaper accounts of Torrey's trial, testimonials of friends, correspondence between Torrey and his abolitionist colleagues, and related ephemera.

Even before transportation to the state penitentiary from the jail where he was held for trial, Torrey railed against the prison reform movement, writing to a friend: "At all events, my physical comforts will not be diminished by the change to the Penitentiary. Ah—the '*reformed*' system of prison discipline, with its horrible secret *scourgings, shower* baths, and six days *starvings,* (which no man wholly escapes)—*these* ARE charming prospects ahead!"[28] Later, writing a public letter to the *Boston Morning Chronicle,* Torrey argued against the principle that silent contemplation of one's guilt bred remorse and penitence: "Did you ever think of the real nature of the *really improved* system of prison discipline? Of its forced silence for years? . . . How certainly a prisoner, by the violation of nearly every great law of his moral, mental and social nature, is *forced down* towards moral imbecility?" (208). Torrey informs readers that even before his conviction he intended to write an essay debunking the claims of prison reformers, hoping to show "that the 'Auburn' or 'Philadelphia' systems of prison discipline, in removing some of the more obvious evils of the old system, and adding some good things, had only *substituted,* for the most part, one evil for another" (208). All of these charges were lodged before Torrey made it to the penitentiary, but incarceration there did not change his opposition to prevailing penal theory. Writing from the penitentiary to his wife, he confirmed that it "is idle to talk of reforming hardened men, here" (221). Later Torrey wrote movingly of the mental torture that incarceration inflicted: "This week, I am not able to read; and my mind begins to act upon itself, as it did before; so that I long to stop *thinking"* (228). Torrey's voice from prison is virtually unique in the antebellum discourse of incarceration insofar as he uses the lived experience of imprisonment to attack the principles of prison reform; other inmates may have denied that conditions within specific penitentiaries were conducive to reform, but they tended not to challenge the underlying theory.[29]

Before and after Torrey, the abolitionist movement recognized the value of publicizing the histories of those who went to prison for acting in accordance with their beliefs.[30] Where the *Memoir of Charles T. Torrey, Who Died in the Penitentiary of Maryland* stands out is in its direct appeal to readers interested in prison reform as well as abolition. Lovejoy drew attention to this confluence of reform movements by including Torrey's sentiments on the Auburn and Pennsylvania systems, as well as through his carefully selected title, which directs readers not merely to consider the suffering Torrey endured for acting on abolitionist principles (emphasis on *"Died"*), but also to recognize the South's perversion of what was supposed to be a reformatory institution (emphasis on *"Penitentiary"*). In other words, in a society already focused on the discourse of prison reform and prepared to confer special authenticity on the testimony of prison inmates, the experience of incarceration in a penitentiary added a value to Torrey's avowal of abolitionism that in some subtle way went beyond simply evincing a willingness to suffer for his beliefs. Sensing the value of this formula, later abolitionists continued to forge closer textual links between the two movements.

George Thompson published *Prison Life and Reflections* in New York in 1848. Thompson, Alanson Work, and James E. Burr were three missionary students in Illinois who conceived a plan in 1841 to rescue slaves from across the Mississippi River in Palmyra, Missouri. After an initial expedition to canvass potential escapees, the three men were caught in Palmyra while putting their plan into execution (evidently, fearful slaves had alerted their masters to the scheme). Held in jail in Palmyra for two months, the three abolitionists were convicted of larceny (for stealing slaves) and issued sentences of twelve years in the state penitentiary in Jefferson City. They began to serve their penitentiary sentence on October 1, 1841; the last of the three to be pardoned, Thompson, was released on June 24, 1846.

Thompson's preface to *Prison Life and Reflections* begins plaintively, "Reader, do you know the heart of a *prisoner*? Are you a friend of *convicts*? If not, you may not be much interested in the following pages—for they tell you much about the inside of a prison, and its suffering inmates."[31] Through his title and opening questions, Thompson, much like the chaplains, stresses his ability to usher readers into a normally unseen world behind prison walls. That penitentiary interiors were anything but invisible, given the thousands of visitors per year who passed through the Eastern State Penitentiary in Philadelphia and the abundance of penitentiary-related material in the era's newspapers and magazines, did not seem to affect the potency of this claim. Thompson further promises to reveal to readers the inner life of the prisoner, a commodity that was highly valued and very much in contention within the arena of competing prison reform schemes, given charges that the separate system irretrievably affected the mental health of inmates. This phrase "the heart of a prisoner" becomes a recurring motif in *Prison Life and Reflections* and comes up again in the volume of poetry based on his carceral experiences which Thompson published the same year.

In accordance with the generic properties of the exposé, Thompson detailed scanty food rations, inadequate medical care, cruel treatment by guards, violations of laws governing inmate treatment, and torturous disciplinary measures in the Missouri Penitentiary, all of which belie the hopeful rhetoric of prison reform. But unlike Torrey, who aimed to discredit the idea of reform through incarceration, Thompson attributed appalling conditions within this particular penitentiary specifically to the influence of slavery. After detailing the extreme suffering of sick inmates forced to work until they fainted, and then denied adequate food and medical attention, he asks:

> Now, to what shall we trace the *cause* of this inhumanity, this driving, this indifference to another's woes? . . . Are the sick thus treated in prisons, where slavery does not exist? It is a well known fact that *slaves* are treated similarly, and worse—half-naked, half-starved, driven early and late, urged on by the lash, their aches and pains disregarded, and when they can *go no longer*, cursed, because they can't work. Yes, to the influence of slavery in hardening the heart . . . must be traced this barbarity. (197)

In Thompson's view, one of the unforeseen by-products of slavery was that it fatally undermined a state's ability to implement the principles of prison reform. The persuasive power of this appeal should not be underestimated, given that prison reform was widely believed to be among the most successful and humane social innovations of the age.

A number of modern commentators have arrived at the analogy Thompson delineated between forced labor in antebellum prisons and on slave plantations.[32] What has perhaps not been noticed, however, is the resulting hybridity of the carceral/slave narrative. Thompson's book borrows a number of tropes from the slave narrative, in particular the influential *Narrative of the Life of Frederick Douglass* (1845), which had been published the year before Thompson's release from prison and which, given the intensity of his commitment to the abolitionist cause, it seems quite possible he would have known. Much in the manner of slave narrators wary of being accused of exaggeration, Thompson defends the strict facticity of the memoir: "You will not charge me with telling something about somebody of whom I know nothing—or with attempting to describe imaginary scenes . . . for 'I speak that I do know, and testify that I have seen,' heard, and experienced" (iii). Like Douglass, Thompson identifies oppressive prison authorities by name, wishing to expose those who "played the part of brutes, or demons" (iv). On Thompson's very first night in his cell, he overhears the screams of inmates being tortured in the guardroom, an initiation into the cruelty of the institution reminiscent of the beating of Aunt Hester that appears in the first chapter of Douglass's *Narrative:* "We laid us down to sleep, but were suffered to indulge ourselves but little in such enjoyment, being awakened and disturbed by the shrieks, and groans, and pleadings of our fellow-prisoners, in the guard room, adjoining our cell. Capt. William Burch, the drunken warden, had come in from his revels, towards midnight . . . and was giving vent to his cruelty by putting them to the torture" (19).

Echoing one of Douglass's major themes, Thompson deplores the hypocrisy of prison guards whose cruelty increases after their religious conversions: "Before Capt. G. [a prison overseer, formerly the warden] was *converted,* he manifested respect for us, but it was after his pretensions to religion, that he treated us with contempt, and seemed to delight in vexing and crossing us, all he could" (340). The breaking up of a Sabbath school, an emblem of the denial of Christianity in a culture that professes to uphold it in Douglass's *Narrative,* causes Thompson and his colleagues particular pain: "We met four or five times in the capacity of a class, and were then forbidden to meet any more, to the great grief of many!" (274).

Both Douglass and Thompson analyze the way that any system conferring absolute power on guards or overseers inherently breeds brutality, a dynamic that Thompson discusses in a section of the book headed "Heart-Hardening Influence of Power" (210). Like many slave narrators, including Douglass, Thompson alludes to the sexual victimization of women; he tells of a "colored woman" who was "placed in the wash-house, to work with two wicked men—if in her cell by day, it was unlocked, so that any prisoner could visit her, or any guard by night!" (288). And just as slaves developed veiled ways of communicating to evade the vigilance of their masters (for example, through the coded messages in slave songs, though this is not detailed in Douglass's *Narrative*), Thompson and his abolitionist colleagues on the outside discover a way to communicate freely despite the strictures of the Auburn regime. When confronted with a subject they are forbidden to write about (such as slavery), the three abolitionists begin to refer to "passages of Scripture expressive of our feelings," knowing the officers who normally censor their letters will not bother to check the references: "In this way we could express ourselves understandingly on almost any subject" (154). Although likenesses between the prison exposé and the slave narrative undoubtedly derive to some extent from the similarity of the systems of forced labor they analyze, Thompson's text betrays a debt to the formulas of the slave narrative that suggests conscious imitation.

Further evidence for the slave narrative–prison exposé relationship emerges from Lewis Paine's *Six Years in a Georgia Prison* (1852). Originally from Rhode Island, Paine went to Georgia in his early twenties to work as a foreman in a factory and later as a schoolteacher. He was captured helping a slave to escape and spent five years and five months, from 1845 to 1851, in the state penitentiary at Milledgeville. Chapters 1 through 10 of Paine's memoir cover his personal history, detailing various abuses within the penitentiary system (inadequate clothing, cruel overseers, corporal punishment). Chapters 11 through 16, however, written, according to Paine, at the solicitation of others, have nothing to do with prison: instead, they expose the various evils of slavery Paine witnessed while residing in the South. Paine details the usual litany of slavery's wrongs: the poor conditions in which the slaves live, their lack of religious training, the cruel severance of family ties, the owners' lack of respect for the sanctity of slave marriages, and the sexual abuse of women slaves. At times the techniques of exposure are exactly parallel; for example, Paine quotes William A. Hotchkiss's *Statute Book of Georgia* first to document abuses in the penal system (where treatment of prisoners deviates from statute law), and later to analyze abuses or paradoxes with regard to slavery (for example, the law illogically allows for the licensing of slave preachers even as it holds slaves' learning to read unlawful).[33]

It may have been Paine's publisher who encouraged the addition of the antislavery chapters. Bela Marsh of Boston had previously published an edition of Richard Hildreth's antislavery novel *The Slave; or, Memoirs of Archy Moore* (1848); abolitionist and legal theorist Lysander Spooner's famous pamphlet denying slavery's legality, *The Unconstitutionality of Slavery* (1846); and slave narratives by Henry Watson (*Narrative of Henry Watson, A Fugitive Slave*, 1850) and William Wells Brown (*Narrative of William W. Brown, A Fugitive Slave*, 1849), among other antislavery titles. In a strategy faintly reminiscent of the chaplains who peddled sermons in the guise of prison memoirs, Marsh and Paine found that the prison exposé and abolitionist tract were compatible enough to rest within the covers of a single volume, even if they failed to achieve the more coherent blending of the two genres that George Thompson managed.

Poetry of Incarceration: The Inmate and Prison Reform Ideology

Since few prisoners possessed the literary skills and social connections to publish memoirs, full-length books about the prison experience from inmates other than abolitionists are rare. The poetry published by antebellum prisoners therefore offers a valuable glimpse into their experiences of incarceration. This poetry must be read carefully, with the mediation of the editors and prison reformers who ushered it into print taken into account, as well as the agendas of the authors themselves. Whereas too naïve an acceptance of the prisoners' expressions of gratitude for the opportunity to reform would be a mistake, a too skeptical appraisal of their sentiments is also potentially misleading. However utopian the premises of penal reform look from the vantage point of the twenty-first century, they must have held out promise to inmates who wanted to believe that their lives could be defined not by their crime and imprisonment but rather by their eligibility for redemption.

In addition to his prose work *Prison Life and Reflections,* George Thompson published a volume of poetry inspired by his time in the Missouri Penitentiary. To judge from the title page of *The Prison Bard: Or Poems on Various Subjects* (1848), Thompson's publisher believed that the author's identity as a prison inmate far eclipsed his commitment to abolition as a claim on the attention of readers. In addition to the title's emphasis on the novelty of a prisoner-poet, the title page identifies Thompson as "for four years and eleven months a prisoner in Missouri, for attempting to aid some slaves to liberty." A separate line redundantly clarifies that the poems were "Written in Prison," a phrase followed by the epigraph "Come ye who love the Saviour's name / And joy His praise to swell / Attend, while I His grace proclaim, / In this our hallowed cell."[34] Hartford publisher William H. Burleigh makes four separate references on the title page to Thompson's incarceration—and only one to his identity as an abolitionist. Thompson picks up this emphasis in his preface, noting that the poems exhibit "the heart of a prisoner," "a more distinct view of my inward soul," and his "*private meditations*" (iii, iv, and v). As both author and publisher realized, a text that promised to deliver the inner life of the prisoner simultaneously satisfied the public's prurient interest in the details of incarceration while constituting a valued contribution to the penal reform debate, in which the psychological state of the prisoner was often a key consideration. *The Prison Bard* is most profitably read, then, within the context of prison reform ideology and the literature associated with it, even as it simultaneously represents the 1840s convergence of prison reform and abolitionism.

Thompson had reported in *Prison Life and Reflections* that the Missouri Penitentiary was an inhospitable climate for moral reform, given the brutality with which prisoners were treated: "This term [reformation] in the mouth of Satan, and applied to this place, is full of meaning—for it does, mostly, reform men from good to bad, and from bad to worse!"[35] These sentiments notwithstanding, *The Prison Bard* includes several poems in which incarceration provides the inmate with an opportunity to reflect on his crimes and achieve moral redemption. Thompson recalls one inmate by name, William Grizzle, a murderer who (a note tells readers) "converted, and toiled with us, in our Prison, more than three years." The lines "O! *happy* brother—what a glorious change! / Here, *suffering pris'ner*—Now, with Jesus reigns" (151–52) nicely condense the carceral conversion narrative into its most abbreviated form. Another inmate is enjoined to recount the story of his prison conversion after release: "Go, tell them all, that you have seen and felt / The evil of your former wicked ways; / That Jesus' love your hardened heart did melt, / And filled your mouth with songs of grateful praise" (110).

Thompson and his abolitionist colleagues took credit for having sparked a revival in the prison (they were training to become missionaries when apprehended); what brutalizing authorities could not accomplish, Thompson implies, was possible given the ministering attentions of the abolitionists. This was the meaning of the phrase "our hallowed cell" in the epigraph: the abolitionists attached this epithet to the cell they shared because it provided an atmosphere of devotion and piety for themselves and, at times, like-minded inmates. But to understand Thompson's poems of conversion, one should also bear in mind that widely circulated narratives about incarceration generally followed a formula of suffering crowned by penitence and triumphant moral renewal. In other words, considerations of literary form that arose from and embodied prevailing beliefs about the effects of incarceration might help to explain the presence of carceral conversion poems within *The Prison Bard,* even if they seem to contradict Thompson's observations about conditions in the Missouri Penitentiary in another forum.

Believing his attempt to help slaves escape morally justifiable, Thompson went to prison without a crime for which to atone. Therefore, *The Prison Bard* includes no poems written in the first person in which Thompson applies the tenets of prison reform to his own experience. In contrast, the first-person poetry of inmates who were committed for crimes that were not politically motivated, and whose effusions about the effects of incarceration reached the public through the mediation of prison reformers, requires a more complex act of interpretation. Poems in this vein naturally invite a certain amount of skepticism regarding the authenticity of the conversion experience recorded and the motives of those who saw the effort into print.

The interpretive value of such skepticism is amply demonstrated in Caleb Smith's brilliant analysis of George Ryno's *Buds and Flowers, of Leisure Hours* (1844), a volume of poetry self-consciously inserted into the antebellum prison reform debate. Writing against the backdrop of Charles Dickens's blistering criticism of Pennsylvania's solitary system of incarceration in *American Notes*, Harry Hawser (Ryno's pseudonym) dedicated his book to Richard Vaux, president of the board of inspectors of the Eastern Penitentiary of Philadelphia, an institution the poet wistfully describes as "a seat on the banks of Repentance." Hawser regards imprisonment as "the happiest event of his life," because it "dissolved improper connections, remodeled his tastes, improved his mind, and, he trusts, made better his heart."[36]

Buds and Flowers is an unqualified defense of the solitary system in place at the Eastern Penitentiary. The poem "Memory" (105), in which incarceration prompts the persona to dwell remorsefully on his past mistakes, represents the successful working of the penitentiary regime, while a devotional poem such as "Wake, Wake the Lyre" (109) records the reawakening of the inmate's spirituality. These lines from "An Inebriate's Solitary Thoughts" (Hawser attributes his criminal past to alcoholism) capture the spirit of the volume: "Come, sweet religion! bland-eyed goddess, come! / . . . Pour out upon this all-polluted heart / The purifying streams of grace, and cleanse / Its inmost recess from the filth of sin" (122).

Contextualizing the poetry through a full explanation of the penal reform debates *Buds and Flowers* addressed and the mass reading public at which it was aimed, Smith notes the significant distance perceptible between persona and historical author. A rougher character than his reputed persona (scarred, tattooed, and described by his keepers as "reckless and hardened," according to Smith), Ryno would be convicted of larceny and sent back to the Eastern Penitentiary five years after his initial release. As Smith notes, the success of *Buds and Flowers* as propaganda required the suppression of the inconvenient facts of Ryno's biography in favor of Harry Hawser's more sentimental personal story. Regarding "Harry Hawser" as a virtual invention of the penal reformers, Smith concludes:

> The peculiar new relationship between the prison interior and the mass public—the reformers' need to answer sensational fiction with an inmate's true testimony—definitively informed the rhetoric and reception of *Buds and Flowers,* making the poet's authenticity a central issue in the meaning and political force of the poetry. This new kind of authenticity, however,

was paradoxically an effect of the inmate's anonymity; it depended on the reformers' capacity to obscure the life of George Ryno behind the screen of Harry Hawser.[37]

With Smith's subtle interrogation of *Buds and Flowers* in mind, I turn now to another book of poetry that arose from the prison reform movement, one perhaps as influential as *Buds and Flowers* and, in its own ways, equally complicated and revealing.

In 1847 Charles Spear edited and published *Voices from Prison,* a selection of poetry written by inmates throughout history, including the contributions of men then serving (or having recently served) in prison. A significantly enlarged third edition was published in 1849; both editions were simultaneously published in London, a reflection of the prison reform movement's international scope.[38] A Universalist minister, Spear was (along with his brother J. M. Spear) the publisher of *Prisoner's Friend,* the Boston-based periodical that devoted itself to the anti-gallows movement as well as to prison reform.[39] *Prisoner's Friend* aligned itself through contributor Louis Dwight with the Auburn system of incarceration. Spear was an enthusiastic and uncritical believer in the premises of penal reform, as the effusive tone that characterizes the volume's paratext makes clear. In an opening "Essay on the Poetry of the Prison," Spear applies the chief principle on which reform ideology was based—the idea that quiet confinement within a cell causes a transformation of the inmate's personality—to the process of artistic composition: "In his solitude [the poet] looks within himself, and his soul, bursting with thought, finds relief in the world of romance and poetry, and his genius, though dead before, breaks forth in the liveliest and sublimest strains of verse."[40] In Spear's eyes, creativity was a proxy for the inmate's reawakened conscience, making artistic production analogous to moral rehabilitation—another strain of evidence confirming the efficacy of penal practice.

The third edition of *Voices from Prison* is organized into five sections: "Distinguished Prisoners" (including, among many others, John Bunyan, Daniel Defoe, and William Lloyd Garrison), "Royal Prisoners" (Queen Elizabeth; Mary, Queen of Scots; Charles I; among others), "State Prisoners" (this section includes writing by contemporary prison inmates, many from the cells of the Massachusetts State Prison), "Music of the Prison," and "Biographical and Critical Notices." The organization appears at first to support the idea expressed in Spear's preface that the prison has "oftener" been the "abode of the innocent and pure" than it has of "the depraved and guilty."[41] After seeing the distinguished names listed in the first two sections, readers will presumably have a less prejudiced view of the state prison inmates whose poems follow; imprisonment has not always signified depravity. Yet the inclusion of contemporary prisoners such as Garrison and Henry Clapp Jr. (an editor confined for libel) in the "Distinguished Prisoners" as opposed to the "State Prisoners" group where the rest of their contemporaries are confined seems to impose a hierarchy in which these contributors are superior to the state prisoners on the grounds of their status as political prisoners rather than common criminals.

The availability of multiple editions of *Voices from Prison* permits us to see Spear's editorial hand at work. The first edition leads off with "Poems by State Prisoners," whereas the third edition places them after poems by "Distinguished Prisoners" and "Royal Prisoners," establishing a new, ennobling framework in which the state prisoners' poems should be read. More telling are editorial changes made to a poem titled "To my Sister, on her Birth-day," authored by S.H. Two stanzas included in the first edition have been redacted from the third. The omitted stanzas include the lines spoken by an inmate, "Where am I now? How changed the scene! / Among the meanest of the mean, / Mixed with the scum of every isle."[42] An endnote glossing this poem in the first edition included Spear's clarification that the poet "speaks too harshly of his companions in crime," as well as fellow inmate C.M.'s opinion that "there is not one in *this prison* who is so totally depraved."[43] The decision to omit the verse from the third edition represents a scrubbing of the poetry to match more closely the sentimental tone of Spear's prefatory essay. Spear evidently decided it better fit his aims to remove the lines than to risk confirming prejudices about the character of penitentiary inmates that the volume as a whole (indeed, the entire prison reform movement) was intended to diminish.

A poem added to the "State Prisoners" section in the third edition is "Prisoner's Lament," by H. Griffin. Awaiting execution, the prisoner asks whether a person gifted with the ability to play music and write poetry should be "rudely blotted from the Book of Life" for a single error.[44] A footnote informs readers that Griffin was executed at Newgate in 1793, after which the poem was discovered in his cell. Although the poem does not quite fit with the rest of the section's contributions by American inmates, Spear obviously added it to support his organization's anti–capital punishment agenda.

If there is a dissenting voice in the third edition of *Voices from Prison,* it belongs to John Quiner of Beverly, Massachusetts. In "The Captive Maniac," for example, Quiner's persona overhears an insane fellow inmate singing a melody from his days as a ship boy. Initially the song calls to the persona's mind the bright scenes of his youth, but he awakens from his reverie to hear, in the poem's despondent final lines, "the maniac's shout, the bitter tear, / And a dark dungeon bed."[45] Why would Spear include a poem that so darkly casts in doubt his cherished notion of the cell as the space of moral redemption? Spear's biographical note explains that "The Captive Maniac" was initially published in the *Essex Register* of Salem, Massachusetts, in 1829. The implication seems to be that Quiner entered prison before the revolution in antebellum penal methods had fully taken hold. Moreover, Quiner was reputed to be "intemperate, and much addicted to stealing," as well as "insane," all of which may serve to explain, in Spear's eyes, his decidedly unhopeful take on incarceration.[46] To offset the impression made by Quiner's lack of sentimentalism, Spear sandwiches his poems between contributions by R.S. and S.H., who express themselves in a sentimental idiom that more reliably promotes the ideology of reform.[47]

One of Spear's most intriguing editorial decisions was the inclusion of an abridged version of a poem by Harry Hawser / George Ryno, "An Inebriate's Solitary Thoughts," attributed to "A Philadelphia Penitentiary Convict." Any biography of the poet is silently omitted from the volume's "Biographical and Critical Notices"; the pseudonym Harry Hawser is conspicuously absent. Whereas Spear claims in his "Concluding Remarks" that *Voices from Prison* is "the first volume the world has ever seen of the Poetry of the Prison," he must have known better if he included a work from the previously published *Buds and Flowers*.[48] It appears that Spear saw nothing to gain from further publicizing this success story from the solitary system, given claims made in *Prisoner's Friend* regarding its debilitating mental effects, and yet he wanted to include "An Inebriate's Solitary Thoughts" on the basis of its poetic merit and promotion of the general idea that incarceration inspired moral reform.

That a poem from a volume explicitly dedicated to the defense of Pennsylvania's solitary system turns up in a volume edited by an opponent of that system is not as extraordinary as it appears. Unpredictable circulation was the rule in antebellum print culture, in which texts, particularly poems, were routinely reprinted by periodical editors without permission or attribution. The precise circumstances under which a handful of prison inmates contributed poetry to the ambitious anthology *Voices from Prison* may be largely lost to history, but their situation in some ways recalls (in intensified form) the position of the antebellum author in general, whose disenfranchisement led Poe to refer to the periodical publishing industry as "The Magazine Prison-House."[49] Prisoner-poets may have had more reason than most writers to complain about a lack of agency when it came to unauthorized reproduction of their intellectual labor (which, however discouraging, probably paled in comparison to the unapologetic exploitation of their physical labor under the contract labor system).

One conclusion that becomes inescapable after reading the antebellum poetry of incarceration is that prisoner-poets were chiefly valued for the ability to write about the prison experience. Most of the state prisoners describe the suffering they endured in prison, the emotions that incarceration inspired, their regrets regarding the pain they imposed on loved ones, and their embrace of the promises of Christianity. Only rarely do the prisoner-poets express themselves on universal subjects such as love, death, nature, and the like outside of the context of confinement. If the popularity of prison reform ideals imbued the prisoner with an unprecedented cultural authority, this was for the most part limited to his observations on matters of criminality, incarceration, and reform. The star contributor to *Voices from Prison*, whose poems verify this observation, is undoubtedly C.M.

A former inmate of the Massachusetts State Prison (an Auburn-style institution considered a triumph of successful prison reform in the late 1840s), C.M. appears first and is given the largest number of pages among poets in the "State Prisoners" section. His contributions also appear in the section on "Music of the Prison," where he is identified, perhaps inadvertently, as Christian Meadows.[50] Meadows's poems include "Temperance Pledge," "The Prisoner at Midnight," "Prisoner and his Mouse," and "Prisoner's Address to his Mother," with one poem on a subject unrelated to incarceration, "Blind Girl." Meadows's immersion in the tenets and language of prison reform (particularly the carceral conversion narrative) can be gauged by "The Prisoner at Midnight," which ends with "The contrite petitioner's prayer"; "The Moonbeam," which visits the prisoner and "reminds me of Him by whose generous will / It visits poor creatures like me"; and "Prisoner's Resolution," where the persona resolves "to do whate'er is right," for which "Heav'n will send us happier days."[51] The biographical notice at the end of the volume informs readers that C.M.'s behavior in prison was "so commendable that the governor and council shortened his term of sentence" and that he is now "an industrious, faithful man."[52] C.M. clearly earns pride of place in the volume by virtue of the fidelity with which he both models and peddles the narrative of reform via incarceration.

Voices from Prison raises complicated questions of agency and authenticity. The volume's efficacy as propaganda depended on antebellum readers' acceptance of the notion that it transparently conveyed the authentic sentiments of state prisoners. But given the way that chaplains and reformers tended to manipulate prisoners' voices to suit their own needs, a modern reader will naturally incline toward skepticism. Smith's exposure of the distance between prisoner-poet Ryno and his reform-friendly poetic persona "Harry Hawser" is called to mind by Meadows's subsequent appearance in the historical record. Like Harry Hawser, the poetic persona of C.M. turns out to be a sentimentalized avatar, one whose façade obscures a real inmate with a messier personal history. In contrast to Spear's portrait of a reformed man leading an industrious and exemplary post-carceral life, Meadows returned to prison within a year or so of the publication of the third edition of *Voices from Prison* as an accomplice of the notorious criminal William Darlington, better known to readers of antebellum crime reports as "Bristol Bill." Meadows appears as a minor character in novelist (no relation to prison bard) George Thompson's *Life and Exploits of the Noted Criminal, Bristol Bill* (1851), a hybrid text combining elements of the Newgate novel and the trial pamphlet, published after the real-life Darlington's arrest and conviction. In *Life and Exploits,* Thompson recounts how Darlington and Meadows were convicted of counterfeiting in Danville, Vermont, on June 21, 1850 (a conviction confirmed in period newspapers), and sentenced to hard labor in the state penitentiary. The identity of this Christian Meadows with the contributor to *Voices from Prison* is beyond dispute; Thompson mentions Meadows's earlier incarceration in the Massachusetts State Prison in *Life and Exploits.* In Thompson's account, Meadows is said to be resigned to his re-confinement, and "it is evident that he has become a repentant man." In the Vermont State Prison, Meadows "calmly bides his fate, and perhaps looks forward, with something like reasonable hope, towards an executive pardon."[53]

Of the few known facts of his biography, Meadows's identity as a counterfeiter serves (almost too conveniently) as a figure for the act of self-invention whereby the real-life Meadows crafted the poetic persona C.M. The mask of the penitent former convict unexpectedly falls away to reveal, it would seem, a Melvillean confidence man who counterfeited carceral conversion discourse skillfully enough to convince not only prison reformer Spear of his penitence, but also the warden of the Massachusetts State Prison and even the governor of Massachusetts, who awarded him a shortened sentence on the basis of his "commendable" deportment. That this model deportment included Meadows's composition of poetry tracing his journey toward repentance seems very likely, given his prominent position within *Voices from Prison.* Editor Spear recounts the inspiring experience of having heard Meadows, while still an inmate, sing a poem he had set to music, "The Prisoner's Address to his Mother," during the Massachusetts State Prison's Independence Day celebration.[54] In light of this information, Meadows's patient, calm demeanor in the Vermont State Prison looks like the guise of a man skilled in manipulating the expectations of credulous prison officials and awaiting the next opportunity to flaunt his penitence in hopes of securing early release—and his poetry in *Voices from Prison* comes across as an act of effrontery, a successful mimicry of penal reform propaganda in the service of securing executive pardon.[55]

A competing narrative—in which Meadows experienced guilt during his initial incarceration in Massachusetts, sincerely devoted himself to repentance under the tutelage of reformers like Charles Spear and warden Frederick Robinson, and inscribed and celebrated that devotion in a set of poems, only to find that the stigma of incarceration so profoundly limited his post-carceral options that he reluctantly returned to a life of crime—cannot be dismissed. Novelist Thompson paints Meadows as a somewhat passive spirit who unfortunately fell into the orbit of "vicious associates," a person whose skill as an engraver "naturally led him, during periods of misfortune, into the crime of bank note counterfeiting," and whose malleable temperament made him an "efficient and dangerous instrument in the hands of his more wily confederates."[56] The historical record appears to support this charitable assessment. By the early 1860s, Meadows had been released from prison and had relocated to upstate New York, where census records and city directories list him as an engraver in possession of considerable personal wealth, suggesting that he did eventually turn his life around.[57]

The true state of Meadows's conscience when he contributed poems to *Voices from Prison* can never be recovered. But his shortened sentence highlights what was potentially at stake for the prisoner-poets when they chose to lend their voices to the prison reform movement. Shifting attention from the motives of prison reformers to the motives of the poets themselves restores to them a degree of agency that might otherwise be overlooked. Take the case of *Voices from Prison* contributor S.H. Though his poem "The Convict to his Bible," a conventional account of the carceral conversion experience, first appears in print (I believe) in the 1847 first edition of *Voices from Prison*, he had at some earlier time sent it to his former prison chaplain—John Luckey of Sing Sing—who read it to that prison's inmates in March 1846. In fact, as part of a quarterly ritual in which he publicly read letters from former inmates who were living successful lives after discharge, Luckey reported having read poems by S.H. on at least two occasions.[58] In *Voices from Prison*, Spear reports that S.H. wrote a letter to "a friend" (perhaps Spear himself, as publisher of *Prisoner's Friend*? Or Luckey?), in which he enclosed "two or three of some hundred poems which [he] composed at [his] work bench."[59] To judge by this evidence, S.H. made a concerted effort to send his poems to figures with the ability to see them into print, letting them know he had more works available for publication. Rather than being the creation of self-interested prison reformers, S.H. may be credited with significant agency in this process of coming into print, having identified Luckey and Spear as his most promising avenues to publication. The appearance in print of "The Convict to his Bible" can therefore be regarded as the desired outcome of an ambitious but socially disadvantaged author carefully cultivating patrons to become a published poet, if only for the gratification of seeing his works in print, or perhaps in hope of inspiring other inmates to follow his course toward a productive post-carceral life. Already discharged, S.H. clearly did not write with the intention of impressing upon prison authorities his eligibility for release, as may have been the case with Meadows.

Prisoner-poets Meadows and S.H. are best understood as "outsider" authors, to use the term coined by Karen A. Weyler in *Empowering Words: Outsiders and Authorship in Early America*. Outsiders are authors "without the advantages of an elite education, social class, or connections, who relied largely on their own labor for subsistence," a definition that easily embraces antebellum prison inmates.[60] In Weyler's analysis, popular genres served as particularly accessible entrance points for outsiders into the world of print, in part because the conventions of these genres were easily comprehensible to authors of limited literacy skills. The "State Prisoners" poets in *Voices from Prison* readily identified the conventions of the carceral conversion narrative and, it appears, shaped their poetry accordingly. In the eighteenth century, outsiders such as Britton Hammon and John Marrant, African Americans taken captive by Native Americans, leveraged personal experience to enter the world of authorship by way of the popular Indian captivity narrative. A similar trajectory was followed by the contributors to *Voices from Prison,* whose experiences as inmates opened up to them the genre of prison-related poetry. Outsider authors often turn to existing social and religious networks to facilitate authorship (as Phillis Wheatley tapped into the Methodist Huntingdon Connexion), a tactic discernible in the letters S.H. sent to prison reformer Luckey. As Weyler pointedly observes of the author-patron relationship, "Collaboration and sponsorship were never disinterested; there was always something at stake for collaborators and sponsors."[61]

The extraordinary history of prisoner-poet Meadows demonstrates what an individual inmate potentially stood to gain from collaboration with the prison reform movement. Like outsider authors before and since, Meadows recognized authorship as "one route to acquiring symbolic and cultural capital," and in his case, the effects of authorship were (at least for a time) life changing.[62] The poetic persona of C.M. apparently represents the creation of an inmate who cannily mastered the tropes of prison reform poetry and then leveraged his position as a contributor to *Voices from Prison* into a successful bid for release. If Meadows's poetry of repentance was taken into consideration in determining his eligibility for early release, as Spear's comments in *Voices from Prison* leads me to believe, this would have to be regarded as a rare and stunning case of an author seizing upon poetry's often professed liberatory power on a practical rather than a merely imaginative level.

In contrast, prisoner-poet S.H. pushed his poems onto patrons in the aftermath of incarceration with no discernible agenda aside from self-expression. The attraction of prison reform ideology for inmates such as S.H. should not be underestimated. One can easily imagine their being drawn to the idea that the subject of incarceration emerges from confinement morally transformed and prepared to return to his community. The rehabilitated inmate of reform literature was a living symbol of the progress of human civilization. ("Look how much more advanced than our forebears we as a society have become by virtue of our humane rehabilitation of prisoners," his experience implicitly suggested.) The principles of prison reform potentially enhanced an inmate's self-worth while promising in the long run to reduce the stigma of incarceration. The conversion experience that prison reform ideology presupposed and promoted in its ubiquitous propaganda (made available to inmates by prison wardens, inspectors, chaplains, prison associations, and reformers like Spear) must have seemed empowering enough to some prisoners to inspire original—and, in some cases, sincere—acts of artistic composition. *Voices from Prison* offers an intriguing test case for assessing dynamics between outsider authors and their patrons in the prison reform movement, revealing poets and reformers separately and self-interestedly attempting to use the cultural capital that proximity to incarceration bestowed upon them to serve (depending on circumstance) overlapping or conflicting agendas.

When Nathaniel Hawthorne exposed for readers the inner life of Hester Prynne to help them determine if the judicial sentence under which she labored had been effective, if the scarlet letter had "done its office," he was participating in a wider cultural discourse.[63] Hawthorne's examination of Hester's psychology paralleled—and to some extent perhaps derived from—antebellum interest in the inner lives of penitentiary inmates. Although the power of Hawthorne's novel lies in his having surpassed in depth and subtlety anything the propaganda of the prison reform movement could boast, *The Scarlet Letter* nonetheless fits alongside a complementary literature of testimony to the effects of the carceral experience. When abolitionist and discharged penitentiary inmate Thompson rhetorically asked readers if they knew "the heart of a prisoner," he obviously believed that his unique ability to reveal it was a strong incentive to continue reading. Interest in prison reform led to a widespread belief that the inmate had something important to tell the rest of society. If in the social realm the stigma of incarceration remained crippling, a history of imprisonment sometimes carried a different, positive valence in the arena of print culture. Chaplains' memoirs, abolitionist prison exposés, and the poetry of incarceration all testify to the value publishers and readers placed on firsthand accounts of the carceral experience.

The authority antebellum Americans conferred upon those who had witnessed incarceration from the inside lent itself to exploitation for a variety of purposes. Some abolitionists recognized a value in aligning their social program with the well-known (and in some quarters, perhaps, more respectable) cause of prison reform. Thompson's *Prison Life and Reflections* represents the most thoughtful product of the convergence of abolition and prison reform, a careful blending of the prison exposé with some of the most rhetorically effective features of the slave narrative as practiced by Frederick Douglass. Meanwhile, American prison chaplains evidently believed that their proximity to the subjects of incarceration offered an unprecedented opportunity to counter the increasing sensationalism of antebellum print culture. In the face of city-mysteries novels, newspaper crime reports, murder trial pamphlets, the flash press, and whatever other lurid subgenres the flourishing antebellum publishing industry could vend to a sensation-addicted reading public, the chaplains wrote books that briefly returned to a model of literary production more than a hundred years out of date, when the life stories of criminals reached the public through the mediation of religious figures for the express purpose of promoting morality, piety, and deference to authority. Chaplains' memoirs drafted the voices of unwitting prisoners into supporting a conservative, evangelical agenda. The chaplains' numerous accounts of conversion experiences on the part of African American inmates collectively suggest that recent assessments may overstate the racialist assumptions supposedly underlying the prison reform movement.

Questions of authenticity, genre, and author-patron interactions must all be factored in to a nuanced interpretation of the poetry of incarceration. *Voices from Prison* arose from self-interested efforts on the part of its outsider authors and reform-minded editor to parlay whatever cultural capital accrued to the converted inmate into serving compatible—or competing—agendas. On the one hand, even granting the volume's frankly propagandistic aims, the possibility remains that some inmates' poems represent the authentic aspirations of prisoners and former prisoners (like S.H.) who, for quite comprehensible personal reasons, sincerely identified with the reformers' humanitarian aims and collaborated with prison reformers to give expression to their reform-friendly sentiments. The case of Christian Meadows, on the other hand, reveals a more complicated and intriguing model of collaboration. In crafting the persona of penitent inmate C.M., Meadows took advantage of the cultural capital that authorship conferred on prisoner-poets to enhance a successful petition for release before returning (temporarily, it appears) to a life of crime. The convergence of the spheres of literature and criminal justice documented in this book opened an avenue to publication—and, it would seem, a path to liberty—that Meadows perceptively exploited, marking him as perhaps the most fascinating figure among a collection of antebellum authors who explored the opportunities latent in their purported ability to take readers inside the American penitentiary.

Conclusion

Christian Meadows, Edgar Allan Poe, and the "Magazine Prison-House"

Attempting to pin down the origins of the novel in English, Lennard Davis notes the persistent link between novels and criminals in eighteenth-century English literature: "The frequency with which the early English novel, newspapers, and ballads focused on the criminal is significant. . . . Indeed, without the appearance of the whore, the rogue, the cutpurse, the cheat, the thief, or the outsider it would be impossible to imagine the genre of the novel."[1] An analogous relationship might be traced in antebellum America between literature and the mechanisms (and personnel) of criminal justice. If the period's literature is not quite unimaginable without the police court, the converted prison inmate, the prison chaplain, the discharged convict, the trial court (along with its extralegal counterpart, the vigilante court), and the angel of the penitentiary, these figures nonetheless appear with sufficient frequency to suggest that they embody some of the culture's most salient preoccupations, related not merely to issues of crime and punishment but also to broader subjects including gender, race, and citizenship.

The emergence of new institutional forms helps to explain why much mid-nineteenth-century American literature transposes British literature's long-standing fascination with criminality into a particular focus on criminal justice. For ideological as well as pragmatic reasons, nineteenth-century Americans established criminal justice practices that did not necessarily trace their origins to colonial precedent: penal codes were rewritten to reduce the number of capital crimes; courts prosecuted crimes that flourished in rapidly growing urban environments; state constitutions were rewritten to accommodate the election of judges; urban police departments were formed; public district attorneys took the place of the colonial era's more informal method of private prosecution; and the penitentiary became society's primary form of criminal punishment. According to criminal law scholar William J. Stuntz, the criminal justice system in the decades preceding the Civil War became "more democratic, more powerful, and more thoroughly under the thumb of local governments" than it had been previously, a set of changes that Stuntz regards as "a revolution in state and local government."[2] Accompanying this revolution in governmental responses to crime were the various technological developments (in areas such as paper manufacturing, steam printing, and distribution networks) that fostered an unprecedented—one might even call it revolutionary—expansion of the American publishing industry, giving rise to an innovative, boisterous print culture that often turned its attention to matters of criminal justice. My goal in these pages has been to examine some effects of these parallel revolutions on a broad spectrum of antebellum American literature.

The discourse surrounding prison reform best exemplifies how, in the unique conditions generated by the expanding antebellum press, innumerable printed sources collectively nurtured a vocabulary of criminal justice–related tropes. Starting in the late eighteenth century, reformers issued theories about prison construction and administration in books and pamphlets, including Benjamin Rush's early and influential *Enquiry into the Effects of Public Punishments upon Criminals, and Upon Society.*[3] As individual states built and managed prisons according to reformers' ideas, official government documents, such as the annual reports of individual prisons submitted to state legislatures, carried out the task of describing and defending certain institutional practices. These reports on prison conditions, disciplinary procedures, budgets, number of inmates received and discharged, and so on often reached a wider public through extracts in newspapers and other periodicals. From such origins—and building upon preexisting popular genres related to criminality, such as the execution sermon and the speeches of condemned criminals—stories of prisons and prisoners proliferated.

With the differentiation of prison reform into the Auburn and Pennsylvania camps, competing reform periodicals emerged to disseminate uplifting stories of incarceration and rehabilitation. Meanwhile, as the United States assumed international leadership in the field of penology, famous literary tourists made pilgrimages to the nation's most prominent penitentiaries; their accounts, including interviews with individual prisoners, invited an expanding circle of readers into an ongoing transatlantic conversation about incarceration. Charles Dickens's skeptical appraisal of the solitary system in use at Philadelphia's Eastern Penitentiary in *American Notes,* in particular, mobilized defensive American reformers to contest his claims with a roster of rehabilitative success stories. Newspapers debated prison reform premises, popular women's magazines lauded female prison reformers, and former prison

chaplains published accounts of their missionary work among the incarcerated, much of this material subject to unfettered circulation under the terms
of what Meredith McGill usefully labels "reprint culture."[4]

Within this print ecosystem, certain images and stories—the carceral
conversion, the angel in the penitentiary, the discharged convict leading a
successful life—became self-selecting memes, multiplying in proportion to
their concurrence with prevailing ideologies. These popular stories migrated
into the period's imaginative literature to be endorsed, adapted, modified, or
challenged according to the political views, artistic choices, reform impulses,
and commercial imperatives of individual authors, editors, and publishers.[5] A
communal, distributed model of authorship recognizes the figures who participated in the composition and circulation of these stories—such as editors
of reform periodicals, newspaper correspondents, and contributors to literary
monthlies—as important collaborators in shaping the period's literary expression alongside those canonical figures, such as Nathaniel Hawthorne, long
recognized by a more romantic, individualistic paradigm.

Given his intensive fictional investment in colonial history, Hawthorne
could have conceived the basic outlines of *The Scarlet Letter* in the absence
of a prison reform movement. But the attention that movement paid to
questions of isolation, reflection, and moral rehabilitation offered him a set
of concepts whose resemblance to Puritan beliefs and practices (especially
admonition) meant that Hester Prynne's seventeenth-century story of crime
and punishment was relevant to some of the most vital cultural conversations
of the mid-nineteenth century. Hawthorne's decision to feature the story of
a discharged convict returning to society after a decades-long incarceration
in his next novel, *The House of the Seven Gables,* cannot be understood independently of the prison reform movement and the distinctive narrative forms
it spawned. Nor were these Hawthorne's only imaginable debts to prison
reform discourse. If the conclusions I draw from surveying the American
reception history of the British Newgate novel (as practiced by Edward Bulwer and Dickens) are valid, then Hawthorne's much-admired breakthrough
in exploring his characters' inner lives in *The Scarlet Letter* can be traced in
part to Americans' infatuation with the principles of penal reform, as reviewers increasingly voiced an expectation that crime novelists depict awakenings
of their primary characters' consciences in alignment with the movement's
central premise.

Prison was not the only criminal justice institution to attract literary and
cultural attention in the middle of the nineteenth century. In urban centers,
various forms of corruption deeply undermined faith in the judicial system.
Meanwhile, the American West saw the emergence of vigilante courts acting
as socially sanctioned adjuncts to the criminal justice system, on the argument

that official courts were inadequate to provide order in lawless territories. Distrust of trial courts and vigilantism were opposing sides of the same coin, partaking of a Jacksonian-tinged argument that authority over legal machinery rightfully belonged to the people rather than to a corrupt or elitist judiciary. Was an ineffectual court system sufficient justification for ordinary citizens to take over the job of punishing criminals? George Lippard and Richard Hildreth offered different answers to this question in novels of the early 1850s. Despite widely varying literary sensibilities, however, the working-class crime novelist–labor organizer and the Boston Brahmin lawyer-historian simultaneously descried and dramatized (with differing levels of approval) a racial component that this debate normally overlooked: vigilantism's unpredictable distribution of civic agency raised the prospect of African American participation in the arbitration of criminal justice and, more broadly, in the democratic process.

In hindsight it may seem paradoxical that the courts charged with funneling convicted criminals into penitentiaries were widely regarded with suspicion, while the prisons themselves were generally, if not quite universally, celebrated for their innovations and successes. How did it happen that antebellum Americans distrusted their courts but lauded their penitentiaries? The distinct circumstances governing each institution's appearance within American print culture begins to suggest an explanation for this differential of confidence. Trial courts achieved their highest visibility among American readers through newspaper reporting of sensational murder trials (along with the pamphlets that aggregated this coverage into a convenient, cheap format). Often this reporting parsed testimony, analyzed evidence, and encouraged speculation about a defendant's guilt or innocence. Individual newspaper editors championed or pilloried defendants according to privately held agendas, or simply with the aim of drumming up controversy to sell newspapers. In cases where evidence was equivocal or editors of competing papers offered different theories about a defendant's guilt (for example, in the heavily sensationalized coverage surrounding the trial of Richard Robinson for the murder of Helen Jewett), any verdict was bound to provoke skepticism. James Fenimore Cooper charged in *The Ways of the Hour* that editors peddled favorable coverage in exchange for bribes by defense lawyers. Add to this sordid picture the belief that courts treated defendants differently according to their social standing, a charge widely bandied about in the antebellum press (and one whose merit is seconded by the judgment of modern historians), and public distrust of antebellum trial courts is not difficult to understand.

The process through which stories about prisons circulated in the antebellum press, however, was often quite different. To the extent they could, advocates of prison reform attempted to control the discourse about incarceration.

Founding periodicals devoted to their cause, they promoted success stories in order to bring public opinion and legislative funding around to their point of view. Moreover, stories about the successes of incarceration flattered Americans' patriotism, reinforced their commitment to Christian principles of sin and redemption, and dovetailed with the discourse of sentimentalism, giving periodical editors overlapping ideological and commercial incentives to select these stories for publishing or reprinting. Even exposés such as those penned by abolitionists incarcerated in southern jails furthered the prison reform agenda, since they were usually couched as indictments of individual prisons, not as attacks on the underlying theory. Specific publishing and reading practices associated with the print culture of criminal justice therefore help to explain why American readers tended to project their collective resentments onto the court system while they (on balance) nurtured faith in the rehabilitative promise of incarceration.

From a twenty-first-century perspective, antebellum American faith in the promise of incarceration was often misplaced. Too much trust was placed in the benignity of prison authorities and too little attention was devoted to the exploitation of convict labor. A troubling strain of voyeurism is present in nineteenth-century stories of incarceration, with the deviant prisoners turned into a spectacle for the entertainment of normative society, a dynamic best represented by the thousands of tourists who annually passed through the doors of the Eastern State Penitentiary in Philadelphia. (In a number of George Thompson's pamphlet novels, his criminal characters express discomfort with the notion that incarceration put them on display for middle-class observers.)[6] Charges of torture tended to be swept under the rug, as when the Pennsylvania legislature attempted to suppress Thomas McElwee's exposé of cruel and unusual punishment at the Eastern State Penitentiary. But these failings existed alongside an earnest public debate about the means, purposes, and efficacy of incarceration, a conversation that twenty-first-century Americans, living in an age of mass incarceration, initially avoided.

The 2010 publication of Michelle Alexander's volume *The New Jim Crow,* however, has inspired renewed public debate about incarceration. Alexander's persuasive thesis, that incarceration is the latest form racial discrimination has taken in an ostensibly post-racial society, challenges twenty-first-century Americans' complacency on the subject of race, even as it looks back to the racial dynamics of incarceration in the nineteenth century. Alexander astutely notes the racial identity of America's first penitentiary inmate: "In fact, the very first person admitted to a U.S. penitentiary was a 'light skinned Negro in excellent health,' described by an observer as 'one who was born of a degraded and depressed race, and had never experienced anything but indifference and harshness.'" She uses this evidence to support the (indisputable) notion that throughout American history "people of color have been disproportionately represented behind bars."[7] It is also worth noting, however, that the Eastern State Penitentiary, to which Prisoner No. 1, Charles Williams, was admitted, was widely regarded as a state-of-the-art institution for rehabilitating prisoners. The observers in question were Gustave de Beaumont and Alexis de Tocqueville, who interviewed Williams, and whose remarks imply that his having previously experienced nothing but indifference and harshness partially exculpates his crimes, and further that he experienced something other than cruelty at the hands of Eastern State Penitentiary authorities. The French observers go on to report that Williams "considers his being brought to the Penitentiary as a signal benefit of Providence" and that he read to them from the Bible to demonstrate his penitence.[8]

However skeptically we may be tempted to evaluate such secondhand reports of inmates' dispositions (this is, after all, yet another iteration of the carceral conversion narrative, which carried its own generic imperatives), to judge by the memoirs of prison chaplains, the African American Williams (who was released after two years, having learned the trade of shoemaking) may have been regarded by at least some of his imprisoning authorities as eligible for moral redemption and reintegration into the community. Without downplaying the racism that permeated American society in the nineteenth century, including its criminal justice procedures, one can also note that some prison reformers explicitly touted the redemptive possibilities of incarceration for black inmates. Nineteenth-century prison reform ideology was undoubtedly misguided in some respects, but I would contend that, contrary to recent scholarly claims, invidious racial distinctions might not have been the source of its most egregious failings.

Even the most perceptive antebellum authors proved capable of exhibiting both skepticism and credulity, at times almost simultaneously, when they approached the subject of criminal justice. In my reading of his newspaper work, Walt Whitman came over time to question the conventions of court reporting in which prostitutes and alcoholics were regarded as fair targets for contempt and ridicule. Whitman's involvement with crime reporting while editing the *Brooklyn Daily Eagle* represents a significant moment in the long foreground preceding the 1855 *Leaves of Grass;* that book's defense of the basic humanity of society's most downtrodden members profited from Whitman's evolving view of the implications of representing criminality in print. Yet when it came to incarceration, Whitman wrote without irony about the "kind and gentle treatment of the American prison."[9]

Contradictory responses to ideological premises sometimes register within a single text. Rebecca Harding Davis conspicuously rejects prison reformers' pieties regarding the penitentiary when Hugh Wolfe (having witnessed the mental and physical ravages wrought by imprisonment on discharged convicts in his community) chooses suicide over incarceration in "Life in the Iron-Mills," and yet she uncritically appropriates the angel-in-the-penitentiary motif at the end of the very same story, where a Quaker reformer modeled on the historical Elizabeth Fry (a sainted figure within American periodical culture) works a sentiment-affirming miracle on the life of Hugh's cousin Deb, a borrowing that sits uneasily with the work's otherwise realist convictions. Among the narrative formulas discussed in this book, angels in the penitentiary may have been among the most seductive, given how economically the trope condensed prevailing beliefs regarding womanhood, Christianity, and the rehabilitative ideal. Varieties of the figure appear in texts authored by Davis, Whitman, Dickens, Frederick Marryat, Harriet Beecher Stowe, Sylvester Judd, E. D. E. N. Southworth, and contributors to periodicals such as *Graham's Lady's and Gentleman's Magazine* and *Godey's Lady's Book*.

A narrative formula like the angel in the penitentiary was by no means bound to a particular gender politics. Novelists Judd and Southworth transformed the motif in accordance with comparatively expansive notions of feminine agency, empowering fictional heroines in *Margaret* and *The Hidden Hand* with sweeping authority over the criminal justice system. Meanwhile, reformer Eliza Farnham followed a trajectory similar to that of Judd's contemporaneous Margaret. Celebrated in the press along conventional angel-in-the-penitentiary lines, Farnham spent the cultural capital thus acquired to launch herself from handmaiden to theorist of prison reform by publishing her illustrated and heavily annotated edition of *Rationale of Crime,* a boldly experimental intervention in the era's penal reform debates.

Similar complexities surface in discourse regarding discharged convicts. Sensational novelists George Thompson and Ned Buntline (ironically, considering their own status as former inmates) were evidently policing a racial boundary when they insisted that the formerly incarcerated were "branded by infamy," permanently marked with a racially coded stigma imparted by the penitentiary. This idea seems to have been associated with the use of a convict-leasing system that, in selling inmates' labor, placed them on a level with slaves as individuals bereft of civil status under the law. And yet the novelists' assertion that the legacy of incarceration lasted beyond the moment of discharge also exposed a critical oversight implicit within prison reformers' optimistic stories of discharged convicts anonymously "passing" back into their communities. The promise of anonymity also carried an injunction to silence, suppressing the discharged convict's testimony about the meaning of his or her experience—or about the cruelties the system condoned. In *The Empire City,* George Lippard took the notion of the penitentiary's permanent stigma in a direction quite different from that of his crime novelist peers, giving Number Ninety-One, a discharged convict prominently bearing the physical scars of incarceration, a platform from which to denounce torture masquerading as discipline in American penitentiaries, provocatively over-turning the arid premises of the decades-long Auburn versus Pennsylvania debate.

To conclude, I turn to a short piece by Edgar Allan Poe that gathers together a few threads from throughout the book. Because of the unauthor-ized and unremunerated circulation of their work made possible by permis-sive domestic and international copyright regulations, antebellum authors frequently perceived themselves at a disadvantage with respect to the editors and publishers who mediated their appearance in print. Addressing this state of affairs, Poe borrowed the language of the prison exposé in his caustic Feb-ruary 1845 *Broadway Journal* article "Some Secrets of the Magazine Prison-House." To illustrate how "poor devil" authors were exploited by editors, Poe offered for readers' consideration the case of an impoverished author who neglects other, more lucrative work to write an article that has been solicited for magazine publication. The author makes repeated and increasingly des-perate pleas to the editor for payment, but dies in the long interval between the article's appearance in print and the editor's dilatory pay schedule, thereby relieving the unscrupulous editor of the necessity to pay at all.[10]

Compelling as the anecdote may be, one wonders with how much fore-thought Poe crafted the implied analogy between unpaid authors and prison inmates. Of course, periodical authors were often poorly paid, if paid at all, and had grounds for complaint when their popular works were subject to virtually unlimited reprinting, often in distorted form, without additional remuneration. ("The Raven," published a few weeks earlier, remained just such a reprint sensation when Poe published "Some Secrets.") But did Poe intend his analogy to imply moral equivalency between these injustices and the unpaid labor that contractors extracted from prison inmates, a system that even contemporary observers sometimes likened to slavery?[11] If the author is the prisoner in this ersatz exposé, what role does the editor/publisher occupy: Warden? Guard? Contractor? The analogy does not stand up to scrutiny. That Poe neglected to develop it beyond the piece's title suggests to me that he used it somewhat offhandedly for its assumed sensational appeal.

The ease with which Poe reached for the rhetoric of the prison exposé illus-trates how temptingly accessible the language of prison reform remained at all times for antebellum authors. The promise of revealing the secrets of the prison-house seems to have become one of the default tactics of attention-seeking authors and publishers at just about the time Poe published "Some Secrets." In the 1840s and 1850s, a few abolitionists shrewdly adopted the lan-guage of the prison exposé to promote their antislavery message, while prison chaplains used similar sensationalist tactics to market their book-length memoirs.

Perhaps Poe's imperfect analogy comparing writers to prisoners and the situation of actual prisoners who also happened to be writers can in some way be regarded as reciprocally illuminating. Poe's invective on behalf of poor-devil authors is softened by his concession that magazine editors themselves had little room for profit under current publishing conditions, and their paying authors at all for contributions argued against their illiberality; moreover, Poe's having passed back and forth across the author-editor divide several times in his career (within months he would take over the editorship of the *Broadway Journal*) further complicates the picture of powerless authors suffering at the hands of nefarious editors. Poe's satire cuts in several directions, impugning tightfisted editors but also politicians who lobby against international copyright provisions and the reading public unwilling to give up its access to cheap reprints. The situation is too complex to allow for the identification of a single villain, which both spoils the prisoner-author analogy and blunts the force of Poe's outrage. "Some Secrets" therefore serves as a helpful reminder that assessing author-editor dynamics in the antebellum era usually requires sensitive parsing of context.

A similar level of sensitivity is called for in attempting to unpack the author-editor dynamic at work in the 1849 poetry anthology *Voices from Prison*. Caleb Smith has persuasively demonstrated that "Harry Hawser," author of the 1844 book of prison-inspired poetry *Buds and Flowers, of Leisure Hours,* was largely the creation of prison reformers, who scrubbed the messy personal biography of actual poet George Ryno to better suit their agenda.[12] I contend that the situation Smith (brilliantly) brings to light, however, is only one possibility for understanding antebellum prisoner-poets, and that individual contributors to *Voices from Prison* can profitably be regarded as something other than the convenient fictions of editor Charles Spear. Because prison reform ideology held out much for antebellum ex-prisoners to embrace, it is worth considering that their poems describing salvation via incarceration may at times have been sincere expressions of their aspirations toward redemption and self-worth. Evidence suggests that some contributors to *Voices from Prison* sought out publication by actively cultivating relationships with those in a position to see their work into print. Not merely the sentimentalized creations of reformers, these outsider authors may have used the authority that antebellum print culture conferred on those who had experienced incarceration in order to elbow their way, against long odds, into print. Formulaic genres such as the carceral conversion poem readily lend themselves to outsider authorship, since they are easily understood and appropriated by writers with modest educational attainments.[13]

Voices from Prison contributor Christian Meadows emerges as one of the most intriguing figures in the foregoing pages. Exemplifying the stakes potentially involved in collaborations between patrons and outsider authors, Meadows appears to have shrewdly mastered the tropes of prison reform poetry with an eye to his liberation from prison, calculatedly and successfully leveraging his position as the most prominent contributor to *Voices from Prison* into an early release. Contributor to an anthology of prison poetry, character in a sensational crime novel, and onetime inmate of both the Massachusetts State Prison and the Vermont State Prison (before moving to upstate New York to pursue a legitimate career as an engraver), Meadows embodies better than anyone else the overlapping spheres of literature, print culture, and the criminal justice system that have been the subject of this book. If analysis of *Voices from Prison* gives us an unexpected purchase on questions of author-editor relationships endemic to the antebellum period (belying the simplistic noble author–exploitative editor dynamic of Poe's short article), it helps to substantiate my claim that attending to the parallel (and related) historical developments of an expanding print culture and an evolving set of criminal justice institutions offers fresh perspectives for the study of antebellum American literature and culture.

Notes

Introduction

1. Ned Buntline, *The Mysteries and Miseries of New York: A Story of Real Life* (1848; repr., New York: W. F. Burgess, 1849). New York's Astor Place Riot of May 10, 1849, was a deadly clash between supporters of rival Shakespearean actors rooted in class and ethnic antagonisms.
2. The city-mysteries genre, which emerged in the 1840s, can be defined as "novels [that] unveiled the city's mysteries by telling tales of criminal underworlds, urban squalor, and elite luxury and decadence." Michael Denning, *Mechanic Accents: Dime Novels and Working-Class Culture in America,* rev. ed. (London: Verso, 1998), 85.
3. George W. Matsell, *Vocabulum; or, The Rogue's Lexicon* (New York: George W. Matsell & Co., 1859).
4. George Thompson, *Life and Exploits of the Noted Criminal, Bristol Bill* (New York: M. J. Ivers & Co., n.d.). David S. Reynolds dates the novel to 1851 in a bibliography appended to an edition of Thompson's writings. George Thompson, *Venus in Boston and Other Tales of Nineteenth-Century City Life,* ed. David S. Reynolds and Kimberly R. Gladman (Amherst: University of Massachusetts Press, 2002), 382.
5. Newgate novels, which emerged in the 1830s in Great Britain, offered exciting stories about the exploits of criminals. Some of these criminals' lives had been previously sketched in collections of criminal biographies known as the *Newgate Calendars,* named after the London prison. Heather Worthington, "The Newgate Novel," in *The Nineteenth-Century Novel, 1820–1880,* vol. 3 of *The Oxford History of the Novel in English,* ed. John Kucich and Jenny Bourne Taylor (London: Oxford University Press, 2012), 122–36.
6. *Voices from Prison: Being a Selection of Poetry from Various Prisoners, Written Within the Cell* (Boston: C. & J. M. Spear, 1847).
7. On Emerson's visit to the New Hampshire State Prison, see Caleb Smith, "Emerson and Incarceration," *American Literature* 78.2 (2006): 207–34.
8. As E. Shaskan Bumas notes, "systems of punishment figure prominently in Hawthorne's romances." E. Shaskan Bumas, "Fictions of the Panopticon: Prison, Utopia, and the Out-Penitent in the Works of Nathaniel Hawthorne," *American Literature* 73.1 (2001): 122.
9. Donald J. McNutt, "'Haunts about Town': Poe's Tales and Eastern State Penitentiary," chap. 3 of *Urban Revelations: Images of Ruin in the American City, 1790–1860* (New York: Routledge, 2006); John Cleman, "Irresistible Impulses: Edgar Allan Poe and the Insanity Defense," *American Literature* 63.4 (1991): 623–40; and Dan Shen, "Edgar Allan Poe's Aesthetic Theory, the Insanity Debate, and the Ethically Oriented Dynamics of 'The Tell-Tale Heart,'" *Nineteenth-Century Literature* 63.3 (2008): 321–45.
10. William J. Stuntz, *The Collapse of American Criminal Justice* (Cambridge: Harvard University Press, 2011), 86.

11. Lawrence Friedman's observations on this point are instructive: "The criminal justice system is an umbrella label for certain people, roles, and institutions in society . . . [which] all deal in some significant way with crime—they define crime; or they detect crime; or they prosecute or defend people accused of crime; or they punish crime." Lawrence Friedman, *Crime and Punishment in American History* (New York: Basic Books, 1993), 4.

12. Caleb Smith, *The Prison and the American Imagination* (New Haven: Yale University Press, 2009); Jeannine Marie DeLombard, *In the Shadow of the Gallows: Race, Crime, and American Civic Identity* (Philadelphia: University of Pennsylvania Press, 2012); and Paul Christian Jones, *Against the Gallows: Antebellum American Writers and the Movement to Abolish Capital Punishment* (Iowa City: University of Iowa Press, 2011).

13. Brook Thomas, *Cross-Examinations of Law and Literature: Cooper, Hawthorne, Stowe, and Melville* (Cambridge: Cambridge University Press, 1987).

14. Colin Dayan, *The Law Is a White Dog: How Legal Rituals Make and Unmake Persons* (Princeton: Princeton University Press, 2011), xii.

15. Laura Hanft Korobkin, *Criminal Conversations: Sentimentality and Nineteenth-Century Legal Stories of Adultery* (New York: Columbia University Press, 1998).

16. Nan Goodman, *Shifting the Blame: Literature, Law, and the Theory of Accidents in Nineteenth-Century America* (Princeton: Princeton University Press, 1998), 10; and Gregg Crane, *Race, Citizenship, and Law in American Literature* (Cambridge: Cambridge University Press, 2002), 10.

17. Friedman identifies "the impulse to *reform* the law, to make it conform to republican ideals," as one of the most important trends in criminal justice during the early nineteenth century. Friedman, *Crime and Punishment in American History,* 62.

18. *The First Booklist of the Library of Congress: A Facsimile* (Washington, D.C.: Library of Congress, 1981), 5.

19. David Brion Davis, *Homicide in American Fiction, 1798–1860: A Study in Social Values* (Ithaca: Cornell University Press, 1957), 7.

20. Louis P. Masur, *Rites of Execution: Capital Punishment and the Transformation of American Culture, 1776–1865* (New York: Oxford University Press, 1989), 77.

21. See David J. Rothman, *The Discovery of the Asylum: Social Order and Disorder in the New Republic* (1971; rev. ed., Boston: Little, Brown, 1991). Readers might expect to find at this point a reference to the work of Michel Foucault, whose analysis of prisons has (to say the least) profoundly influenced literary criticism. While the present volume relies on multiple histories of penal reform, including *Discipline and Punish,* the questions I ask tend not to center on the issues of knowledge, surveillance, and social control that concern Foucault. The very ubiquity of prison-related stories that I find in nineteenth-century print culture nonetheless serves to confirm Foucault's observations about how the innovative penal regimes of the eighteenth and nineteenth centuries depended on new public awareness of criminal justice practices. Michel Foucault, *Discipline and Punish: The Birth of the Prison,* trans. Alan Sheridan (New York: Vintage Books, 1979).

22. Christopher J. Beshara, "Moral Hospitals, Addled Brains and Cranial Conundrums: Phrenological Rationalisations of the Criminal Mind in Antebellum America," *Australasian Journal of American Studies* 29.1 (2010): 37 and 38.

23. M. B. Sampson, *Rationale of Crime and Its Appropriate Treatment, With Notes and Illustrations by E. W. Farnham* (New York: D. Appleton & Company, 1846), xiii.

24. "The Rationale of Crime," *United States Magazine, and Democratic Review* 20 (January 1847): 50. For a representative negative review, see "Crime, Criminals and Phrenology," *New York Observer and Chronicle,* November 7, 1846.

25. Isaac Ray, *A Treatise on the Medical Jurisprudence of Insanity* (New York: Da Capo Press, 1983). See also John Starrett Hughes, *In the Law's Darkness: Isaac Ray and the Medical Jurisprudence of Insanity in Nineteenth-Century America* (New York: Oceana Publications, 1986).

26. "The Trial of Abner Rogers," *Law Reporter* 7 (February 1845): 449–61.

27. Thomas Maeder, *Crime and Madness: The Origins and Evolution of the Insanity Defense* (New York: Harper & Row, 1985), 33.

28. "Art. I—1. *A Treatise on the Medical Jurisprudence of Insanity,*" *North American Review* 60 (January 1845): 1–37.

29. Robert Ferguson, *Law and Letters in American Culture* (Cambridge: Harvard University Press, 1984).

30. James D. Rice, "The Criminal Trial before and after the Lawyers: Authority, Law, and Culture in Maryland Jury Trials, 1681–1837," *American Journal of Legal History* 40.4 (1996): 459.

31. As I discuss in chapter 2, one finds these criticisms of the judicial system in the pages of the *National Police Gazette.*

32. For discussions of the tug-of-war between judges and juries in antebellum trial courts, see Lawrence M. Friedman, *A History of American Law* (New York: Simon and Schuster, 1978); and Kermit L. Hall, *The Magic Mirror: Law in American History* (New York: Oxford University Press, 1989).

33. Robert M. Cover discusses Massachusetts juries that refused to enforce the Fugitive Slave Law in *Justice Accused: Antislavery and the Judicial Process* (New Haven: Yale University Press, 1975). See chap. 11, "Positivism and Crisis: The Fugitive Slave Law, 1850–1859."

34. Jeannine Marie DeLombard, *Slavery on Trial: Law, Abolitionism, and Print Culture* (Chapel Hill: University of North Carolina Press, 2007), 21. Robert Ferguson similarly refers to "a general loss of faith in the lawyer and his republic of laws." Ferguson, *Law and Letters,* 203.

35. Paul Boyer, *Urban Masses and Moral Order in America, 1820–1920* (Cambridge: Harvard University Press, 1978), 67.

36. Samuel Walker, *Popular Justice: A History of American Criminal Justice* (New York: Oxford University Press, 1980), 56.

37. Edwin Chadwick, *Report on the Sanitary Condition of the Labouring Population of Great Britain* (Edinburgh: Edinburgh University Press, 1965), 198.

38. Henry Mayhew, *London Labour and the London Poor,* 4 vols. (New York: Augustus M. Kelley, 1967).

39. "Art. VI.—Reformatory Schools for the Children of the Perishing and Dangerous Classes," *North American Review* 79 (October 1854): 411.

40. John H. Griscom, M.D., *The Sanitary Condition of the Laboring Population of New York* (New York: Harper & Brothers, 1845), 22 and 23.

41. William E. Channing, D.D., *The Works of William E. Channing,* 6 vols. (Boston: James Munroe and Company, 1848), 4:108 and 100.

42. "Starting in the mid-1820s and quickening in ensuing decades, the pace of change in print culture accelerated, in tandem with dramatic innovations in transportation and communications." Robert A. Gross, "An Extensive Republic," in *A History of the Book in America,* vol. 2, *An Extensive Republic: Print, Culture, and Society in the New Nation, 1790–1840,* ed. Robert A. Gross and Mary Kelley (Chapel Hill: University of North Carolina Press, 2010), 34.

43. Karen Halttunen, *Murder Most Foul: The Killer and the American Gothic Imagination* (Cambridge: Harvard University Press, 1998).

44. Dan Schiller, *Objectivity and the News: The Public and the Rise of Commercial Journalism* (Philadelphia: University of Pennsylvania Press, 1981).

45. Ned Buntline, *The Convict; or, The Conspirators' Victim. A Novel, Written in Prison* (1851; repr., New York: Dick & Fitzgerald, 1863); Eleazer Smith, *Nine Years Among the Convicts; or, Prison Reminiscences* (Boston: J. P. Magee, 1856).

46. Harry Hawser, *Buds and Flowers, of Leisure Hours* (Philadelphia: Geo. W. Loammi Johnson, 1844); George Thompson, *The Prison Bard: or Poems on Various Subjects* (Hartford: William H. Burleigh, 1848).

47. George Thompson, *Prison Life and Reflections; or, A Narrative of the Arrest, Trial, Conviction, Imprisonment, Treatment, Observations, Reflections, and Deliverance of Work, Burr, and Thompson* (New York: Printed by S. W. Benedict, 1848).

48. "Art. V.—Prison Discipline in America," *North American Review* 66 (January 1848): 145–90. Three articles on the subject appeared in the *United States Magazine, and Democratic Review:* "The Clinton State Prison, Clinton County, New York," 17 (November 1845): 345–52; "Prison Discipline," 19 (August 1846): 219–40; and "The Rationale of Crime," 20 (January 1847): 49–55.

49. "Congress," *The Independent*, February 27, 1851, 35.

50. The phrase comes from an article in the periodical press describing discharged convicts. See C. S., "Discharged Convicts. No. VIII," *Prisoner's Friend*, February 25, 1846, 30.

51. Karen A. Weyler, *Empowering Words: Outsiders and Authorship in Early America* (Athens: University of Georgia Press, 2013).

52. The memorandum books of prison chaplain Jared Curtis offer an unvarnished account of interactions between a reformer and the inmates under his charge. Curtis balances sincere belief in the reformative ideal with unsentimental (though generally charitable) assessments of each inmate's personal character. *Buried from the World: Inside the Massachusetts State Prison, 1829–1831; The Memorandum Books of the Rev. Jared Curtis*, ed. Philip F. Gura (Boston: Massachusetts Historical Society, 2001).

53. Russ Castronovo, *Propaganda 1776: Secrets, Leaks, and Revolutionary Communications in Early America* (New York: Oxford University Press, 2014), 60.

54. Ryan Cordell, "Reprinting, Circulation, and the Network Author in Antebellum American Newspapers," *American Literary History* 27.3 (2015): 420.

55. Smith writes: "According to Jefferson's categories, blacks were not endowed with the essential capacity necessary for penitentiary discipline, the power of reflection. . . . In the poetics of the penitentiary, 'individuals of the African variety' could be weakened and killed by solitude, but never redeemed." Smith, *The Prison and the American Imagination*, 104 and 105.

56. DeLombard, *In the Shadow of the Gallows*, 114.

57. Richard Hildreth, *Atrocious Judges: Lives of Judges Infamous as Tools of Tyrants and Instruments of Oppression* (New York: Miller, Orton & Mulligan, 1856), 9; James Fenimore Cooper, *The Ways of the Hour* (Upper Saddle River, NJ: The Gregg Press, 1968), 279.

1. "The Best Side of a Case of Crime"

1. Dan Schiller, *Objectivity and the News: The Public and the Rise of Commercial Journalism* (Philadelphia: University of Pennsylvania Press, 1981), 57.

2. The tone of Bennett's populist railing against the legal system is nicely captured in an article from 1843: "One of the most deplorable features in the administration of justice in the present day, is said to be the fatal influence, which supposed wealth, troops of friends, and assumed respectability, exercise over the movements of our courts of justice, and particularly with grand juries. Petty criminals are pursued with commendable zeal, and even all those who are without influence or connection with Wall Street, seem to receive some attention." "Wall Street Morals and Finance—The Duty of Grand Juries," *New York Herald*, January 11, 1843.

3. David Ray Papke, *Framing the Criminal: Crime, Cultural Work and the Loss of Critical Perspective, 1830–1900* (Hamden, Conn.: Archon Books, 1987), 43.

4. Alexander Saxton, *The Rise and Fall of the White Republic: Class Politics and Mass Culture in Nineteenth-Century America* (London: Verso, 1991), 100.

5. I use the term "artisan republican" (perhaps somewhat loosely) here to denote a style of political affiliation among members of the working and middling classes rooted in values of public good, virtue, independence, citizenship, and equality and opposed to concentrations of wealth in the hands of a social elite associated with corruption, vice, and class

privilege. See Sean Wilentz, *Chants Democratic: New York City and the Rise of the American Working Class, 1788–1850,* 20th anniversary ed. (Oxford: Oxford University Press, 2004), 14. As Wilentz notes, the language of republicanism was subject to appropriation by various groups during the antebellum period in support of conflicting economic and political agendas.

6. James Stanford Bradshaw, "George W. Wisner and the *New York Sun," Journalism History* 6.4 (1979–80): 118.

7. Both quotations are from John D. Stevens, *Sensationalism and the New York Press* (New York: Columbia University Press, 1991), 22–23.

8. Quoted in Hans Bergmann, *God in the Street: New York Writing from the Penny Press to Melville* (Philadelphia: Temple University Press, 1995), 21.

9. Isaac C. Pray, *Memoirs of James Gordon Bennett and His Times* (New York: ARNO & the New York Times, 1970), 183.

10. Papke claims that the *Herald* "abandoned the [Police Court] column in the process of re-gearing itself following the fire" of 1835. Papke, *Framing the Criminal,* 41. But such reporting had obviously been resurrected by the early 1840s, under the title "City Intelligence."

11. "City Intelligence," *New York Herald,* January 19, 1842.

12. "City Intelligence," *New York Herald,* January 6, 1842.

13. Bergmann, *God in the Street,* 22.

14. "City Intelligence," *New York Herald,* June 21, 1842.

15. "City Intelligence," *New York Herald,* April 19, 1842.

16. "City Intelligence," *New York Herald,* January 18, 1842.

17. "City Intelligence," *New York Herald,* February 15 and 28, 1842.

18. Carol Stabile, *White Victims, Black Villains: Gender, Race, and Crime News in U.S. Culture* (New York: Routledge, 2006), 22.

19. "City Intelligence," *New York Herald,* August 7, 1842.

20. "City Intelligence," *New York Herald,* May 27, 1842.

21. "City Intelligence," *New York Herald,* May 28, 1842.

22. That these cases specifically involve Irish immigrants may speak to the perception during this period that the Irish were less "white" than other immigrant groups and therefore somehow akin to African Americans. As David Roediger notes, "In short, it was by no means clear that the Irish were white." David Roediger, *The Wages of Whiteness: Race and the Making of the American Working Class,* rev. ed. (London: Verso, 1999), 134.

23. "City Intelligence," *New York Herald,* January 1, 1842.

24. "City Intelligence," *New York Herald,* January 1 and March 9, 1842.

25. These weekly papers directed primarily at young men described the sexual underworld of New York, reporting on the activities of prostitutes and their patrons. They regarded culturally unsanctioned sexual practices (interracial sex, homosexuality) with particular horror. The editors of a volume on the flash press offer several examples of "the racial stereotyping and vehement racism of the flash press editors." Patricia Cline Cohen, Timothy J. Gilfoyle, and Helen Lefkowitz Horowitz, eds., *The Flash Press: Sporting Male Weeklies in 1840s New York* (Chicago: University of Chicago Press, 2008), 187.

26. Charles Dickens, *American Notes and Pictures from Italy* (London: Oxford University Press, 1966), 92.

27. "City Intelligence," *New York Herald,* March 12, 1842.

28. For example, under the heading "Three Men at a Molasses Jug" in the "City Intelligence" column of February 3, 1842, Chauncey Bailey, Lewis Thurston, and Robert Smith are reported as having been locked up for contriving to steal two gallons of molasses. Two days later, the "Special Sessions" column reports that Bailey was found guilty and sentenced to the penitentiary for sixty days, while the other two defendants were acquitted. "City Intelligence," *New York Herald,* February 3, 1842; and "Special Sessions," *New York Herald,* February 5, 1842.

29. "City News," *Spirit of the Times*, February 7, 1842. George Lippard's early journalism was published on a website sponsored by the University of California, Los Angeles. The site, from which all quotes from Lippard's journalism are taken, has since been removed.

30. "City Police," *Spirit of the Times*, February 26, 1842.

31. "City Police," *Spirit of the Times*, March 3, 1842.

32. Timothy Helwig, "Denying the Wages of Whiteness: The Racial Politics of George Lippard's Working-Class Protest," *American Studies* 47.3–4 (2006): 88.

33. "City Police," *Spirit of the Times*, March 19, 1842.

34. Schiller, *Objectivity and the News*, 49.

35. "Our Talisman, No. 2," *Spirit of the Times*, January 12, 1842.

36. Helwig, "Denying the Wages of Whiteness," 93.

37. "Our Talisman, No. 3," *Spirit of the Times*, January 18, 1842.

38. "Our Talisman, No. 1," *Spirit of the Times*, January 11, 1842.

39. "Our Talisman, No. 9," *Spirit of the Times*, February 17, 1842.

40. "Our Talisman, No. 4," "Our Talisman, No. 5," and "Our Talisman, No. 6," *Spirit of the Times*, January 20, 22, and 26, 1842.

41. George Lippard, *The Quaker City; or, The Monks of Monk Hall*, ed. David S. Reynolds (Amherst: University of Massachusetts Press, 1995), 205.

42. George Lippard, *The Empire City; or, New York by Night and Day, Its Aristocracy and Its Dollars* (1850; repr., Philadelphia: T. B. Peterson & Brothers, 1864), 53.

43. Lippard, *The Quaker City*, 339.

44. Reynolds, introduction, ibid., xl.

45. George Lippard, *The Nazarene; or, The Last of the Washingtons* (1846; repr., Philadelphia: T. B. Peterson, 1854), 147.

46. Lippard, *The Empire City*, 147.

47. Walt Whitman, *Leaves of Grass*, 150th anniversary ed., ed. David S. Reynolds (New York: Oxford University Press, 2005), 10.

48. "City Intelligence," *Brooklyn Daily Eagle*, July 13, 1846.

49. Thomas L. Brasher, *Whitman as Editor of the "Brooklyn Daily Eagle"* (Detroit: Wayne State University Press, 1970), 141.

50. "Local Intelligence," *Brooklyn Daily Eagle*, February 27, 1847.

51. "Local Intelligence," *Brooklyn Daily Eagle*, October 22, 1846. According to Whitman's report, the woman petitioned the court successfully for support of her child by the defendant.

52. "City Intelligence," *Brooklyn Daily Eagle*, July 15, 1846. Whitman said this by way of explaining an earlier, inaccurate report in the *Eagle* regarding two married women who had run off together with their (also married) lovers.

53. "City Intelligence," *Brooklyn Daily Eagle*, September 7, 1846.

54. Brasher, *Whitman as Editor of the "Brooklyn Daily Eagle,"* 164.

55. "City Intelligence," *Brooklyn Daily Eagle*, March 9 and 11, 1846. In the second article, Whitman corrects the man's name to Richard Moore, but he is clearly referring to the same person.

56. "Local Intelligence," *Brooklyn Daily Eagle*, August 7 and 9, 1847. This was not the only instance of Whitman relegating race to parentheses. He described Eliza Underhill as "(colored)" in a report of black-on-white crime. "Local Intelligence," *Brooklyn Daily Eagle*, December 26, 1846.

57. "Local Intelligence," *Brooklyn Daily Eagle*, November 30 and December 1, 1847.

58. "Infernal Outrage!" *Brooklyn Daily Eagle*, April 3, 1846. This paragraph on the rape of a white woman actually appears above the day's "City Intelligence" column. "Local Intelligence," *Brooklyn Daily Eagle*, December 26, 1846.

59. Although Whitman did not sensationalize (or even discuss) interracial sexuality in his *Eagle* crime reports, he did depict an interracial marriage (one that disastrously ended in the Creole wife's suicide) in his 1842 temperance novel *Franklin Evans*. Walt Whitman,

Franklin Evans, or, The Inebriate: A Tale of the Times, ed. Christopher Castiglia and Glenn Handler (Durham: Duke University Press, 2007).

60. Jerome Loving attributes to Whitman a change of heart about African Americans dating from December 1847, near the end of his editorial tenure with the *Eagle* and after his attendance at an abolitionist lecture: "Whitman, it seems, had suddenly broken away from the nineteenth-century stereotypes about the slave as less than human to see blacks in the context of citizenry and the social roles he had championed for whites in his editorials throughout the 1840s." Jerome Loving, *Walt Whitman: The Song of Himself* (Berkeley: University of California Press, 1999), 112. A rare use of the word "nigger" to describe an African American appears in one earlier column, where Whitman describes "a crazy nigger who called himself Sambo Poney, a waif and stray from Squankum, N.J. [who] got into the clutches of the police, and steps were taken to send him back." "City Intelligence," *Brooklyn Daily Eagle,* September 11, 1846.

61. "City Intelligence," *Brooklyn Daily Eagle,* June 11, 1846.

62. "City Intelligence," *Brooklyn Daily Eagle,* June 17, 1846.

63. "City Intelligence," *Brooklyn Daily Eagle,* June 5, 1846.

64. "Local Intelligence," *Brooklyn Daily Eagle,* April 21, 1847.

65. For example, Whitman reports, "Officer Combs yesterday arrested a German, named George Fruch . . . who was charged with having threatened the life of his wife." Or, a few days later, "A party of Germans, men and women, were yesterday arrested for taking fruit from an orchard at Gowanus." This neutral tone was characteristic of Whitman's handling of immigrant violators. "City Intelligence," *Brooklyn Daily Eagle,* October 7 and 12, 1846.

66. "Local Intelligence," *Brooklyn Daily Eagle,* August 4, 1847.

67. "Local Intelligence," *Brooklyn Daily Eagle,* September 16, 1847. Whitman first chronicled the young man's discovery by his sister in the "Local Intelligence" column of September 14.

68. "Oppress not the Hireling!" *Brooklyn Daily Eagle,* April 3, 1846.

69. "City Intelligence," *Brooklyn Daily Eagle,* April 13 and June 11, 1846.

70. "Local Intelligence," *Brooklyn Daily Eagle,* October 14, 1847.

71. "City Intelligence," *Brooklyn Daily Eagle,* April 24, 1846.

72. Brasher covers Whitman's support of the temperance movement in *Whitman as Editor of the "Brooklyn Daily Eagle,"* 157–61. The version of *Franklin Evans* published in the *Eagle* actually downplayed the work's original temperance theme. Although Whitman late in life disavowed his novel as "damned rot," he apparently found the temperance movement of the 1840s attractive for its populist message of working-class uplift. Quoted in David S. Reynolds, *Walt Whitman's America: A Cultural Biography* (New York: Alfred A. Knopf, 1995), 97.

73. According to Christopher Castiglia and Glenn Handler, "the Washingtonians were led by working men and women who were themselves suffering drinkers." Castiglia and Handler, introduction to Whitman, *Franklin Evans,* xxxiv.

74. "City Intelligence," *Brooklyn Daily Eagle,* April 13, 1846.

75. "City Intelligence," *Brooklyn Daily Eagle,* April 18, 1846.

76. "Prisons," *Brooklyn Daily Eagle,* June 30, 1846.

77. "Memorial—Capital Punishment," *Brooklyn Daily Eagle,* January 5, 1847.

78. "City Intelligence," *Brooklyn Daily Eagle,* August 11, 1846. Whitman ungenerously went on to complain that conditions were "too *luxurious,*" a situation that would be remedied by the construction of a "projected workhouse."

79. "The Officers of Our State Prisons," *Brooklyn Daily Eagle,* March 10, 1846. For Whitman's support of shooting home burglars, see "Local Intelligence," *Brooklyn Daily Eagle,* October 28, 1846.

80. M. B. Samspon, *Rationale of Crime and Its Appropriate Treatment* (New York: D. Appleton & Company, 1846), 71.

81. "Notices of New Books," *Brooklyn Daily Eagle,* November 9, 1846.

82. "The Officers of Our State Prisons," *Brooklyn Daily Eagle,* March 10, 1846.
83. "A Letter from Sing Sing," *Brooklyn Daily Eagle,* May 1, 1846. Whitman also defended Farnham in an editorial a few months later. "The Attacks on Mrs. Farnham," *Brooklyn Daily Eagle,* September 2, 1846.
84. "Local Intelligence," *Brooklyn Daily Eagle,* September 9, 1847.
85. The two brief quotes are from "Local Intelligence," *Brooklyn Daily Eagle,* October 27 and December 13, 1847.
86. "Local Intelligence," *Brooklyn Daily Eagle,* October 7, 1847.
87. "Local Intelligence," *Brooklyn Daily Eagle,* November 22, 1847.
88. "City Intelligence," *Brooklyn Daily Eagle,* June 1, 1846.
89. "City Intelligence," *Brooklyn Daily Eagle,* June 3, 1846.
90. "City Intelligence," *Brooklyn Daily Eagle,* June 20, 1846.
91. "City Intelligence," *Brooklyn Daily Eagle,* October 10, 1846.
92. "Local Intelligence," *Brooklyn Daily Eagle,* November 13, 1846.
93. "Local Intelligence," *Brooklyn Daily Eagle,* April 30, 1847.
94. Whitman, *Leaves of Grass,* 31, 17, 46, 75.
95. Ibid., 16.
96. Paul Christian Jones, *Against the Gallows: Antebellum American Writers and the Movement to Abolish Capital Punishment* (Iowa City: University of Iowa Press, 2011), 124. Jones mentions, for example, the poems "You Felons on Trial in Courts" from the 1867 *Leaves of Grass* and "The Singer in the Prison" from the 1871–72 edition. Whereas Jones attributes the poet's sympathy for criminals to his involvement in the movement against capital punishment, Whitman's advocacy of prison reform in his newspaper writing was probably as influential in shaping his thoughts on criminality.

2. Race, Vigilantism, and the Diffusion of Civic Authority

1. Nathaniel Hawthorne, *The Blithedale Romance,* vol. 3 of *The Centenary Edition of the Works of Nathaniel Hawthorne* (Columbus: Ohio State University Press, 1964), 214–15.
2. Karen Halttunen, *Murder Most Foul: The Killer and the American Gothic Imagination* (Cambridge: Harvard University Press, 1998), 36 and 96.
3. Dan Schiller, *Objectivity and the News: The Public and the Rise of Commercial Journalism* (Philadelphia: University of Pennsylvania Press, 1981), 134–36 (police corruption), 137–38 (executive pardons), and 139 (judges' compromises with felons).
4. "Corruption of Police Officers," *National Police Gazette,* August 14, 1847.
5. Probius, "The Probity of Grand Juries," *National Police Gazette,* July 3, 1847.
6. Schiller writes, "The penny journals appropriated vast reaches of republican rhetoric." Schiller, *Objectivity and the News,* 48.
7. Isaac C. Pray, *Memoirs of James Gordon Bennett and His Times* (1855; repr., New York: Arno Press and the New York Times, 1970), 301.
8. "The Present Bailing System," *National Police Gazette,* July 31, 1847.
9. Timothy J. Gilfoyle, "'America's Greatest Criminal Barracks': The Tombs and the Experience of Criminal Justice in New York City, 1838–1897," *Journal of Urban History* 29.5 (2003): 543.
10. "Our Criminal Courts," *New York Daily Times,* December 7, 1855.
11. Allen Steinberg, *The Transformation of Criminal Justice: Philadelphia, 1800–1880* (Chapel Hill: University of North Carolina Press, 1989), 162.
12. Harry Hawser, "Our City Not a Paradise," in *Buds and Flowers, of Leisure Hours* (Philadlphia: Geo. W. Loammi Johnson, 1844), 56.
13. Mark DeWolfe Howe, "Juries as Judges of Criminal Law," *Harvard Law Review* 52.4 (1939): 615.
14. Lawrence M. Friedman, *A History of American Law* (New York: Simon and Schuster, 1978), 251.

15. Kermit L. Hall, *The Magic Mirror: Law in American History* (New York: Oxford University Press, 1989), 173.

16. Clay S. Conrad, *Jury Nullification: The Evolution of a Doctrine* (Washington, D.C.: Cato Institute, 2014), 65.

17. Robert M. Cover, *Justice Accused: Antislavery and the Judicial Process* (New Haven: Yale University Press, 1975).

18. Conrad, *Jury Nullification*, 77.

19. Lysander Spooner, *An Essay on the Trial By Jury* (Boston: John P. Jewett and Company, 1852), 10.

20. Richard Hildreth, *Atrocious Judges: Lives of Judges Infamous as Tools of Tyrants and Instruments of Oppression* (New York: Miller, Orton & Mulligan, 1856), 34.

21. Ned Buntline, *The Mysteries and Miseries of New York* (1848; repr., New York: W. F. Burgess, 1849), pt. 5, 126.

22. Ned Buntline, *The Convict; or, The Conspirators' Victim* (1851; repr., New York: Dick & Fitzgerald, 1863).

23. James Fenimore Cooper, *The Ways of the Hour* (Upper Saddle River, NJ: Gregg Press, 1968), 143, 133, and 140.

24. Francis Bowen, "Art. V.—*The Ways of the Hour; A Tale*," *North American Review* 71 (July 1850): 121–35; "The Administration of the Law," *Western Law Journal* 3 (October 1850): 1–24. Both reviewers found horse-shedding and pillowing interesting enough to quote at length from the chapter in which the practices appear.

25. L. Ray Gunn, "Politics and Policy," chap. 23 in *The Empire State: A History of New York*, ed. Milton M. Klein (Ithaca: Cornell University Press with the New York State Historical Association, 2001), 392.

26. Cooper, *The Ways of the Hour*, 133.

27. John P. McWilliams Jr., *Political Justice in a Republic: James Fenimore Cooper's America* (Berkeley: University of California Press, 1972), 380.

28. Cooper, *The Ways of the Hour*, 476.

29. Robert Ferguson, *Law and Letters in American Culture* (Cambridge: Harvard University Press, 1984), 203.

30. Friedman makes the same point: "This [uncertainty over whether legally codified criminal penalties would be carried out] was one reason for the periodic outbursts of lynching and vigilantes." Friedman, *A History of American Law*, 254.

31. Leonard L. Richards, *"Gentlemen of Property and Standing": Anti-Abolition Mobs in Jacksonian America* (New York: Oxford University Press, 1970).

32. Abraham Lincoln, "The Perpetuation of Our Political Institutions," quoted in Richard Maxwell Brown, *Strain of Violence: Historical Studies of American Violence and Vigilantism* (New York: Oxford University Press, 1975), 3.

33. David Grimsted, *American Mobbing, 1828–1861: Toward Civil War* (New York: Oxford University Press, 1998), 109.

34. According to Christopher Waldrep: "In the 1830s, opponents of slavery launched a campaign to label episodes of white southerners' most murderous racial violence as lynchings. Abolitionists worked to redefine *lynching* and to shift ordinary northerners' views of white southerners." Christopher Waldrep, "Word and Deed: The Language of Lynching, 1820–1953," in *Lethal Imagination: Violence and Brutality in American History*, ed. Michael A. Bellesiles (New York: New York University Press, 1999), 236.

35. P.P., "Uses and Abuses of Lynch Law," *American Whig Review* 5 (May 1850): 462.

36. Brown, *Strain of Violence*, 94.

37. Mary Floyd Williams, *History of the San Francisco Committee of Vigilance of 1851: A Study of Social Control on the California Frontier in the Days of the Gold Rush* (1921; repr., New York: Da Capo Press, 1969), 144–45.

38. Ibid., 205.

39. An article in *The Independent* maintained that every one of San Francisco's five daily

papers "approved and supported the Vigilance Committee from the first." S.H.W., "Letter from California," *The Independent . . . Devoted to the Consideration of Politics, Social and Economic Tendencies,* September 4, 1851. Historian Mary Floyd Williams agrees, noting that "the newspapers united in approving the work of the Committee." Williams, *History of the San Francisco Committee of Vigilance,* 217.

40. Christopher Waldrep, *The Many Faces of Judge Lynch: Extralegal Violence and Punishment in America* (New York: Palgrave Macmillan, 2002), 61.

41. Of the vigilante groups operating in the West in the 1850s, Friedman writes, "Some of them, hungry for legitimacy, parodied the regular written law; they had their own 'judges' and 'juries,' their own quick and summary trials." Friedman, *A History of American Law,* 506.

42. Frank Soulé, John H. Gihon, M.D., and James Nisbet, *The Annals of San Francisco* (New York: D. Appleton & Company, 1854), 318 and 350.

43. Orestes Brownson attacked "the doctrine that in the mob . . . resides the power which creates legislatures and courts of justice" and worried that the spirit animating the San Francisco Committee of Vigilance was "strong, fearfully strong, in our midst." "Art. III.," *Brownson's Quarterly Review* 5 (October 1851): 494–95.

44. David Walker, *David Walker's Appeal, In Four Articles,* ed. Charles M. Wiltse (New York: Hill and Wang, 1965), 8.

45. The quotation is from J. Clay Smith Jr., *Emancipation: The Making of the Black Lawyer, 1844–1944* (Philadelphia: University of Pennsylvania Press, 1993), 94; see also 96 (Allen's appointment as justice of the peace and Morris admitted to the bar) and 392 (Vashon).

46. Jeannine Marie DeLombard, *Slavery on Trial: Law, Abolitionism, and Print Culture* (Chapel Hill: University of North Carolina Press, 2007), 130.

47. Smith, *Emancipation,* 2.

48. Detailing all three cases of slave rescues, Stanley W. Campbell notes that African Americans "would continue to play a prominent part in almost every instance where a fugitive slave was rescued or where attempts were made to effect a rescue." Stanley W. Campbell, *The Slave Catchers: Enforcement of the Fugitive Slave Law, 1850–1860* (Chapel Hill: University of North Carolina Press, 1968), 151.

49. "Congress," *The Independent,* February 27, 1851, 35.

50. Wai-Chee Dimock, *Residues of Justice: Literature, Law, Philosophy* (Berkeley: University of California Press, 1996), 176.

51. George Lippard, *The Empire City; or, New York by Night and by Day* (1850; repr., Philadelphia: T. B. Peterson & Brothers, 1864). Subsequent references to this edition are given parenthetically in the text.

52. George Lippard, *New York: Its Upper Ten and Lower Million* (Cincinnati: H. M. Rulison, 1853), 162. Subsequent references are given parenthetically in the text.

53. This reader is explicitly white and male: the narrator charges him with hypocrisy in denouncing slavery while ignoring the plight of "white men, (nearer to you in equality of organization certainly than black men)" who work in factories. Lippard, *New York,* 206.

54. Jeannine Marie DeLombard, *In the Shadow of the Gallows: Race, Crime, and American Civic Identity* (Philadelphia: University of Pennsylvania Press, 2012).

55. William J. Mahar notes that various mock lectures and sermons, including burlesques of courtroom rhetoric and political oratory, were "important ingredients" in the minstrel repertory. William J. Mahar, *Behind the Burnt Cork Mask: Early Blackface Minstrelsy and Antebellum American Popular Culture* (Urbana: University of Illinois Press, 1999), 59.

56. For a reading of this scene crediting Lippard with a progressive racial politics, see Timothy Helwig, "Denying the Wages of Whiteness: The Racial Politics of George Lippard's Working-Class Protest," *American Studies* 47.3–4 (2006): 87–111.

57. One critic's observation that *The Slave* "has never received the attention it deserves" remains more or less true, forty years after it was made. Nicholas Canady Jr., "The Antislavery Novel Prior to 1852 and Hildreth's *The Slave* (1836)," *CLA Journal* 17.2 (1973–74): 178. Three more recent studies, however, have focused on issues of race, sexuality, and

nationalism in Hildreth's fiction: Werner Sollors, *Neither Black Nor White Yet Both: Thematic Explorations of Interracial Literature* (Oxford: Oxford University Press, 1997); Cassandra Jackson, *Barriers between Us: Interracial Sex in Nineteenth-Century American Literature* (Bloomington: Indiana University Press, 2004); and Eve Allegra Raimon, *The "Tragic Mulatta" Revisited: Race and Nationalism in Nineteenth-Century Antislavery Fiction* (New Brunswick: Rutgers University Press, 2004).

58. Mark Randall Gruner, "Letters of Blood: Antislavery Fiction and the Problem of Law" (Ph.D. diss., University of California at Los Angeles, 1993).

59 Donald E. Emerson, *Richard Hildreth*, Johns Hopkins University Studies in Historical and Political Science (Baltimore: Johns Hopkins University Press, 1946), 124 and 126.

60. Arthur M. Schlesinger Jr., "The Problem of Richard Hildreth," *New England Quarterly* 13.2 (1940): 223–45.

61. Emerson, *Richard Hildreth*, 42. On sympathy for the judiciary in the *Boston Atlas*, see 46.

62. Richard Hildreth, *The White Slave; or, Memoirs of a Fugitive* (1852; repr., New York: Arno Press and the New York Times, 1969), 195. All quotes from *The Slave* and *The White Slave* come from this edition: when he published *The White Slave*, Hildreth merely added chapters to *The Slave*. Subsequent references are given parenthetically in the text.

63. Jean Fagan Yellin notes that the "landscape through which Archy searches is the America of 1835 and 1836," documenting several historical events dramatized in the novel. Jean Fagan Yellin, *The Intricate Knot: Black Figures in American Literature, 1776–1863* (New York: New York University Press, 1972), 109.

64. Hildreth wrote in an introduction to an 1856 edition of the novel that it was the success of *Uncle Tom's Cabin* that prompted a Boston bookseller to inquire about publishing a new edition of *The Slave*, "at whose suggestion the concluding portion of it, which the author had long revolved in his mind, was now written." Richard Hildreth, *Archie Moore: The White Slave; or, Memoirs of a Fugitive* (New York: Augustus M. Kelley, 1971), xxi. (Hildreth inconsistently spelled his protagonist's name as both Archie and Archy.)

65. David Brion Davis, *Homicide in American Fiction, 1798–1860: A Study in Social Values* (Ithaca: Cornell University Press, 1957), 284.

66. Yellin notes the similarity of this incident to the case of Sharkey, who was himself a justice of the peace in Mississippi. Yellin, *The Intricate Knot*, 110. For a discussion of Sharkey's persecution at the hands of a vigilance committee, see Clement Eaton, *The Freedom-of-Thought Struggle in the Old South* (New York: Harper Torchbooks, 1964), 98–99.

67. Richard Hildreth, "Has Slavery in the United States a Legal Basis?" *Massachusetts Quarterly Review* 3 (June 1848): 291.

68. Emerson, *Richard Hildreth*, 130.

69. Gary L. Collison, "The Boston Vigilance Committee: A Reconsideration," *Historical Journal of Massachusetts* 12.2 (1984): 112.

70. Gruner, "Letters of Blood," 40.

71. It is worth noting that jury nullification traditionally applied to criminal, not civil, prosecutions. Montgomery is not the victim of government tyranny. Despite this qualification, I think Hildreth's faith in the institution of the jury remains a key element of the scene. Agrippa's later incarnation as a representative of the government (a deputy marshal) may help to support such a reading.

72. Gary Collison, "'This Flagitious Offense': Daniel Webster and the Shadrach Rescue Cases, 1851–1852," *New England Quarterly* 68.4 (1995): 609–25.

73. Hildreth, "Has Slavery in the United States a Legal Basis?" 274.

74. Biographer Martha M. Pingel regards Hildreth's confidence that "civilization is on the whole progressing" as a fundamental belief underlying his philosophical writings, especially the *Theory of Morals* and *Theory of Politics*. Martha M. Pingel, *An American Utilitarian: Richard Hildreth as a Philosopher* (New York: Columbia University Press, 1948), 10.

75. Gregg Crane, *Race, Citizenship, and Law in American Literature* (Cambridge: Cambridge University Press, 2002), 123.

76. Alexander Saxton, *The Rise and Fall of the White Republic: Class Politics and Mass Culture in Nineteenth-Century America* (London: Verso, 1990), 239.

77. Stowe's plantation court is not unlike the maroon community in *The White Slave:* "There are certain rules for the order and well-being of the plantation, which all agree to abide by; and, in all offences, the man is tried by a jury of his peers." In *Dred,* however, the plantation court is set up on the initiative of benevolent slave owner Edward Clayton, and is somewhat condescendingly credited with manifesting "a good deal of shrewdness and sense" alongside "a good many droll scenes." Harriet Beecher Stowe, *Dred* (New York: Penguin Books, 2000), 309. Delany invests his Cuban Grand Council (a legislative rather than a judicial body), in contrast, with considerable dignity, but of course it acts outside of a U.S. context and does not envision the same level of cross-racial cooperation as one finds in *The White Slave.* Martin R. Delany, *Blake; or, The Huts of America* (Boston: Beacon Press, 1970), esp. chap. 61, "The Grand Council."

78. Smith, *Emancipation,* 98.

79. Derrick Bell writes of the *Brown* decision, "Again and again, perceived self-interest by whites rather than the racial injustices suffered by blacks has been the major motivation in racial-remediation policies." Derrick Bell, *Silent Covenants: Brown v. Board of Education and the Unfulfilled Hopes for Racial Reform* (New York: Oxford University Press, 2004), 59.

80. Black abolitionist William C. Nell discussed precedents for African American citizenship in a variety of contexts, including examples of black men who had obtained passports, voted, and practiced as attorneys. William C. Nell, *The Colored Patriots of the American Revolution* (New York: Arno Press and the New York Times, 1968). See chap. 1 of the appended section "Conditions and Prospects of Colored Americans," 311–42.

3. Carceral Conversions

1. William Gilmore Simms, *Martin Faber; The Story of a Criminal and Other Tales* (1837; repr., New York: Arno Press, 1976), viii.

2. Ibid., 150.

3. Nina Baym, *Novels, Readers, and Reviewers: Responses to Fiction in Antebellum America* (Ithaca: Cornell University Press, 1984), 177.

4. Simms, *Martin Faber,* x.

5. It must be noted that in his very influential analysis, Michel Foucault disputes the idea that penal reform had its origins in a newly refined sensibility with regard to torture, imputing it instead to industrial capitalism's requirement for stricter social control: "The true objective of the reform movement, even in its most general formulations, was not so much to establish a new right to punish based on more equitable principles, as to set up a new 'economy' of the power to punish, to assure its better distribution, so that it should be neither too concentrated at certain privileged points, nor too divided between opposing authorities; so that it should be distributed in homogenous circuits capable of operating everywhere, in a continuous way, down to the finest grain of the social body." Michel Foucault, *Discipline and Punish: The Birth of the Prison,* trans. Alan Sheridan (New York: Vintage Books, 1979), 80.

6. David J. Rothman, *The Discovery of the Asylum: Social Order and Disorder in the New Republic,* rev. ed. (Boston: Little, Brown, 1990), xxv. For a dissenting view that stresses the European origins of the penitentiary concept and compares incarceration with slavery as analogous forms of coerced labor in early America, see Adam Jay Hirsch, *The Rise of the Penitentiary: Prisons and Punishment in Early America* (New Haven: Yale University Press, 1992). A more recent account that stresses the concept of "contractual penal servitude" (58), or contracting prison labor out to private corporations, is Rebecca M. McLennan, *The Crisis of Imprisonment: Protest, Politics, and the Making of the American Penal State, 1776–1941* (Cambridge: Cambridge University Press, 2008).

7. Gustave de Beaumont and Alexis de Tocqueville, *On the Penitentiary System in the United States and Its Application in France* (Carbondale: Southern Illinois University Press, 1964), 84.

8. Rothman, *The Discovery of the Asylum,* 87.

9. McLennan, *The Crisis of Imprisonment,* 67.

10. Martineau wrote of the Pennsylvania system, "I am persuaded that this is the best method of punishment which has yet been tried." Harriet Martineau, *Society in America,* vol. 3 (London: Saunders and Otley, 1837), 182. Marryat agreed, writing, "The best system is that acted upon in the Penitentiary at Philadelphia, where there is solitary confinement, but with labour and exercise." Capt. Marryat, C.B., *A Diary in America; with Remarks on its Institutions,* vol. 2 (Philadelphia: Carey & Hart, 1839), 54. In his comments excoriating the cruelty of the Pennsylvania system, Dickens offered a backhanded endorsement of the Auburn system: "All the instances of reformation that were mentioned to me, were of a kind that might have been—and I have no doubt whatever, in my own mind, would have been—equally well brought about by the Silent System." Charles Dickens, *American Notes* (London: Oxford University Press, 1966), 110.

11. Martineau's *Society in America* was published in New York by its English publishers, Saunders and Otley, in 1837 and reprinted by Thomas W. White in Richmond, Virginia, in 1838. A number of American publishers, including Carey & Hart of Philadelphia and Appleton of New York, issued editions of Marryat's *Society in America* shortly after its London publication. Harper & Brothers and Lea and Blanchard, among other publishers, issued editions of Dickens's *American Notes* in 1842.

12. "The Clinton State Prison, Clinton County, New York," *United States Magazine, and Democratic Review* 17 (November 1845): 345.

13. Martineau, *Society in America,* 3:181.

14. Dickens, *American Notes,* 52.

15. Orlando F. Lewis, *The Development of American Prisons and Prison Customs, 1776–1845* (Montclair, N.J.: Patterson Smith, 1967), 236.

16. "Art. V.—Prison Discipline in America," *North American Review* 66 (January 1848): 145–90.

17. The three articles are "The Clinton State Prison, Clinton County, New York," *United States Magazine, and Democratic Review* 17 (November 1845): 345–52; "Prison Discipline," 19 (August 1846): 219–40; and "The Rationale of Crime," 20 (January 1847): 49–55.

18. Lewis, *The Development of American Prisons,* 227.

19. W. David Lewis, *From Newgate to Dannemora: The Rise of the Penitentiary in New York, 1796–1848* (Ithaca: Cornell University Press, 1965), 124.

20. Emma C. Embury, "The Interesting Stranger; or, Diamond Cut Diamond," *Graham's Lady's and Gentleman's Magazine* 19 (November 1841): 205–9.

21. Negley K. Teeters and John D. Shearer, *The Prison at Philadelphia, Cherry Hill; The Separate System of Penal Discipline, 1829–1913* (New York: Columbia University Press, 1957), 196 and 200.

22. Daniel A. Cohen, *Pillars of Salt, Monuments of Grace: New England Crime Literature and the Origins of American Popular Culture, 1674–1860* (New York: Oxford University Press, 1993), 167.

23. C. D. Cleveland, "Religious and Moral Instruction in Philadelphia County Prison," *Pennsylvania Journal of Prison Discipline and Philanthropy* 1 (January 1845): 79–80.

24. "A Letter from Sing Sing," *Brooklyn Daily Eagle,* May 1, 1846.

25. "Murderers in the Massachusetts State Prison," *Prisoner's Friend* 1 (September 1845): 23.

26. George Baker, "The New York State Prison," *Prisoner's Friend* 9 (May 1849): 380.

27. "A Baptism in Prison," *New York Evangelist,* January 16, 1841, 12.

28. H. Green, "Charlestown and State Prison," *Christian Reflector,* March 23, 1842.

29. "Universalism in the Murderer's Cell," *Trumpet and Universalist Magazine,* June 4, 1842.

30. O., "Who, On Earth, Should Despair! Reading a Tract the Means of Hopeful Conversion," *New York Evangelist,* November 14, 1840, 183.

31. Mrs. C. Latham, "The Jailer's Daughter," *Godey's Magazine and Lady's Book* 35 (July 1847): 27 and 29.

32. Martineau, *Society in America*, 3:184.

33. Emma C. Embury, "The Prisoner: A Sketch," *Godey's Lady's Book, and Ladies' American Magazine* 21 (October 1840): 148–49.

34. "Lives of the Felons: No. 11, John A. Murrell the Great Western Land Pirate," *National Police Gazette*, April 24, 1847, 258.

35. Marryat, *A Diary in America*, 2:55.

36. "The Convict's Daughter," *Godey's Magazine and Lady's Book* 30 (January 1845): 21–27.

37. J., "The Solitary Convict," *Godey's Magazine and Lady's Book* 33 (July 1846): 30.

38. Herman Melville, *Typee: A Peep at Polynesian Life* (New York: Library of America, 1982), 150.

39. Quoted in Lewis, *The Development of American Prisons*, 73.

40. The warden in question was Gershom Powers. Quoted in Lewis, *From Newgate to Dannemora*, 115. The chaplain at Sing Sing in the 1840s, John Luckey, wrote of the complete isolation of prisoners in place when he began working at the prison in 1839: "No communications were allowed between the prisoners and their friends, neither personally nor by letter; and so thoroughly was this arrangement carried out that a convict from his commitment to his release was as completely cut off from his family as if dead." John Luckey, *Life in Sing Sing Prison, As Seen in a Twelve Years' Chaplaincy* (New York: N. Tibblas & Co., 1860), 18.

41. The story has enjoyed a small renaissance of critical attention, specifically for its examination of citizenship and nationhood. In separate treatments, Robert S. Levine and Carrie Hyde both note how the story traces the origins of patriotism/nationalism in dispossession, with implications for the citizenship of onetime outcasts. Robert S. Levine, "Edward Everett Hale's and Sutton E. Griggs's Men Without a Country," in *Jim Crow, Literature, and the Legacy of Sutton E. Griggs*, ed. Tess Chakkalakal and Kenneth W. Warren (Athens: University of Georgia Press, 2013), 69–87; Carrie Hyde, "Outcast Patriotism: The Dilemma of Negative Instruction in 'The Man Without a Country,'" *ELH* 7 (2010): 915–39.

42. John R. Adams, *Edward Everett Hale* (Boston: Twayne Publishers, 1977), 27.

43. According to the Internet Movie Database, four film versions of the story were made, the latest a 1973 television adaptation.

44. Edward Everett Hale, *The Man Without a Country* (Boston: Roberts Brothers, 1897), 23 and 26. Subsequent references are given parenthetically in the text.

45. In one exposé, a former inmate of Auburn Prison charges that a warden withheld a pardon from an inmate for three years after its issue because the warden suspected the inmate of an "intrigue" with his (the warden's) daughter. This inmate exposes numerous abuses at the prison, including torture of rebellious inmates, poor diet, negligent medical care, and false bookkeeping to defraud the state. W. A. Coffey, *Inside Out; Or, An Interior View of the New-York State Prison* (New York: James Costigan, 1823).

46. Brook Thomas attributes the story's popularity in part to readers' sympathy with Nolan as a victim of excessive punishment. Brook Thomas, *Civic Myths: A Law-and-Literature Approach to Citizenship* (Chapel Hill: University of North Carolina Press, 2007), 98.

47. For an excellent account of the voluminous wartime literature, see Alice Fahs, *The Imagined Civil War: Popular Literature of the North and South, 1861–1865* (Chapel Hill: University of North Carolina Press, 2001).

48. E. D. E. N. Southworth, *The Hidden Hand; or, Capitola the Madcap* (New Brunswick: Rutgers University Press, 1988), 215. Subsequent references are given parenthetically in the text.

49. Rebecca Harding Davis, "Life in the Iron-Mills," *Atlantic Monthly* 7 (April 1861): 445. Subsequent references are given parenthetically in the text.

50. Henry D. Thoreau, *Walden,* ed. J. Lyndon Shanley (Princeton: Princeton University Press, 1971), 74 and 76.

51. It was around this period that Emerson, too, began to look with renewed skepticism at the premises of penal reform, even as he adapted the idea of the solitary individual in a cell as an idealized image of the contemplative life. In the words of Caleb Smith, "Emerson's writing engages the ideology of prison reform, and his protest matters: reclaimed as an inversion of the penitentiary model of correction, 'Self-Reliance' invites us toward a renewed critique of that model, even as Emerson yields to his faith in some of its fundamental notions." Caleb Smith, "Emerson and Incarceration," *American Literature* 78.2 (2006): 226.

52. Henry David Thoreau, "Resistance to Civil Government," in *Reform Papers,* ed. Wendell Glick (Princeton: Princeton University Press, 1973), 80 (dimensions of the jail), 83 (meals), and 82 (verses and reform tracts).

53. Thoreau, "Resistance to Civil Government," 82–83.

54. Jason Haslam, "'They Locked the Door on My Meditations': Thoreau and the Prison House of Identity," *Genre* 35.3–4 (2002): 466.

55. Nathaniel Hawthorne, *The Scarlet Letter,* Centenary Edition, vol. 1 (Columbus: Ohio State University Press), 1962, 47. Subsequent references are given parenthetically in the text.

56. Hirsch, *The Rise of the Penitentiary,* 7.

57. Foucault remarks on the speed with which prisons came to seem inevitable: "One can understand the self-evident character that prison punishment very soon assumed. In the first years of the nineteenth century, people were still aware of its novelty; and yet it appeared so bound up and at such a deep level with the very functioning of society that it banished into oblivion all the other punishments that the eighteenth-century reformers had imagined. It seemed to have no alternative, as if carried along by the very movement of history." Foucault, *Discipline and Punish,* 232.

58. Robert Shulman, "The Artist in the Slammer: Hawthorne, Melville, Poe and the Prison of Their Times," *Modern Language Studies* 14.1 (1984): 82.

59. Caleb H. Snow, *History of Boston* (Boston: Abel Bowen, 1825), 116. Hawthorne's debt to Snow (among others) is discussed in Charles Ryskamp, "The New England Sources of *The Scarlet Letter,*" *American Literature* 31.3 (1959): 257–72.

60. Drawing from the *Records of the Governor and Colony of the Massachusetts Bay,* edited by Nathaniel Shurtleff and published in 1853–54, Hirsch notes that Puritan authorities opened a jail in Boston in 1635. Obviously, given the publication date, these records were not available to Hawthorne when he was composing *The Scarlet Letter.* Hirsch, *The Rise of the Penitentiary,* 6. The Plymouth Colony Records, with which Hawthorne was not familiar (they were published in Boston in 1855), include entries providing for the construction of a prison as early as 1637. *Records of the Colony of New Plymouth in New England,* ed. Nathaniel B. Shurtleff, *Court Orders,* vol. 1, *1633–1640* (1855; repr., New York: AMS Press, 1968), 75.

61. For example, one finds a memorable scene in which Quaker Mary Prince abuses Governor John Endecott from a prison cell: "Mary Prince called to him from a window of the prison, railing at and reviling him, saying Woe unto thee, thou art an oppressor." Imprisonment, though, serves merely to confine Prince and other Quakers until a trial, when the sentence of banishment is passed. Thomas Hutchinson, *The History of the Colony of Massachusetts-Bay* (1764; repr., New York: Arno Press, 1972), 197.

62. Sargent Bush Jr. traces an influence from the prison reform movement of the 1840s to *The Scarlet Letter* on the basis of an article about prisons (with an image of a rosebush) that appeared in an 1843 issue of the *Salem Gazette.* Sargent Bush Jr., "Hawthorne's Prison Rose: An English Antecedent in the *Salem Gazette,*" *New England Quarterly* 57.2 (1984): 256–57.

63. George Lee Haskins, *Law and Authority in Early Massachusetts: A Study in Tradition and Design* (New York: Macmillan, 1960), 204.

64. John Winthrop, *The Journal of John Winthrop, 1630–1649*, ed. Richard S. Dunn, James Savage, and Laetitia Yeandle (Cambridge: Belknap Press of Harvard University Press, 1996), 386–87 and 469.

65. On the subject of public confession as a key element in the transgressor's experience of penitence in Puritan Boston, see Ernest W. Baughman, "Public Confession and *The Scarlet Letter*," *New England Quarterly* 40.4 (1967): 532–50.

66. Caleb Smith, *The Prison and the American Imagination* (New Haven: Yale University Press, 2009), 15. Smith reads *The Scarlet Letter* as an allegory contrasting the ineffective public punishment issued to Hester with the redemptive private anguish suffered by Dimmesdale, which is more in keeping with the principles of the antebellum penal reform movement.

67. Shulman, "The Artist in the Slammer," 86.

68. "Thus in the 1790s, convicts for the first time began to wear uniforms in order to render it more difficult for an escaped inmate to disappear into a town. . . . Massachusetts, among the more security conscious systems, devised a more bizarre one, half red and half blue." Rothman, *Discovery of the Asylum*, 90. W. David Lewis points out that a hallmark of the Auburn system of incarceration was "black-and-white striped outfits which made [inmates] look grotesque and ridiculous." Lewis, *From Newgate to Dannemora*, 92.

69. Quoted in Lewis, *The Development of American Prisons*, 73.

70. Rothman, *Discovery of the Asylum*, 95.

71. Of course, opinion was not monolithic on this subject. An article in the *United States Magazine, and Democratic Review*, in a wide-ranging discussion of prison discipline, included the statement that the "separate system, or isolation . . . is repugnant to one of the strongest instincts of our nature. Man is eminently a social being; it is not therefore surprising that absolute seclusion not only causes present wretchedness, but not unfrequently leads to mental alienation and imbecility, perhaps the greatest of human calamities." This issue of the magazine also included a piece edited by Hawthorne, "Papers of an Old Dartmoor Prisoner." R., "Prison Discipline," *United States Magazine, and Democratic Review* 19 (August 1846): 137–38.

72. Brook Thomas, "Citizen Hester: *The Scarlet Letter* as Civic Myth," *American Literary History* 13.2 (2001): 184.

73. Untitled review, *The Knickerbocker; or, New York Monthly Magazine* 2 (October 1833): 317; "The Author of 'Martin Faber,' 'Guy Rivers,' and 'The Yemassee,'" *Southern Literary Journal and Magazine of Arts* 1 (September 1835): 42.

74. Simms, *Martin Faber*, 14.

75. "Martin Faber, or the History of a Criminal," *Atkinson's Saturday Evening Post*, October 26, 1833, 639.

76. Acknowledging the difficulty of defining as a genre a group of novels that do not always closely resemble one another, Keith Hollingsworth writes that the "sole common feature" of the Newgate novel was that "an important character came (or, if imaginary, might have come) out of the Newgate Calendar." Keith Hollingsworth, *The Newgate Novel, 1830–1847: Bulwer, Ainsworth, Dickens, and Thackeray* (Detroit: Wayne State University Press, 1963), 14. For a more recent overview of the genre, see Heather Worthington, "The Newgate Novel," in *The Nineteenth-Century Novel, 1820–1880*, vol. 3 of *The Oxford History of the Novel in English*, ed. John Kucich and Jenny Bourne Taylor (Oxford: Oxford University Press, 2012), 122–36.

77. An anonymous reviewer of several Simms novels denied the originality that Simms had claimed for his works, noting: "'Eugene Aram' and 'Miserrimus' were written with feelings of the same kind. Originality in the structure of such a tale is out of the question—models enough for it may be found in the 'Newgate Calendar.'" "The Author of 'Martin Faber,' 'Guy Rivers,' and 'The Yemassee,'" 41.

78. "Eugene Aram," *The Ariel: A Semimonthly and Miscellaneous Gazette,* March 3, 1832, 356.

79. An excerpt of the *New-York Commercial Advertiser* review, from which this quotation is taken, appeared in the *Philadelphia Album and Ladies' Literary Portfolio,* March 3, 1832, 70.

80. Hollingsworth quotes from the chief British attack on *Eugene Aram's* moral tendencies, which appeared in *Fraser's Magazine:* "Finally, we dislike altogether this awakening sympathy with interesting criminals, and wasting sensibilities on the scaffold and gaol. It is a modern, a depraved, a corrupting, taste." Hollingsworth, *The Newgate Novel, 1830–1847,* 93.

81. "Article 2," *Philadelphia Album and Ladies' Literary Portfolio,* March 17, 1832, 85.

82. Robert Dale Owen, "Letter 14. To Amos Gilbert. Bulwer's *Eugene Aram,*" *Free Enquirer,* April 7, 1832, 187.

83. J.B.S., "Thoughts on Bulwer's Novels," *Casket* 4 (April 1830): 173–74; and J., "Art. IV.—Falkland," *American Quarterly Review* 8 (September 1830): 99–100.

84. "Art. III.—Paul Clifford," *Christian Examiner and General Review* 9 (September 1830): 46 and 52–53.

85. Sean Grass, *The Self in the Cell: Narrating the Victorian Prisoner* (New York: Routledge, 2003), 8. To differentiate my argument from Grass's, Grass is concerned primarily with the narrative techniques that evolved from Victorian attempts to narrate prisoners' lives, whereas I am concerned with the emergence and embrace of psychological interiority by reviewers and authors alike as a valued feature of novels concerned with crime.

86. Baym, *Novels, Readers, and Reviewers,* 94.

87. Christopher Castiglia, *Interior States: Institutional Consciousness and the Inner Life of Democracy in the Antebellum United States* (Durham: Duke University Press, 2008).

88. Thomas Augustus Worrall, "The Literature and Liberties of the Age," *North American Magazine* 3 (December 1833): 112.

89. "Novel Reading—And the Novels of 1832," *American Monthly Magazine* 1 (April 1833): 103.

90. J.S.D., "Art. II—*Oliver Twist,*" *Christian Examiner and General Review* 27 (November 1839): 173.

91. "Article 12," *Atkinson's Saturday Evening Post,* February 9, 1832, 2.

92. "The Writings of 'Boz,'" *Yale Literary Magazine* 6 (December 1840): 61.

93. Philip F. Gura, *Truth's Ragged Edge: The Rise of the American Novel* (New York: Farrar, Straus and Giroux, 2013), 189.

94. "Book Notices," *Portland Transcript,* March 30, 1850; and Henry Fothergill Chorley, "*The Scarlet Letter: A Romance,*" *Athenaeum,* June 15, 1850, in John L. Idol Jr. and Buford Jones, *Nathaniel Hawthorne: The Contemporary Reviews* (Cambridge: Cambridge University Press, 1994), 121 and 127.

95. Evert A. Duyckinck, "*The Scarlet Letter,*" *Literary World* 6 (March 1850), in Idol and Jones, *Hawthorne: Contemporary Reviews,* 122. Lewis Gaylord Clark's review repeats verbatim Duyckinck's judgment on the novel anatomizing the human heart. Lewis Gaylord Clark, "The Scarlet Letter," *Knickerbocker* 35 (May 1850), in Idol and Jones, *Hawthorne: Contemporary Reviews,* 126.

96. Anne W. Abbot, "The Scarlet Letter," *North American Review* 71 (July 1850), in Idol and Jones, *Hawthorne: Contemporary Reviews,* 130.

97. Edwin Percy Whipple, "Review of New Books," *Graham's Magazine* 36 (May 1850), in Idol and Jones, *Hawthorne: Contemporary Reviews,* 125.

98. Orestes Augustus Brownson, "The Scarlet Letter," *Brownson's Quarterly Review* 4 (October 1850), in Idol and Jones, *Hawthorne: Contemporary Reviews,* 144 and 146.

99. "The Reveries of a Bachelor, by Ik Marvel," *Yale Literary Magazine* 16 (April 1851): 246.

100. "Notices of New Works," *The Albion, A Journal of News, Politics and Literature,* December 14, 1850, 597; "Reveries of a Bachelor," *American Whig Review* 7 (January 1851): 94.

101. "Our Young Authors," *Putnam's Monthly Magazine of American Literature, Science, and Art* 1 (January 1853): 77.

4. The Angel in the Penitentiary

1. Capt. Marryat, C.B., *A Diary in America; with Remarks on its Institutions,* vol. 2 (Philadelphia: Carey & Hart, 1839), 60.
2. Ibid., 55.
3. Charles Dickens, *American Notes* (London: Oxford University Press, 1966), 99.
4. Ibid., 104.
5. Ibid., 109.
6. Cindy Weinstein, *Family, Kinship, and Sympathy in Nineteenth-Century American Literature* (Cambridge: Cambridge University Press, 2004), 5.
7. On conditions in the Walnut Street Prison endured by Carson, see Daniel E. Williams, "'The Horrors of This Far-Famed Penitentiary': Discipline, Defiance, and Death during Ann Carson's Incarcerations in Philadelphia's Walnut Street Prison," in *Buried Lives: Incarcerated in Early America,* ed. Michele Lise Tarter and Richard Bell (Athens: University of Georgia Press, 2012), 203–30.
8. Ann Carson, *The History of the Celebrated Mrs. Ann Carson* (Philadelphia: Published by the Author, 1822), 298 and 300.
9. Ibid., 306 (solitary confinement for not attending worship) and 303 (accuses fellow prisoners of hypocrisy in professions of religion). The general tone of Carson's depiction of women inmates is echoed by contemporary W. A. Coffey, who published an exposé of conditions in New York's Auburn prison in 1823. Coffey found the convict women beyond hope of reform, "more depraved than the men," in part on the grounds of sexual behavior that was "agonizing to every fibre of delicacy and virtue, and sickening to the bosom of chastity and love." W. A. Coffey, *Inside Out; Or, An Interior View of the New-York State Prison* (New York: James Costigan, 1823), 61.
10. Mrs. M. Clarke, *The Memoirs of the Celebrated and Beautiful Mrs. Ann Carson,* 2nd ed., vol. 2 (Philadelphia, 1838), 78.
11. Carson, *History of the Celebrated Mrs. Ann Carson,* 298.
12. Clarke, *Memoirs of the Celebrated and Beautiful Mrs. Ann Carson,* 2:167 and 175.
13. Susan Branson, *Dangerous to Know: Women, Crime, and Notoriety in the Early Republic* (Philadelphia: University of Pennsylvania Press, 2008).
14. Joanne Dobson, "Reclaiming Sentimental Literature," *American Literature* 69 (1997): 267.
15. "Reformation of Females," *Prisoner's Friend* 3 (February 1851): 252–54.
16. Eliza Farnham, "Report of the Matron of the Female Department at Sing-Sing," quoted in Margaret Fuller, "Prison Discipline," in *Margaret Fuller's New York Journalism: A Biographical Essay and Key Writings,* ed. Catherine C. Mitchell (Knoxville: University of Tennessee Press, 1995), 107.
17. "Reformation of Females," 252–54.
18. "Article VIII," *Prisoner's Friend,* April 30, 1845, 19.
19. Eliza Farnham, "Case of Destitution of Moral Feelings," *Boston Medical and Surgical Journal,* October 21, 1846, 237–38.
20. Charles Spear, ed., *Voices from Prison: Being a Selection of Poetry from Various Prisoners, Written Within the Cell* (Boston: C. & J. M. Spear, 1847).
21. "Article XIII. Elizabeth Fry," *Prisoner's Friend* 2 (December 1849): 182–83.
22. "Active Benevolence," *Prisoner's Friend,* January 22, 1845, 13. A lengthy article in the *Pennsylvania Journal of Prison Discipline and Philanthropy* includes a laudatory account of Fry's activities expressing the same conceit of her mystical power over prisoners: "She entered fearlessly the room where a hundred and sixty women and children surrounded her in the wildest disorder. But her noble air and pious expression exacted respect from these abandoned creatures." "Female Convicts," *Pennsylvania Journal of Prison Discipline and Philanthropy* 1 (April 1845): 99.
23. "Elizabeth Fry," *Prisoner's Friend* 9 (December 1856): 110.

24. See "Female Convicts," 97–117. The two journals drew from a common (unattributed) source, as some of the descriptions of Fry are identically phrased.

25. Lydia H. Sigourney, "On Seeing Mrs. Fry at Newgate Prison," *Godey's Lady's Book, and Ladies' American Magazine* 24 (April 1842): 189.

26. Mrs. C. Latham, "The Jailer's Daughter," *Godey's Magazine and Lady's Book* 35 (July 1847): 21, 27, 28, and 29.

27. J. S. Freligh, "Alethe," *Graham's Lady's and Gentleman's Magazine* 18 (May 1841): 216, lines 12–14 and 19–22.

28. H.C., "For Better, for Worse," *Godey's Lady's Book and Magazine* 57 (September 1858): 257, lines 21–22.

29. Ann S. Stephens, "The Wife," *Graham's Lady's and Gentlemen's Magazine* 24 (November 1843): 246.

30. Paul Christian Jones, "'I Put My Fingers Around My Throat and Squeezed It, To Know How It Feels': Antigallows Sentimentalism and E. D. E. N. Southworth's *The Hidden Hand*," *Legacy: A Journal of American Women Writers* 25.1 (2008): 45.

31. E. D. E. N. Southworth, "The Thunderbolt to the Hearth," *National Era*, October 21, 1847, 1–2.

32. Francis B. Dedmond, *Sylvester Judd* (Boston: Twayne Publishers, 1980), 53.

33. Sylvester Judd, *Margaret: A Tale of the Real and Ideal, Blight and Bloom,* ed. Gavin Jones (Amherst: University of Massachusetts Press, 2009), 47. Subsequent references are given parenthetically in the text.

34. Margaret Fuller, "The Great Lawsuit. Man versus Men. Woman versus Women," *The Dial: A Magazine for Literature, Philosophy, and Religion* 4 (July 1843): 32. In a review, Fuller praised *Margaret*'s "naïve discussion of the leading reform movements of the day in their rudimentary forms." Quoted in Dedmond, *Sylvester Judd,* 80.

35. Gavin Jones, introduction to Judd, *Margaret,* viii.

36. Glenn Hendler, *Public Sentiments: Structures of Feeling in Nineteenth-Century American Literature* (Chapel Hill: University of North Carolina Press, 2001), 24.

37. Harriet Beecher Stowe, *Dred: A Tale of the Great Dismal Swamp,* ed. Robert S. Levine (New York: Penguin Books, 2000), 441 and 544.

38. Fuller, "Prison Discipline," 110.

39. E. D. E. N. Southworth, *The Hidden Hand; or, Capitola the Madcap,* ed. Joanne Dobson (New Brunswick: Rutgers University Press, 1988), 439 and 448. Subsequent references are given parenthetically in the text.

40. In his relevant and convincing interpretation of this scene, Paul Christian Jones notes that Southworth "inextricably links the fate of Donald, the condemned individual, with that of Capitola." In Jones's reading, the scene and the novel serve Southworth's lifelong interest in opposing the death penalty. Jones, "Antigallows Sentimentalism and E. D. E. N. Southworth's *The Hidden Hand*," 55.

41. E. D. E. N. Southworth, *The Lost Heiress* (Philadelphia: Deacon & Peterson, 1854), and *The Gipsy's Prophecy: A Tale of Real Life* (Philadelphia, T. B. Peterson & Brothers, 1861), 201.

42. Paul Christian Jones, *Against the Gallows: Antebellum American Writers and the Movement to Abolish Capital Punishment* (Iowa City: University of Iowa Press, 2011), 152.

43. Michele Ann Abate, "Launching a Gender B(l)acklash: E. D. E. N. Southworth's *The Hidden Hand* and the Emergence of (Racialized) White Tomboyism," *Children's Literature Association Quarterly* 31.1 (2006): 51. Gillian Silverman offers a similar assessment in noting that "Southworth's vision often fell well short of feminist critique," and that her novels "are populated less by independent female thinkers than by models of classic domestic femininity." Gillian Silverman, "Sympathy and Its Vicissitudes," *American Studies* 43.3 (2002): 20.

44. Cindy Weinstein, "'What Did You Mean?' The Language of Marriage in *The Fatal Marriage* and *Family Doom*," in *E. D. E. N. Southworth: Recovering a Nineteenth-Century*

Popular Novelist, ed. Melissa J. Homestead and Pamela T. Washington (Knoxville: University of Tennessee Press, 2012), 268.

45. Rebecca Harding Davis, "Life in the Iron-Mills," *Atlantic Monthly* 42 (April 1861): 449. Subsequent references are given parenthetically in the text.

46. Adam Silver, "'Unnatural Unions': Picturesque Travel, Sexual Politics, and Working-Class Representation in 'A Night Under Ground' and 'Life in the Iron-Mills," *Legacy* 20.1 and 2 (2003): 112.

47. Jill Gatlin, "Disturbing Aesthetics: Industrial Pollution, Moral Discourse, and Narrative Form in Rebecca Harding Davis's 'Life in the Iron Mills,'" *Nineteenth-Century Literature* 68.2 (2013): 229.

48. For an argument against trying to resolve any generic tensions in "Life in the Iron-Mills," see Dana Seitler, "Strange Beauty: The Politics of Ungenre in Rebecca Harding Davis's *Life in the Iron Mills*," *American Literature* 86.3 (2014): 523–49.

49. "The Attacks on Mrs. Farnham," *Brooklyn Daily Eagle,* September 2, 1846.

50. "A Letter from Sing Sing," *Brooklyn Daily Eagle,* May 1, 1846.

51. Fuller, "Prison Discipline," 106.

52. John Hallwas, introduction to *Life in Prairie Land,* by Eliza Farnham (Urbana: University of Illinois Press, 1988), xvi.

53. Janet Floyd, "Dislocations of the Self: Eliza Farnham at Sing Sing Prison," *Journal of American Studies* 40.2 (2006): 317.

54. Another antebellum figure who qualified as an angel in the penitentiary was Dorothea Dix, who devoted herself to the subject of prison reform before turning to the treatment of the mentally ill, for which she is now better known. Abolitionist George Thompson, who served time in Missouri for trying to liberate slaves from that state, wrote these lines in tribute to Dix after she donated a library to the Missouri Penitentiary: "Bright Angel of Mercy, in pure virtue drest, / By whose deeds of pity the prisoner is blest / . . . The hearts of poor prisoners *here* you have cheered, / To thousands, the name of 'Miss Dix' is endeared." George Thompson, "Address to Miss Dix," in *The Prison Bard; Or Poems on Various Subjects* (Hartford: William H. Burleigh, 1848), 206–7.

55. M. B. Sampson, *Rationale of Crime and Its Appropriate Treatment, With Notes and Illustrations by E. W. Farnham* (New York: D. Appleton & Company, 1846), xiv.

56. Madeleine B. Stern, "Mathew B. Brady and the *Rationale of Crime:* A Discovery in Daguerreotypes," *Quarterly Journal of the Library of Congress* 31.3 (1974): 126–35.

57. Farnham's efforts met resistance from New York prison authorities, who were troubled by her attempts to adapt the principles of phrenology to penal reform measures. An excellent account of Farnham's career at Sing Sing is found in W. David Lewis, *From Newgate to Dannemora: The Rise of the Penitentiary in New York, 1796–1848* (Ithaca: Cornell University Press, 1965), chap. 10, "Radicalism and Reaction," 230–55.

5. "Branded with Infamy"

1. It must be acknowledged that although Hawthorne avoids the term "penitentiary," he does use the terms "prison" and "imprisonment" in the novel. The penitentiary to which Clifford Pyncheon would presumably have been sent was formally known as the Massachusetts State Prison.

2. David J. Rothman, *The Discovery of the Asylum: Social Order and Disorder in the New Republic,* rev. ed. (Boston: Little, Brown, 1990), xxv.

3. Larry E. Sullivan, *The Prison Reform Movement: Forlorn Hope* (Boston: Twayne Publishers, 1990), 13.

4. "Art. V.—Prison Discipline in America," *North American Review* 66 (January 1848): 165.

5. Harriet Martineau, *Society in America,* vol. 2 (New York: Saunders and Otley, 1837), 283.

6. Capt. Marryat, C.B., *A Diary in America, with Remarks on its Institutions,* vol. 2 (Philadelphia: Carey & Hart, 1839), 58 and 60–62.

7. Charles Dickens, *American Notes and Pictures from Italy* (London: Oxford University Press, 1966), 99, 102–4 and 109.

8. William Peter, "17.—Mr. Dickens' report of his visit to the Eastern Penitentiary," *Pennsylvania Journal of Prison Discipline and Philanthropy* 1 (January 1845): 86–87.

9. W. David Lewis, *From Newgate to Dannemora: The Rise of the Penitentiary in New York, 1796–1848* (Ithaca: Cornell University Press, 1965), 213.

10. C.S., "Discharged Convicts. No. VIII," *Prisoner's Friend,* February 25, 1846, 30.

11. "The Massachusetts State Prison," *Prisoner's Friend,* August 6, 1845, 73.

12. James B. Finley, *Memorials of Prison Life* (Cincinnati: L. Swormstedt & A. Poe, 1853), 209. Fellow chaplain Eleazer Smith devoted a whole chapter of his prison memoir to the subject of how the community should deal with discharged convicts. Eleazer Smith, *Nine Years Among the Convicts: Or, Prison Reminiscences* (Boston: J. P. Magee, 1856), chap. 19, "Discharged Convicts."

13. O'Sullivan is listed as one of the organization's two secretaries in an article describing its foundation: "Prison Reform Meeting," *Christian Register,* December 21, 1844, 201.

14. "First Report of the Prison Association of New York," *Pennsylvania Journal of Prison Discipline and Philanthropy* 1 (January 1845): 32–33.

15. Lewis, *From Newgate to Dannemora,* 225.

16. George E. Baker, "The New York State Prison: Article CXXVII ORIGINAL," *Prisoner's Friend* 1 (May 1849): 377.

17. Orlando F. Lewis, *The Development of American Prisons and Prison Customs, 1776–1845* (1922; repr., Montclair, NJ: Patterson Smith, 1967), 323.

18. "Letter from Mrs. Child," *Prisoner's Friend,* January 8, 1845, 6.

19. "Prison Discipline," *United States Magazine, and Democratic Review* 19 (August 1846): 133. Child's letter to the *Boston Courier* with the story of Mary Norris was also reprinted in the *Cincinnati Weekly Herald and Philanthropist,* January 1, 1845, 9, and *The Youth's Companion,* September 3, 1846, 20.

20. "Reform of Prisons and Their Inmates," *Christian Reflector,* December 19, 1844, 202.

21. Lydia Maria Child, "The Irish Heart. A True Story," *Columbian Lady's and Gentleman's Magazine* 4 (July 1845): 17–21.

22. Emma C. Embury, "The Convict's Daughter," *Godey's Magazine and Lady's Book* 30 (January 1845): 24.

23. Ned Buntline, *The Convict; or, The Conspirators' Victim. A Novel, Written in Prison* (1851; repr., New York: Dick & Fitzgerald, 1863).

24. George Thompson, *My Life: or, The Adventures of Geo. Thompson,* in *Venus in Boston and Other Tales of Nineteenth-Century City Life,* ed. David S. Reynolds and Kimberly R. Gladman (Amherst: University of Massachusetts Press, 2002), 370.

25. Prison officials in Thompson's Jack Harold crime novels are often, though not uniformly, cruel and self-interested. Thompson took special pleasure in satirizing prison chaplains. In *The Outlaw,* Harold easily gulls the greedy Mr. Spoons into helping secure his temporary release from prison for a share in the supposedly buried spoils of Harold's criminal exploits. In *Road to Ruin,* the Reverend Mr. Varnish attempts to seduce an attractive young female inmate he is supposed to be counseling to repent. George Thompson, *The Outlaw; or, The Felon's Fortunes* (New York: Frederic A. Brady, n.d.), and *Road to Ruin; or, The Felon's Doom* (New York: Frederic A. Brady, n.d.). The novels probably date from the early 1850s.

26. Thompson, *The Outlaw,* 24.

27. George Thompson, *Life and Exploits of the Noted Criminal, Bristol Bill* (New York: M. J. Ivers & Co., n.d.), 90.

28. George Lippard, *The Nazarene; or, The Last of the Washingtons* (1846; repr., Philadelphia: T. B. Peterson, 1854), 147.

29. George Lippard, *The Killers: A Narrative of Real Life in Philadelphia* (Philadelphia: Hankinson and Bartholomew, 1850), 25 and 31.

30. C. S., "Discharged Convicts. No. VIII.," 30.
31. George Thompson, *Venus in Boston; A Romance of City Life*, in *Venus in Boston and Other Tales*, 87.
32. Thompson, *Life and Exploits*, 31.
33. Ned Buntline, *The Mysteries and Miseries of New York* (New York: W. F. Burgess, 1849), pt. 2, 84.
34. U.S. Constitution, art. 13, sec. 1.
35. Caleb Smith, *The Prison and the American Imagination* (New Haven: Yale University Press, 2009), 12.
36. Colin Dayan, *The Law Is a White Dog: How Legal Rituals Make and Unmake Persons* (Princeton: Princeton University Press, 2011), 61.
37. Rebecca M. McLennan, *The Crisis of Imprisonment: Protest, Politics, and the Making of the American Penal State, 1776–1941* (Cambridge: Cambridge University Press, 2008), 4 and 63.
38. David Roediger writes, "White workers could, and did, define and accept their class position by fashioning identities as 'not slaves' and 'not Blacks.'" David Roediger, *The Wages of Whiteness: Race and the Making of the American Working Class*, rev. ed. (London: Verso, 1999), 13.
39. George Lippard, *The Quaker City; or, The Monks of Monk Hall*, ed. David S. Reynolds (Amherst: University of Massachusetts Press, 1995), 529–30.
40. George Lippard, *The Empire City* (1850; repr., Philadelphia: T. B. Peterson & Brothers, 1864), 49. Subsequent references are given parenthetically in the text.
41. H. Bruce Franklin, *The Victim as Criminal and Artist: Literature from the American Prison* (New York: Oxford University Press, 1978), 141.
42. Quoted in Lewis, *From Newgate to Dannemora*, 129.
43. In the words of the *North American Review*, "The only question that remains, and it is a grave one, is whether [prisoners] should work together . . . during the daytime . . . or whether they should be confined by day, as well as by night, each to his separate cell." "Art. V.—Prison Discipline in America," *North American Review* 66 (January 1848): 147.
44. Negley K. Teeters and John D. Shearer, *The Prison at Philadelphia, Cherry Hill: The Separate System of Penal Discipline, 1829–1913* (New York: Columbia University Press, 1957), 95, 98, and 101.
45. C.S., "Massachusetts State Prison," *Prisoner's Friend*, November 12, 1845, 130.
46. "The Officers of Our State Prisons," *Brooklyn Daily Eagle*, March 10, 1846.
47. Dix wrote: "I am convinced that, with due care, and under proper direction, the shower bath, (not the douche, or bolt bath,) is a very effectual means of procuring submission to proper rules and regulations. It is a mode of discipline which may be, and which has been abused, but so has and may be every other form of punishment which the law allows." Dorothea Dix, *Remarks on Prisons and Prison Discipline in the United States* (Boston: Munroe & Francis, 1845), 25.
48. According to David J. Rothman, "The whip was commonplace in the prisons of New York, Massachusetts, and Ohio; Pennsylvania tied an iron gag on disobedient inmates, and Maine had recourse to the ball and chain." David J. Rothman, "Perfecting the Prison: United States, 1789–1865," in *The Oxford History of the Prison: The Practice of Punishment in Western Society*, ed. Norval Morris and David J. Rothman (New York: Oxford University Press, 1995), 121. On the basis of his reading of legislative investigations into practices at Sing Sing, W. David Lewis states succinctly, "Excessive severity seems at times to have degenerated into pure sadism." Lewis, *From Newgate to Dannemora*, 151.
49. Michael Meranze, *Laboratories of Virtue: Punishment, Revolution, and Authority in Philadelphia, 1760–1835* (Chapel Hill: University of North Carolina Press, 1996), 318.
50. McLennan, *The Crisis of Imprisonment*, 80. W. David Lewis provides another valuable account of workingmen's objections to penal labor. Lewis, *From Newgate to Dannemora*, chap. 8, "Prisons, Profits, and Protests," 178–200.

51. Sean Wilentz, *Chants Democratic: New York City and the Rise of the American Working Class, 1788–1850* (New York: Oxford University Press, 1984), 237.

52. Lewis, *The Development of American Prisons and Prison Customs,* 135.

53. Teeters and Shearer, *The Prison at Philadelphia,* 148.

54. Lewis, *The Development of American Prisons and Prison Customs,* 73.

55. H. Green, "Charlestown and State Prison," *Christian Reflector,* March 23, 1842, 3.

56. "Moral Improvement of Convicts," *New York Evangelist,* July 9, 1846, 110.

57. Dix, *Remarks on Prisons and Prison Discipline,* 22.

58. P.H.S., "The Massachusetts State Prison," *Prisoner's Friend,* August 6, 1845, 73.

59. See, for example, C.S., "Massachusetts State Prison," 130. C.S. (undoubtedly publisher Charles Spear) includes a complete chart of transgressions committed and lashes assigned in April, May, and June of 1844 and 1845. In 1850 the periodical again defended the reforms of Warden Robinson and complained that corporal punishment, though much more infrequently used, was still among the disciplinary measures in place at the prison. "Article XII. The Massachusetts State Prison, 1849," *Prisoner's Friend* 2 (April 1850): 372–75.

60. "Massachusetts," *Niles' National Register,* January 24, 1846, 330–31.

61. Nathaniel Hawthorne, *The House of the Seven Gables,* in *Collected Novels* (New York: Library of America, 1983), 441. Subsequent references are given parenthetically in the text.

62. For a provocative interpretation situating Clifford's unstable psychological state within the emergent field of mental health reform in the 1840s, see Stephen Knadler, "Hawthorne's Genealogy of Madness: *The House of the Seven Gables* and Disciplinary Individualism," *American Quarterly* 47.2 (1995): 280–308.

63. Although I do not endorse their line of interpretation, I should note here that Hawthorne's ambiguous staging of this scene has led at least three commentators to speculate that Judge Pyncheon's death involves some degree of complicity or agency on the part of other characters. Paul J. Emmett, "The Murder of Judge Pyncheon: Confusion and Suggestion in *The House of the Seven Gables,*" *Journal of Evolutionary Psychology* 24.2–3 (2003): 189–95; Clara B. Cox, "'Who Killed Judge Pyncheon?' The Scene of the Crime Revisited," *Studies in American Fiction* 16.1 (1988): 99–103; and Alfred H. Marks, "Who Killed Judge Pyncheon? The Role of the Imagination in *The House of the Seven Gables,*" *PMLA* 71.3 (1956): 355–69.

64. In Brook Thomas's influential analysis, "Hawthorne's tale questions the impersonal authority not only of texts but of all three branches of the United States government, a questioning perhaps influenced by Hawthorne's dismissal from the post of customs officer as the result of the spoils system." Brook Thomas, "*The House of the Seven Gables:* Reading the Romance of America," *PMLA* 97.2 (1982): 200. In a reading that does not otherwise engage with my own, Christopher Castiglia notes that "*The House of the Seven Gables* is obsessed with law." Christopher Castiglia, "The Marvelous Queer Interiors of *The House of The Seven Gables,*" in *The Cambridge Companion to Nathaniel Hawthorne,* ed. Richard H. Millington (Cambridge: Cambridge University Press, 2004), 186.

65. Barry L. Salkin describes the pardoning power as "one of the most troublesome aspects of criminal administration in antebellum Pennsylvania," and notes that "charges of pardon-buying" were common during the administration of Governor David Porter in the early 1840s. Barry L. Salkin, "The Pardoning Power in Antebellum Pennsylvania," *Pennsylvania Magazine of History and Biography* 100.4 (1976): 507 and 511.

66. For a helpful overview of criticism on the novel's ending, see Bernard Rosenthal, introduction to *Critical Essays on Hawthorne's* The House of the Seven Gables (New York: G. K. Hall & Co., 1995), 13–15. Rosenthal sums up the critical consensus: "For the most part, and on a variety of grounds, critics have continued to see the ending as a symptom of larger difficulties in *The House of the Seven Gables*" (14).

67. Toni Morrison, *Playing in the Dark: Whiteness and the Literary Imagination* (New York: Vintage Books, 1992), 46.

68. In chronological order of publication, the relevant commentators are Shawn Michelle Smith, *American Archives: Gender, Race, and Class in Visual Culture* (Princeton: Princeton University Press, 1999); Paul Gilmore, *The Genuine Article: Race, Mass Culture, and American Literary Manhood* (Durham: Duke University Press, 2001); Robert S. Levine, *Dislocating Race and Nation: Episodes in Nineteenth-Century American Literary Nationalism* (Chapel Hill: University of North Carolina Press, 2008); David Anthony, *Paper Money Men: Commerce, Manhood, and the Sensational Public Sphere in Antebellum America* (Columbus: Ohio State University Press, 2009); and Jeffory A. Clymer, *Family Money: Property, Race, and Literature in the Nineteenth Century* (New York: Oxford University Press, 2013).

69. Shawn Michelle Smith notes that Jaffrey "has been politically allied with Southern pro-slavery politicians." Smith, *American Archives*, 40. The textual evidence for this claim (not noted by Smith) seems to be the narrator's observation that when Jaffrey does not turn up at the dinner where he is expected, his political friends will conclude "that the Free Soilers have him" (588).

6. Voices from Prison

1. Karen Halttunen, "Gothic Mystery and the Birth of the Asylum: The Cultural Construction of Deviance in Early-Nineteenth-Century America," in *Moral Problems in American Life: New Perspectives on Cultural History*, ed. Karen Halttunen and Lewis Perry (Ithaca: Cornell University Press, 1998), 42.

2. H. Bruce Franklin, *The Victim as Criminal and Artist: Literature from the American Prison* (New York: Oxford University Press, 1978); see especially pages 131–32 on political prisoners and 134 for a paragraph on prison poet George Ryno. (Franklin spells the name "Reno.")

3. Michele Lise Tarter and Richard Bell, introduction to *Buried Lives: Incarcerated in Early America*, ed. Michele Lise Tarter and Richard Bell (Athens: University of Georgia Press, 2012), 5.

4. Candy Gunther Brown, *The Word in the World: Evangelical Writing, Publishing, and Reading in America, 1789–1880* (Chapel Hill: University of North Carolina Press, 2004), 92.

5. Rev. James B. Finley, *Memorials of Prison Life* (Cincinnati: L. Swormstedt & A. Poe, 1853); Eleazer Smith, *Nine Years Among the Convicts; or, Prison Reminiscences* (Boston: J. P. Magee, 1856); John Luckey, *Life in Sing Sing State Prison, As Seen in a Twelve Years' Chaplaincy* (New York: N. Tibbals & Co., 1860).

6. Finley, *Memorials of Prison Life*, 4, 82, 116, and 31.

7. Smith, *Nine Years Among the Convicts*, 125, 130, and vi.

8. Daniel A. Cohen, *Pillars of Salt, Monuments of Grace: New England Crime Literature and the Origins of American Popular Culture, 1674–1860* (New York: Oxford University Press, 1993), 23.

9. Worldcat lists nine separate editions of Finley's *Memorials of Prison Life* between 1850 and 1861, including one published in New York, and three editions of Luckey's *Life in Sing Sing State Prison* between 1856 and 1866.

10. Finley, *Memorials of Prison Life*, 286–87.

11. Luckey, *Life in Sing Sing*, 67.

12. Caleb Smith, "Harry Hawser's Fate: Eastern State Penitentiary and the Birth of Prison Literature," in Tarter and Bell, *Buried Lives*, 252.

13. Former New York police commissioner George W. Matsell capitalized on interest in criminals' speech with his *Vocabulum; or, The Rogue's Lexicon* (New York: Published by George W. Matsell & Co., 1859).

14. Finley, *Memorials of Prison Life*, 117.

15. Smith, *Nine Years Among the Convicts*, 87.

16. Luckey, *Life in Sing Sing State Prison*, 243–44.

17. Rebecca M. McLennan, *The Crisis of Imprisonment: Protest, Politics, and the Making of the American Penal State, 1776–1941* (Cambridge: Cambridge University Press, 2008), 4.

18. Finley, *Memorials of Prison Life,* 202.

19. Luckey, *Life in Sing Sing State Prison,* 50–51.

20. Luckey comes across as a sympathetic figure in the history of penal practice in New York. He worked hard to acquire a prison library for Sing Sing's inmates, and he took greater interest in their personal lives than most prison chaplains: "He frequently accompanied ex-convicts back to the city [of New York], helped them to find jobs, tried to protect them from the blandishments of former associates in crime, and made periodic checks on their progress in free life." W. David Lewis, *From Newgate to Dannemora: The Rise of the Penitentiary in New York, 1796–1848* (Ithaca: Cornell University Press, 1965), 213. The argument that his use of prisoners' voices in *Life in Sing Sing State Prison* is exploitative stands alongside recognition of the humane values otherwise evident in his chaplaincy.

21. Caleb Smith, *The Prison and the American Imagination* (New Haven: Yale University Press, 2009), 104–5.

22. C. D. Cleveland, "Religious and Moral Instruction in Philadelphia County Prison," *Pennsylvania Journal of Prison Discipline and Philanthropy* 1 (January 1845): 77.

23. Smith, *Nine Years Among the Convicts,* 187 and 190.

24. Jeannine Marie DeLombard, *In the Shadow of the Gallows: Race, Crime, and American Civic Identity* (Philadelphia: University of Pennsylvania Press, 2012), 103.

25. Quoted in Philip F. Gura, ed., *Buried from the World: Inside the Massachusetts State Prison, 1829–1831; The Memorandum Books of the Rev. Jared Curtis* (Boston: Massachusetts Historical Society, 2001), 220, 225, 16 (Stevens), and 120 (Johnson).

26. Luckey, *Life in Sing Sing State Prison,* 89 and 342.

27. Stanley Harrold, "On the Borders of Slavery and Race: Charles T. Torrey and the Underground Railroad," *Journal of the Early Republic* 20.2 (2000): 287.

28. J. C. Lovejoy, *Memoir of Rev. Charles T. Torrey, Who Died in the Penitentiary of Maryland* (Boston: John P. Jewett & Co., 1847), 170. Subsequent references are given parenthetically in the text.

29. For example, former convict James R. Brice wrote a scathing exposé of conditions at Sing Sing, claiming that inmates were underfed and flogged without provocation. He also charged contractors with enriching themselves on the backs of prison laborers, diverting profits from the state's coffers. Yet even Brice subscribed to the prevailing theory of prison reform: "Now, what is the object of punishment? Surely it is to reform the offender—to reclaim him, and bring him back into the paths of duty, from which he has swerved. . . . But the sufferings of the convicts in this prison . . . are they not unjust, inhuman and uncharitable, as well as unlawful?" James R. Brice, *Secrets of the Mount-Pleasant State Prison, Revealed and Exposed* (Albany: Printed for the Author, 1839), 72.

30. Examples include *Trial and Imprisonment of Jonathan Walker, At Pensacola, Florida, for Aiding Slaves to Escape from Bondage* (Boston: Published at the Anti-Slavery Office, 1845); and *Personal Memoir of Daniel Drayton, For Four Years and Four Months A Prisoner (For Charity's Sake) in Washington Jail* (Boston: B. Marsh, 1854).

31. George Thompson, *Prison Life and Reflections; or, A Narrative of the Arrest, Trial, Conviction, Imprisonment, Treatment, Observations, Reflections, and Deliverance of Work, Burr, and Thompson* (New York: Printed by S. W. Benedict, 1848), iii. Subsequent references are given parenthetically in the text.

32. Torrey recognized the analogy between the legal standing of the slave and that of the penitentiary inmate, noting astutely, "I am civilly (most uncivilly I think it) dead to the world, while in these tombs." Lovejoy, *Memoir of Rev. Charles T. Torrey,* 239. James R. Brice made the same comparison: "Thus they [inmates] are bargained for and sold to these contractors, the same as horses, or slaves in the southern states." Brice, *Secrets of the Mount-Pleasant State Prison,* 66. Among modern prison historians, the connection between slavery and incarceration is most fully explored in Adam Jay Hirsch, *The Rise of*

the *Penitentiary: Prisons and Punishment in Early America* (New Haven: Yale University Press, 1992). Caleb Smith also sees the "civil death of the prisoner" as a "counterpart to what the sociologist Orlando Patterson has described as the 'social death' of the slave." Smith, *The Prison and the American Imagination*, 41.

33. Lewis W. Paine, *Six Years in a Georgia Prison* (Boston: Bela Marsh, 1852), 53 and 145–46.

34. George Thompson, *The Prison Bard: Or, Poems on Various Subjects* (Hartford: William H. Burleigh, 1848), title page. Subsequent references are given parenthetically in the text.

35. Thompson, *Prison Life and Reflections*, 300–301.

36. Harry Hawser, *Buds and Flowers, of Leisure Hours* (Philadelphia: Geo. W. Loammi Johnson, 1844), dedication and preface (both unpaginated). Subsequent references are given parenthetically in the text.

37. Smith, "Harry Hawser's Fate," 250 and 252.

38. It cannot be claimed, however, that the three editions are necessarily an index of the volume's runaway popularity. A circular listed in Worldcat contains Spear's plea for donations to offset the debt incurred through publication of *Voices for Prison,* suggesting that the volume was not remunerative to its publisher and perhaps was never intended to be.

39. For a discussion of Charles Spear's career as a reformer, especially in regard to the anti-capital punishment movement, see Louis P. Masur, *Rites of Execution: Capital Punishment and the Transformation of American Culture, 1776–1865* (New York: Oxford University Press, 1989), 124–40.

40. Charles Spear, ed., *Voices from Prison; A Selection of Poetry Written Within the Cell, By Various Prisoners,* 3rd ed. (Boston: Published by the Author, 1849), vi.

41. Ibid.

42. "To my Sister, on her Birth-day," in Charles Spear, ed., *Voices from Prison: Being a Selection of Poetry from Various Prisoners, Written within the Cell,* 1st ed. (Boston: C. & J. M. Spear, 1847), 25. Unattributed in the first edition, the poem is attributed to S.H. in the third.

43. Spear, *Voices from Prison,* 1st ed., 117.

44. H. Griffin, "Prisoner's Lament," in Spear, *Voices from Prison,* 3rd ed., 205.

45. John Quiner, "The Captive Maniac," in Spear, *Voices from Prison,* 3rd ed., 179.

46. Spear, *Voices from Prison,* 3rd ed., 292. John Quiner appears among the inmates interviewed by Jared Curtis at Massachusetts State Prison. On March 10, 1829, Curtis recorded Quiner's own admission that intemperance had produced "a partial insanity," in which state he committed his crime. Curtis regarded Quiner as a "man of sense" who spoke of his parents with "deep feeling" and was resolved to do well. Quoted in Gura, *Buried from the World,* 2.

47. R.S. writes a Christian-themed poem called "Good Time Coming," while S.H. is the author of the editorially sanitized "To my Sister on her Birth-day" as well as "The Convict to his Bible" and "The Convict Son to his Mother." Spear, *Voices from Prison,* 3rd ed., 174–76 (R.S.) and 183–90 (S.H.).

48. Spear, *Voices from Prison,* 3rd ed., 200 and 298.

49. Edgar Allan Poe, "Some Secrets of the Magazine Prison-House," *Broadway Journal,* February 15, 1845, 103–4.

50. In the "Music of the Prison" section, the poem "O where are his Joys?" is set to music, with the attribution "Words by Christian Meadows." In the biographical and critical notices, however, Spear preserves C.M.'s anonymity, writing that he "preferred not to have his history spread before world's eye." Spear, *Voices from Prison,* 3rd ed., 231 and 291.

51. C.M., "The Prisoner at Midnight," "The Moonbeam," and "Prisoner's Resolution," in Spear, *Voices from Prison,* 3rd ed., 163, 164, and 165–66.

52. Spear, *Voices from Prison,* 3rd ed., 291.

53. George Thompson, *Life and Exploits of the Noted Criminal, Bristol Bill* (New York: M. J. Ivers & Co., n.d.), 96. The first half of *Life and Exploits* is a clearly fictionalized account of Bristol Bill's adventures in England. But once the scene shifts to Bill's later adventures in the United States, Thompson apparently relies heavily on nonfictional sources such

as newspaper accounts and court documents. For Meadows's previous incarceration, see ibid., 92. Conviction of Bristol Bill and Christian Meadows is confirmed in newspapers including the *New York Evangelist,* June 27, 1850, and *Maine Farmer,* June 27, 1850.

54. Spear, *Voices from Prison,* 3rd ed., 290–91.

55. One thinks here of chap. 61 of *David Copperfield* (1850), in which the villainous Uriah Heep fulsomely (and manipulatively) credits the penitentiary with having reformed him. Charles Dickens, *David Copperfield* (Oxford: Oxford University Press, 1997), 834.

56. Thompson, *Life and Exploits,* 73 and 92.

57. The 1860 U.S. Census Record lists Christian Meadows as a forty-six-year-old engraver residing in Buffalo, New York, in possession of $1,000 worth of real estate and $500 in personal property. City directories locate him in Rochester in 1863 and Buffalo in 1867, both records identifying his profession as "engraver."

58. In his 1860 *Life in Sing Sing State Prison,* Luckey reproduces the quarterly report he read to inmates on March 1, 1846, on the activities of their discharged peers. In this report, he reminds inmates of "one of the original poems of this young man I not long since read to you" and proceeds to read S.H.'s "The Convict to his Bible." Luckey, *Life in Sing Sing State Prison,* 341.

59. Spear, *Voices from Prison,* 3rd ed., 292.

60. Karen A. Weyler, *Empowering Words: Outsiders and Authorship in Early America* (Athens: University of Georgia Press, 2013), 4.

61. Ibid., 6.

62. Ibid.

63. Nathaniel Hawthorne, *The Scarlet Letter,* in *Collected Novels* (New York: Library of America, 1983), 261.

Conclusion

1. Lennard J. Davis, *Factual Fictions: The Origins of the English Novel* (New York: Columbia University Press, 1983), 125.

2. William J. Stuntz, *The Collapse of American Criminal Justice* (Cambridge: Harvard University Press, 2011), 86 and 90.

3. Benjamin Rush, *An Enquiry into the Effects of Public Punishments Upon Criminals, and Upon Society* (Philadelphia: Joseph James, 1787).

4. Meredith L. McGill, *American Literature and the Culture of Reprinting, 1834–1853* (Philadelphia: University of Pennsylvania Press, 2003).

5. On the subject of porous generic boundaries, Jennifer Rae Greeson notes the surprising influence of city-mysteries fiction on Harriet Jacobs in "The 'Mysteries and Miseries' of North Carolina: New York City, Urban Gothic Fiction, and *Incidents in the Life of a Slave Girl,*" *American Literature* 73.2 (2001): 277–309. I demonstrated similar generic permeability in an article tracing the motif of a man being nailed into a crate and shipped to freedom, moving from Henry Box Brown's 1849 slave narrative into sensational novels by George Lippard and George Thompson. Carl Ostrowski, "Slavery, Labor Reform, and Intertextuality in Antebellum Print Culture: The Slave Narrative and the City-Mysteries Novel," *African American Review* 40.3 (2006): 493–506. Kathryn Conner Bennett characterizes E. D. E. N. Southworth's fiction as "insistently hybrid," crafted from a mixture of sentimental and sensational discourses, an observation that may apply to a number of the period's popular authors. Kathryn Conner Bennett, "Illustrating Southworth: Genre, Conventionality, and *The Island Princess,*" in *E. D. E. N. Southworth: Recovering a Nineteenth-Century Popular Novelist,* ed. Melissa J. Homestead and Pamela T. Washington (Knoxville: University of Tennessee Press, 2012), 100.

6. For example, in *Road to Ruin,* Kate objects to being put on display in prison, "for she particularly disliked to be made the object of an idle curiosity, and many persons had contrived, on various pretexts, to gain admission to her cell merely for the purpose of

beholding the beautiful woman who was condemned to death." George Thompson, *Road to Ruin; or, The Felon's Doom* (New York: Frederic A. Brady, n.d.), 70.

7. Michelle Alexander, *The New Jim Crow: Mass Incarceration in the Age of Colorblindness* (New York: New Press, 2010), 182.

8. Negley K. Teeters, "The Early Days of the Eastern State Penitentiary at Philadelphia," *Pennsylvania History* 16.4 (1949): 282.

9. "A Letter from Sing Sing," *Brooklyn Daily Eagle,* May 1, 1846.

10. Edgar Allan Poe, "Some Secrets of the Magazine Prison-House," *Broadway Journal,* February 15, 1845.

11. Rebecca M. McLennan, *The Crisis of Imprisonment: Protest, Politics, and the Making of the American Penal State, 1776–1941* (Cambridge: Cambridge University Press, 2008). As early as 1839, James Brice complained that the convict labor system described by McLennan put the convicts of Sing Sing on a level with slaves: "Thus [prisoners] are bargained for and sold to these contractors, the same as horses, or slaves in the southern states." James Brice, *Secrets of the Mount-Pleasant State Prison, Revealed and Exposed* (Albany: Printed for the Author, 1839), 66.

12. Caleb Smith, "Harry Hawser's Fate: Eastern State Penitentiary and the Birth of Prison Literature," in *Buried Lives: Incarcerated in Early America,* ed. Michele Lise Tarter and Richard Bell (Athens: University of Georgia Press, 2012), 231–58.

13. Karen A. Weyler, *Empowering Words: Outsiders and Authorship in Early America* (Athens: University of Georgia Press, 2013), 9.

Index

CARL OSTROWSKI was born in Detroit and graduated from Wayne State University. He earned an MA at the University of Tennessee and a PhD (in English) at the University of South Carolina. His book on the early history of the Library of Congress, *Books, Maps, and Politics: A Cultural History of the Library of Congress, 1783–1861,* earned the 2007 Eliza Atkins Gleason Book Award from the Library History Round Table of the American Library Association. He has published articles on nineteenth-century American literature and culture in a number of journals, including *American Periodicals, ESQ: A Journal of the American Renaissance, and African American Review.* A professor of English at Middle Tennessee State University in Murfreesboro, Ostrowski lives in Nashville with his wife and son.